W9-ASO-937

BLACK MAFIA

 **ETHNIC SUCCESSION
IN ORGANIZED CRIME**

FRANCIS A. J. IANNI

SIMON AND SCHUSTER □ NEW YORK

SBN 671-21764-X
Library of Congress Catalog Card Number: 74-113
Designed by Irving Perkins
Manufactured in the United States of America

1   2   3   4   5   6   7   8   9   10

ACKNOWLEDGMENTS

WHILE I am solely responsible for the data and interpretations that are presented in this book, a number of other people were involved in the project. First thanks must go to the National Institute of Law Enforcement for the grant (NI-71-076-G, Ethnic Succession and Network Formation in Organized Crime) that made the study possible and to Annelise Anderson and Martin Danziger, who were respectively the project monitor and institute director during the period of the grant. Elizabeth Reuss-Ianni and Kelly Snodgrass worked with me and the field assistants in organizing the data from the field reports, and Ms. Reuss-Ianni also did extensive field work, particularly in Paterson, New Jersey, after the formal period of field research was completed. She also interviewed a number of government law enforcement officials, scholars and specialists in the field of organized crime.

Much of the data and some of the analyses presented here were originally part of the final report on the NILE grant, which was published in abridged form by that agency. Suzy Fisher, Jeffrey Lewis and Ms. Reuss-Ianni worked on that report with me. Mercer L. Sullivan worked on various drafts of the material on prostitution and prisons, translating field notes into episodes. Henry Roth and Lester Smith also worked on drafts of episodes. Among the various organized crime specialists we talked with about the research and findings, Professor Donald Cressey, of the University of California at Santa Barbara; Arthur Grubert, chief of the Intelligence Division, William McCarthy, deputy commissioner for Organized Crime Control, both of the New York City Police Department; John McDowell, assistant United States Attorney, Strike Force on Organized Crime, St. Louis, Missouri; and Ralph Salerno, chief rackets investigator, Queens County (New York) District Attorney's office, were particularly helpful.

I am greatly indebted to a number of colleagues for their advice and criticism while I was developing the manuscript. My colleagues Lawrence Cremin and Edmund Gordon read sections of the manuscript in various stages of development and offered ideas and suggestions. Thomas Plate, Spenser Jameson, Eli Ginsberg, Elizabeth Reuss-Ianni, Irving Horowitz, Howard Becker and

Noel Chrisman read the manuscript in its entirety, and their criticisms re-shaped portions of it. Robert Stewart, my editor at Simon and Schuster, worked very closely with me and not a few of the ideas in the book emerged from long conversations in which his insight helped resolve a number of conceptual and stylistic problems. Helen Hardy, my administrative assistant, organized me and a number of typists to complete the manuscript. Finally, my deepest thanks go to "Buddha and the Seven Thieves," the field assistants, whose willingness to undertake considerable risks was more responsible for the success of the project than anything I might have done.

The fact that the National Institute of Law Enforcement furnished financial support to the activity described in this publication does not necessarily indicate their concurrence in the statements or conclusions contained therein.

For Elizabeth, my main man

CONTENTS

9

INTRODUCTION

IN THE summer of 1969 during my field study of the Italian-American organized crime "family" to which I gave the pseudonym "Lupollo" in my book *A Family Business,*[1] I stumbled onto a problem that at that time was largely ignored but is now beginning to attract some public notice. In the course of trying to determine what the future of the Lupollos might be—whether the family would continue in organized crime or turn to more legitimate occupations—I discovered that each succeeding generation of the family had been moving quietly but certainly out of crime. I had managed to trace the family history back seventy years through four generations and could see that from the second generation on, fewer and fewer sons had gone into criminal careers. Now, in the fourth generation, only four of the twenty-seven males were involved in organized crime. If the Lupollos were typical of other Italian-American organized crime families—and later on in the study we learned that they were—then their exodus should have resulted in some decline in organized crime activities in America. Yet organized crime has continued to flourish: the "numbers game" and other forms of illegal gambling are still widespread and are now estimated to gross $50 billion yearly with $15 billion in profits; drug traffic is increasing at an alarming rate and now represents a $75-billion-a-year industry; prostitution rings, which produce an estimated $2 billion a year for organized crime, are endemic in metropolitan neighborhoods where they operate side by side with the organized sale of pornography; and other activities such as loan

[1] Francis A. J. Ianni, *A Family Business: Kinship and Social Control in Organized Crime* (New York: Russell Sage–Basic Books, 1972).

11

sharking, hijacking and the sale of stolen goods are conservatively estimated as worth $100 billion every year. If the Italians were moving or being forced out of organized crime, who was replacing or displacing them in what is obviously a major sector of the American economy?

The answer to that question began to emerge as the research progressed. I learned that the Lupollos had lost all of their gambling activities in Harlem to blacks. In Brooklyn the family was trying to hold on to at least some control over its once vast gambling empire through a franchise arrangement with blacks and Puerto Ricans in which the Lupollos supplied the working capital and the necessary police and political protection in return for a share of the profits. By the time I completed my research in 1970 the pattern was so clear that I was able to report in *A Family Business* that as the Italians move or are forced out of organized crime, they are being replaced or displaced by blacks and in some cases by Puerto Ricans. Following my study of the Lupollos, I spent eighteen months studying the emerging but as yet not clearly identifiable process of succession of blacks and Puerto Ricans in organized crime in the United States. What I put forward here as the major conclusion of this new study is the thesis that if this pattern continues, we shall witness over the next decade the systematic development of what is now a scattered and loosely organized pattern of emerging black control in organized crime into a black Mafia.

Toward the end of the Lupollo study, I asked Phil Alcamo, one of the leaders of the family, if my observation about the declining role of the Italians and the emergence of blacks in organized crime was an accurate one. Phil agreed it was and went on to tell me how the Lupollos, at least, were accommodating to this change with a mixture of resentment and resignation:

Things here in Brooklyn aren't good for us now. This neighborhood right here used to be all Italian and the people looked up to us because we kept things quiet here. We tried fighting them for a while but there is no way to win. Lindsay and the other politicians are scared of them and they will give them anything they want to get their votes. A couple of years ago it really got bad and there was a lot of knifing and fighting between colored gangs and some of the Italian boys. Mayor Lindsay had to get somebody to Joey Gallo who ran things in the neighborhood, and tell him it was a bad thing and would he help stop it. But Joey didn't need Lindsay to tell him anything. Joey was always crazy but he was smart, too. When he was in Green Haven [prison] he saw that the blacks were going to take over on the street in Brooklyn so he began making contact with them even then. One night, when the Italian boys were getting ready to go after the coloreds, he drove up to a bunch of them who were getting organized near a school yard. They all knew who he was. He asked them what the beef was and one of them said, "Those fucking niggers are trying to take over everything in the whole neighborhood and we're going to kill a couple and put some manners on the rest of them." Joey went up to the guy and said, "You don't call them niggers anymore, they're colored people. And if you keep up this kind of shit the cops are going to come in and that's not good for us or for them." Joey turns around and starts walking back to his car when some kid yells out "They're *still* fucking niggers." Joey turns around, walks back and picks up the kid, throws him against the fence, knocks him down and then kicks him a couple of times while he's laying there moaning. Then Joey looks down at him and at the other guys and says, "I said *colored people*" and gets back into his car. There wasn't any trouble for a while after that but it's going to start again someday. They're going to keep taking over but if you watch the way they run things in Harlem now you know it's not going to be the same. A lot of times they refuse to pay off, even to their own people. In the thirty years we were in East Harlem we always paid off, even when we knew we were being taken. Now nobody knows what is going to happen, but what the Hell, those guys want to make a little, too. We're moving out and they're moving in. I guess it's their turn now.

What Phil was describing was the most salient but overlooked fact about organized crime as a way of life in the United States: there is a complex but demonstrable relationship among ethnicity, politics and organized crime in American cities. Daniel Bell, for example, describes the transfer from one wave of European immigrants to another as a "queer ladder of social mobility" out of the slums that had organized crime as the first few rungs.[2] The Irish came first, and early

---

[2] Daniel Bell, "The Myth of the Cosa Nostra," *The New Leader,* 46 (December 23, 1963), 12–15.

in this century they dominated crime as well as big-city political machinations. As they came to control the political machinery of large cities they won wealth, power and respectability through subsequent control of construction, trucking, public utilities and the waterfront. By the 1920s and the period of prohibition and speculation in the money markets and real estate, the Irish were succeeded in organized crime by the Jews, and Arnold Rothstein, Lepke Buchalter and Gurrah Shapiro dominated gambling and labor racketeering for over a decade. The Jews quickly moved into the world of business and the professions as more legitimate avenues to economic and social mobility. The Italians came next, and what Phil had been telling me—and what is now becoming increasingly obvious—was that as the Italians are leaving or are being pushed out of organized crime they are being replaced by the next wave of migrants to the city: blacks and Puerto Ricans.

Ethnic groups move in and out of organized crime and their time in control comes and goes. Even the specific crimes may change, as bootlegging is replaced by drug pushing and prostitution gives way to pornography. But organized crime as an American way of life persists and transcends the involvement of any particular group and the changing social definitions of what is illegal and what is not.

Criminologists have usually used the term "organized crime" to distinguish the professional from the amateur in crime and to indicate that the criminal activity involved is structured by cooperative association among a group of individuals. Thus, any gang or group of criminals organized formally or informally to extort money, shoplift, steal automobiles or rob banks is part of organized crime regardless of its size or of whether it operates locally or nationally. In recent years, however, governmental commissions and agencies have used a different definition of organized crime, based on the notion of a nationwide conspiracy involving thousands of criminals, mostly Italian-American, organized to gain control over whole sectors of both legitimate and illegitimate enterprise in order to amass huge profits. In both cases the definitions focus on the criminals themselves and they differ mainly in terms of size and complexity of organization (relatively small local groups as contrasted to a national syndicate) and the nature of the crimes involved (crimes in which there is a perpetrator and a victim and crimes in which illegal goods and services are supplied to those willing to pay for them). In my own work, I have preferred to focus not on the aggregation of individuals who join together to perform specific criminal acts or on particular types of crime. Rather, I have defined organized crime as an integral part of the American social system that brings together a public that demands certain goods and services that are defined as illegal, an organization of individuals who produce or supply those goods and services, and corrupt public officials who protect such individuals for their own profit or gain.

It was toward the end of the Lupollo study that I became convinced that organized crime was a functional part of the American social system and should be viewed as one end of a continuum of business enterprises with legitimate business at the other end. But if this is so, why then is organized crime so universally condemned while it is so widespread and so patently tolerated by the public and protected by the authorities? It seemed obvious that this contradiction is a structural means of resolving some of the conflicts, inconsistencies and ambiguities that plague us because our desires and our morals are so often in opposition. Organized crime, then, could be more than just a way of life; it could be a viable and persistent institution within American society with its own symbols, its own beliefs, its own logic and its own means of transmitting these attributes systematically from one generation to the next. I realized, of course, that I couldn't generalize about a major social phenomenon in American society from one case and some rather scanty information on how that case fits into the total picture. To really understand organized crime as an American institution would require looking at organized crime in other groups as well, finding out what is common and what different in the experience of these groups, what similar adaptations to common problems have been made and what distinctive patterns are peculiarly associated with particular groups.

Anthropologists have a method for defining the basic structures of institutions by looking at the same institution in a number of cultures. From these comparative ethnographies it is possible to determine what is common to an institution no matter where it is found. It is also possible to find what is uncommon or idiosyncratic to a particular culture and then to construct a typology of cultures that have similar patterns for particular institutions. It seemed to me that a comparative field study of some ethnic group in organized crime other than Italian-Americans was essential to isolate the basic structure of organized crime in American society.

It was too late to study the Irish and Jewish experience in organized crime except through historical accounts or through the recollections of the aging members of these ethnic groups who had lived through that period. My three years with the Lupollos had convinced me that blacks and Puerto Ricans were involved in organized crime in significant enough numbers that it would be possible to look at the formation and behavior of organized crime groups among them as a comparison to the Italian-American experience. I knew from the outset that the problems we had anticipated and found in studying the Lupollos were quite simple compared to those I would find in attempting to carry out field research among black and Puerto Rican organized crime groups. I could be certain of hostility and perhaps outright refusal on the part of the black and Puerto Rican communities, to say nothing of the organized crime groups themselves, to be subjected to such study. This meant that participant observation in the sense that I had lived among the Lupollos was impossible. The only solution was to find a number of "native" informants who could and would become field assistants and do the actual observing and interviewing.

Finding "natives" in this new study, however, was doubly difficult because it meant that the field assistants had to be not only black or Puerto Rican but knowledgeable about and acceptable in organized crime circles as well. After some exhausting and often discouraging attempts to locate, interview and check out the qualifications and records of a number of former and even practicing criminals through contacts with prison officials, parole officers and police officials, I came upon an organization of former offenders that was developing educational and occupational programs for ex-convicts. Over the course of a few weeks I was able to locate and recruit eight black and Puerto Rican ex-convicts who were members of this organization and who had been involved in organized crime activities—running numbers, pushing dope, or hijacking goods—prior to their imprisonment. All were now on parole and, although they were no longer involved in crime, were known to crime activists and had easy access to crime circles in ghetto areas of the city where they had once been active. Each field assistant was to work in his own neighborhood except in the two cases where the assistants had moved to a new location after release from prison. In these two cases, they were to return to their old neighborhood. This arrangement eventually meant that we were able to do field work in East and Central Harlem in Manhattan, the Red Hook and Bedford-Stuyvesant sections in Brooklyn, and in Paterson, New Jersey.

During the eighteen months in which we looked at emerging groups of black and Puerto Rican organized crime operatives, we gathered a substantial amount of information. Organizing that information so that it would tell us what these new groups look like, how they operate, how they are related to the social world around them and how we might predict their future presented many problems I had not encountered in studying the Lupollos. I have already mentioned the problem of the cultural distance between these groups and my own life experiences. The use of field assistants who were native to those cultures and to the culture of organized crime did, I am certain, reduce much of that deficit, but I am just as certain that it did not erase it. Another problem, similar to one that I faced with the Lupollos, was the question of confidentiality, because we did acquire information that could be harmful to any number of people, including the field assistants and myself. Research into organized crime is always a precarious business because the nature of the inquiry puts a major strain on interpersonal relationships with informants and may even endanger one's life when it leads to an exploration of information people do not want made public. My major interest in research in organized crime has always been its organization rather than solely in criminal behavior, so much of the potentially harmful or dangerous information we gathered is not really pertinent. Some of it, however, is important to understanding how groups of crime activists organize and operate and how they relate to each other and to the community. Where I have included such information in this book I have stuck by the bargain I struck at my first meeting with the field assistants and we have altered names and situations just enough to "put some shade" on the people involved. In no case, however, have we invented any characters or events or altered events or people to the point where there is a distortion of how that event or person fits into a group.

There are two other major differences between this study and my earlier work with the Lupollos that affect how I report what we learned. When I described the life of the Lupollo family, it was with some confidence that the reader was at least generally familiar with the world in which they live. The subject of Italian-American involvement in organized crime has long been a popular one in the media, and even if it was a somewhat distorted picture, the general outlines and recent history of that involvement are fairly well known to the public. Such is not the case with the much newer and certainly much less frequently described world of black and Hispanic organized crime.

The other problem is a related one but is somewhat more difficult to deal with. In studying the Lupollos I concentrated on the long-term study of one family and from that experience I generalized some notions about the involvement of Italian-Americans in organized crime. I knew what a "family" was in organized crime, and while I carefully avoided letting that knowledge structure my search for the rules that organized the family, at least I knew where to look for them. On the other hand, I learned very early that there is as yet no black or Puerto Rican equivalent for the Italian-American crime family. The period of black and Hispanic control over organized crime is not yet here, and the organizational pattern is therefore far less standardized than among the Italians. There are, however, a number of patterns of organization that are found with enough frequency among the black and Hispanic groups we observed that I shall describe them as types of behavioral organization. It is a major finding of our study, and so a major thesis of this book, that those forms of behavioral organization will in time form the basis of syndicate formation—the development of a Mafia, if you will—among black and Hispanic organized criminals just as the crime family evolved among the Italians. It is, however, still an emerging one and there is a distinct danger of trying to describe it by analogizing it to what I know about the structure and organization of the Lupollos. There are, as you will see, some similarities that grow out of the constant nature of organized crime as it has become institutionalized in American society and, possibly, out of the fact that some black and even more Hispanic groups have learned their organizational patterns from the Italians who preceded them in organized crime. But there are some important differences as well, and these differences are of at least equal importance in understanding what black and Hispanic organized crime syndicates will look like when their period of control finally arrives.

Because we did not have a model such as the crime family to follow in observing and analyzing the structure of criminal interaction among blacks and Hispanics, we used an anthropological technique known as network charting to construct models of such groups in the field. These network "maps" were extremely important in our work because they allowed us to focus our observations and interviewing on a known number of people that we felt certain were functioning as a group. We identified a number of such networks during the study. With what we learned about the day-to-day activities of the people who were operating as members of the group, we were able to set up a tentative classification along a continuum that we feel shows how these presently scattered and as yet unorganized networks may well eventually develop into an interrelated complex of crime groups who will control organized crime in the years to come. From the various networks we observed, I have selected those that I feel describe the locales, events, people and patterns of organization in sufficient depth to give the reader a feeling for what it is like to be a part of this world and to illustrate various stages in network development. (These all appear in Appendix B.)

The first section of the book describes two very different black crime networks. One is a very loosely organized network in the Central Harlem area of New York City—a pimp and his prostitutes, a band of thieves which steals goods "downtown" and then sells them in Harlem and a ring of dope pushers—each with its own leader and operatives.

This network illustrates the lowest but, for the present at least, most common level of organization among black crime activists. The second network is a complexly structured but well articulated one we found in Paterson, New Jersey, which describes the emergence of a militant black criminal empire out of the wreckage of the crumbling Italian dynasty to which it still maintains some links. This network, particularly when it is compared to the one in Central Harlem, presents a vivid picture of how the presently loosely structured networks of black crime operatives may well become organized into a true black Mafia.

In the second section, I first describe the historical and cultural background of organized crime in the United States, which serves to shape and organize the coming era of black and Hispanic control. Then I have selected two networks for inclusion, each of which illustrates one of the two major types of social relationships—the childhood gang and the prison—which we found are now serving to organize blacks into criminal networks.

The third section of the book deals with two very special cases we uncovered in our field research. The first of these is a Spanish-speaking network in which a number of different criminal activities operating out of three different areas—West Harlem, East Harlem and the Red Hook section of Brooklyn—are held together by the bonds of kinship and childhood friendship. In this network we are also introduced to "the Cuban connection," the new Cuban-dominated system of importing, buying and selling drugs, which seems certain to replace the existing European connections in the next few years. Finally, I describe the quasi-legal gypsy cab industry in New

York City and its mixture of legal, semilegal and openly illegal activities that illustrate our confusion over what is "business" and what is "crime."

Each of these networks is unique and a little world of its own, but each in its own way reflects something of the emerging pattern of black and Hispanic control over organized crime in the United States. In describing the various networks I have tried to maintain the sense of realism of our recorded interviews by leaving them in the language of the people involved, in order to give some feeling for the immediacy and wholeness of what was happening, being described or being thought about. The stories that describe life in the networks have remained faithful to the actual events upon which they are based and the only deviations are those necessary to protect the identity of the people involved and are never introduced for some purpose of dramatic or even conceptual impact.

In the final chapter of the book I have attempted to answer the questions that led me to undertake this study. Some of the answers are still in a preliminary stage and will require further research and examination. Some, however are sufficiently developed for me to offer them as conclusions that lead both to a different definition of organized crime in American society and to some recommendations about what can be done to control it.

In the appendices, I have included a note on the research methods used in this study, and network charts and casts of characters for each of the organized crime groups described in the book.

The first network I have selected for inclusion represents the lowest level of network cohesion in that it is actually a description of three sets of criminal ventures each of which is a separate operation and is joined with others by the pattern of friendships among the leaders of each group. The first of these is a prostitution ring headed by a very successful pimp, Reginald Martin, a twenty-eight-year-old black male who lives in Central Harlem but whose prostitutes ply the rich downtown trade in the area of 42nd Street and in parts of the fashionable East Side. Reggie has personal friendships with two males who are part of two other crime groups. His childhood friend Calvin Meadows is the manager of an illegal after-hours club, which is owned by Thomas Irwin, a forty-five-year-old black entrepreneur who sells stolen goods as part of a legitimate dry cleaning business. Irwin is a good example of such entrepreneurs in that he employs a number of thieves, or "boosters," to steal goods downtown for resale in his community. As his business grew, he branched out, almost reluctantly, into gambling and the illegal sale of alcohol. He is, in his own view, a businessman who is almost forced into crime by the circumstances of his environment. Finally, there is James Mitchell, another childhood friend of Reggie's, who is a large-scale narcotics dealer with an extensive ring of pushers working for him. Mitchell also operates seemingly legitimate boutiques, in one of which Reggie Martin is a partner. As we examine the relationships among Reggie, Jimmy and (through Calvin Meadows) Thomas Irwin, however, it becomes apparent that each is the leader of a separate ring of crime operatives— Reggie with his prostitutes, Irwin with his thieves and Mitchell with his pushers—but that the three operations are interconnected and do exchange goods and services.

In describing this network, I have presented a brief description of part of a day in the life of each of the three leaders of these separate operations and then proceeded to show how they are interconnected. The events described all took place on Wednesday, July 14, 1971.

PART ONE

✠

THE NETWORK

1

A DAY IN CENTRAL HARLEM

CENTRAL HARLEM is compressed between El Barrio of East Harlem, with its rapidly expanding Puerto Rican population and its few remaining pockets of Italians, and West Harlem, with its mixture of blacks, Puerto Ricans, Cubans and the white high-rise dwellers along the river. To the south it stops at 110th Street, where Central Park begins, but the northern boundary falls indistinctly somewhere around 155th Street. Within this area live 300,000 blacks but it is not really a community in the sense of people living and working in the same area. It is actually a number of communities. There are vast areas of tenements, there is an Afro-American bazaar along 125th Street and there are blocks of brownstones as well as high-rise apartments. There are also sections where the affluent live. In the 1930s and 1940s the prestige area for wealthy blacks was Sugar Hill along Edgecombe Avenue between 145th and 155th Streets. By the 1950s and 1960s it was the Riverton Houses at 135th Street and Fifth Avenue and the Lenox Terrace area. Today, and in recent years, wealthy blacks have been leaving Harlem for Westchester, suburban New Jersey, Queens, Riverdale and any number of upper-middle-class suburbs just as the Jews and the Italians had moved before them. So by July 1971, while the Lenox Avenue area was still a

25

better place to live, its former image of affluence was already beginning to disappear.

By 10 A.M. the traffic along Lenox Avenue is already brisk. The
iron grills are pulled back from the windows of the new, flat-roofed
retail strip on the east side of the boulevard. The contrast between
these stores and the littered streets, aging tenements and vacant lots
of the neighborhood is typical of Harlem's tension between flash and
filth. Inside the stores, merchants are readying themselves for the
day's business. Already the wide sidewalks are filled with all sorts of
people, on their way somewhere or just hanging out.

Just a few hours before, however, while the storefronts were ar-
mored and many of those now on the streets were behind locks, this
same area was a scene of strange grandeur. In front of Hall's, a bar
on Lenox near 134th Street, a series of automobiles—heavily cus-
tomized El Dorados and Lincolns—cruised and parked. The occupants were no less flamboyant than their vehicles—black men in
wide-brimmed hats, diamond rings, custom-tailored suits and platform shoes; black and white women in wigs, satin hot pants, heavy
make-up, and low-cut blouses: the pimps and prostitutes of Harlem.

REGINALD MARTIN

When the street sounds finally make their way through the second-
story window at 138th and Lenox, Reginald Martin, at twenty-eight
one of Harlem's most successful and respected pimps, looks at the
time and grumbles himself awake. He was out until three o'clock that
morning picking up his prostitutes from work and returning them to
their apartments. Normally, he would sleep at least until noon, but
one of his girls is to be released from the Women's House of Detention on Riker's Island at 11:30, and Reggie has to drive out and
pick her up.

One of the marks of Reggie's success as a pimp is that driving his
women about in his car is one of the few tasks of any sort that life is
likely to demand of him. He was not out the previous evening follow-

ing the prostitutes' rounds, either to protect them or to make sure they turned over all the money from their tricks. He expects his women to pursue their profession ambitiously, handle themselves and the inevitable hazards of the streets and turn over to him all of their earnings. Though Reggie originally made his money and reputation on the streets of Harlem, his current stable consists of eight women, all white, who work the rich territories of the East Side of Manhattan and the sin strip that stretches out in the midtown area around 42nd and Broadway.

Reggie drags his powerful, lithe body out of bed and across the rich bedroom carpet toward the shower. Before he went to sleep, he washed and braided his hair to ensure that his Afro would stand out full today. Keeping his head dry, he washes himself meticulously as the first step in the elaborate grooming and adorning of his body. Stepping out of the shower, he dries himself with a large, clean towel left for him by one of his prostitute-"wives" when she cleaned his apartment the day before. Next he shaves, applies deodorant and cologne and checks his fingernails.

Moving now to the closet, Reggie pulls open the door and surveys the contents: custom-tailored suits of every description, some with wide lapels, others with short jackets and elaborate zippers, jump-suits, suits with long vests, silk suits, leather ensembles, caftans, shirts with balloon cuffs and twelve-inch collar points and dozens of pairs of shoes and boots. Like all the accouterments of his flamboyant life style, Reggie's clothes are also essential tools of his profession. His status among the pimps and hustlers of Harlem, New York, perhaps even the nation, is of the first order. His appearance therefore must be absolutely exemplary in every detail. Consequently, Reggie spends a good deal of time and money on a distinctive wardrobe. Most of his suits are hand-made to his own design by a tailor on Amsterdam Avenue who specializes in clothing for pimps. Some of his suits, however, he buys from a dry cleaning shop just a few blocks away from his apartment where clothing stolen from exclusive shops down-town is sold at a considerable reduction. His shirts, cuff links, ties, belts and shoes come from a men's clothing boutique on the East Side in which Reggie is a silent partner. When he goes out recruiting or "copping" for women to add to his stable, the charisma of his looks is his first attraction, and he does not expect to be upstaged by anybody.

Checking outside, Reggie finds the same bright and warm weather the city has been having all week. Accordingly he selects and dons a lightweight patterned jumpsuit, which he leaves unzipped to his navel. His shoes are high-heeled and made of patchwork suede. Around his neck and down over his bare chest he wears a series of gold chains. Before he leaves the house, jeweled rings, a gold watch and the mandatory wide-brimmed hat slanting steeply across his forehead will complete his attire. He used to wear a ruby earring, but he's gotten out of that lately.

Beginning now to come fully awake, Reggie stands in front of his three-way mirror, yawns and surveys himself front and back. Satisfied, he loosens one braid and combs it out carefully. He undoes each braid and spends fully twenty minutes picking his hair straight up from the top of his head until it forms a full, perfect globe.

Not the least of Reggie's care for his appearance is the exercise he takes daily. Before he began pimping, Reggie's only major interests were sports. He is extremely proud of his trim, relaxed body and pays as assiduous care to his health as to his appearance. Normally, he would drive down to the YMCA in the early afternoon to work out, perhaps shoot baskets with some of his fellow "players" (as pimps refer to themselves) and relax for a while in the steam room. The visit to Riker's preempts his workout for today, however, and Reggie sits down for a bite before setting out.

As he breakfasts (on a bean pie and coffee) at a large glass table, Reggie is thinking about the new prospect he is going to encounter shortly. One of his "wives," Ginger, age twenty-two, is finishing a prostitution sentence today. While she was inside, however, she wrote Reggie that she had met and befriended another white woman, Patricia Quinn, age twenty-one, who is also being released today. Reggie has been sending Patricia letters and money orders and intends to invite her to join his stable of prostitutes this morning. He does not think about what he will say or do to her, however, for he comes on very naturally when he performs this recruitment part of his business. He knows he can rely on his style and charm and his experience and understanding of women. Reggie is a prototype of the "sweet mack," the new-style pimp who prefers psychology and the promise of profit to violence in manipulating his women. He certainly knows how to lift his hand against man or woman if need be. Since he has kept a stable of white women, however, he has very seldom found this necessary.

Reggie goes downstairs to the street and around the corner toward where his car is parked. On the way he greets his neighbors who are stoop-sitting to escape the oppressive heat inside. When Reggie reaches his car, he finds it surrounded, as always, by a group of small boys. The car is a 1971 white El Dorado, which he purchased through a company in New Jersey that specializes in customizing. The top bears an elaborate chrome design. Reggie previously owned an "EL D" with a suede top but found it a nuisance not to be able to drive in bad weather. The interior is upholstered in imitation leopard skin and contains a stereo system and a telephone. As Reggie approaches, the boys swarm around him begging to be taken for a ride. The first to reach him is Larry, a tall, brown-skinned child who seems always to wear a huge grin. He extends his palm, which Reggie slaps. As the others compete for his attention, Danny, a clever, impish kid of ten, grabs Reggie's arm and skillfully removes his wristwatch. Reggie pretends not to notice. A few seconds later, Danny holds up the watch with a sly smile and says, "Hey, Reggie, look. Man, I told you I was a professional." Reggie feigns anger. "Boy, you think you're bad, but ain't nobody ever showed me for a chump." He regains his watch and throws his palms out. Immediately small fists begin sparring against his hands. Danny, always a step ahead, fakes a karate kick and almost falls.

Ignoring his idolators' pleas to ride, Reggie pulls out across 138th Street and all the way to Morningside Avenue. When he reaches 125th Street, he turns left toward the Triborough Bridge. He slows down almost immediately and honks for the attention of an old friend he has spotted. He rolls down the window. "Calvin, what's happening, man?" Calvin Meadows, twenty-eight, grew up in the same block with Reggie. He is manager of an illegal after-hours club and he often steers customers to Reggie's girls, for which he receives a standard fee of $5 per customer. "Reggie, my man, I am hanging on this corner like a stewed chicken and would just love to go anywhere in that air conditioned hog of yours."

"Get in man, I'm out to Riker's. One of my bitches is walking today."

As they drive east across 125th Street, the retail section that unfolds before them represents a number of conflicting interests. The larger stores, such as Blumstein's, are still Jewish-owned, as much of ghetto retailing once was. The numerous bars and night clubs once controlled by or paying protection to white organized crime are beginning to have new black ownership. Many of the newest establishments are franchised fast-food operations such as Kentucky Fried Chicken that compete with the locally owned fast-food and take-out operations, some of which have always been around and some of which have recently been opened by Black Muslims. The trend in black retailing is also evident in the smaller shops such as record stores, beauty parlors, clothing boutiques and the Africa-oriented bazaars and bookstores.

Reggie and Calvin pass the Apollo Theatre between Eighth and Seventh Avenues and chat about the current bill, a rock and roll revival with Anthony and the Imperials, the Drifters and the Shirelles. One of Reggie's prime social obligations is to visit the Apollo on occasion with some of his women on his arm. His women in turn vie jealously for the privilege of accompanying him. Across the street from the Apollo are two men's clothing stores whose lavish window displays are filled with ready-made versions of players' finery. Along the south side of 125th Street, all the way from Eighth to Seventh Avenue and beyond are street stalls selling wigs, clothing and cheap jewelry and cosmetics. There has been considerable tension recently between these sidewalk vendors, who bring in their stands in the mornings by van and station wagon, and the store owners who sell competing wares but must defray considerably higher overhead. The stores have now begun putting out their own sidewalk wig stands. In places, the wide sidewalks have become aisles.

On the other side of Seventh Avenue rears a huge symbol of Harlem's growing contact with the outside world, the high-rise state office building that is finally under construction after a variety of community protests. Almost the entire north side of the block has been razed for this project. The building itself is set back from the street and has no windows lower than the third floor. When it is finally occupied, those who work inside will be able to drive to work and never venture into the surrounding neighborhood. Every aspect of the planning and construction is that of a fortress.

The final ingredients in the 125th Street mix are the religious and cultural centers. A red awning across the sidewalk marks the National Black Theatre. A huge second-story loft houses Olatunji's center for African dance, music, language and culture. Such centers are undergoing a financial crisis at this time. The interest of the foundations and the government in the rediscovery and revitalization of black culture is waning as the economy begins to tighten up.

The eastern end of 125th Street contains a number of Pentecostal storefront churches in various states of repair. Some are quite large, and many are covered with signs bearing extensive evangelical messages. Just before the elevated railroad bridge crosses over the street on Park Avenue is the His Holiness African Pentecostal Church with its large sign proclaiming: DOPE PUSHERS, WHITE AND BLACK, BEWARE—GET OUT OF HARLEM AND STAY OUT!!! Residents of the area know the space under the tracks as a nest for junkies.

On passing this sign, Calvin asks Reggie what he has done about Debbie, one of his wives who had become addicted to heroin. Reggie replies, "I dropped that bitch so fast she didn't know what happened. I didn't even go through no whipping her around. That is one thing that don't come *near* my family."

Although Reggie smokes marijuana and occasionally snorts cocaine, a status drug and a favorite with pimps, he bears a firm hatred toward heroin. He has never used it himself and will not countenance it for his women. His reasons are based on health, business and personal experience. Personally, his pride in his body, his love of athletics and his health fanaticism have always kept him away from the needle. From a business perspective, Reggie has built his reputation as a pimp on having the cleanest girls in town. His prostitutes are well known for being unhooked flatbackers, that is, they are nonaddicts and they make their money exclusively by performing sexual acts and not by any supplementary crimes such as shoplifting. There are many prostitutes who are addicts. Making another person dependent for a fix is a sure way to exert complete control. Prostitution operations that are run this way, however, are messy. Reggie knows that addict-streetwalkers are unreliable and bring much lower prices. He also takes pride in being able to dominate his women simply by the force of his personality. This is the surest and safest as well as the most prestigious way to operate. Though Reggie is constantly harassed by the police, he has never done time, since it is virtually impossible to convict a pimp without a prostitute's testimony that she has given her money to him. He can also credit his freedom to his avoidance of involvement in any crimes besides prostitution.

Finally, Reggie's hatred of hard drugs also stems from a bitter personal experience. He was led into the Life himself by a childhood sweetheart who chose him, helped him build his first stable and taught him his game. In the opinion of many of his friends, much of his success in controlling his women is the result of his having originally learned prostitution from a woman's point of view. Ironically, his mentor was the only addict who ever worked for him. She eventually died in her early twenties of an overdose.

At the end of 125th Street rises the steel latticework of the Triborough Bridge. The El Dorado swooshes into the curved entrance ramp and pulls up at the toll booth. The attendant is engaged in conversation with his sergeant, who is picking up money. Both of them ignore the El Dorado for a moment. The attendant remarks loudly to the sergeant, "Do I charge this boy for a car, or is there a special rate for nigger whorehouses on wheels?" Since display is the essence of the player's life, Reggie is used to the hostility and harassment that his flaunting provokes in other men. He remains silent, unconcerned, pays his toll and pulls out. Once on the bridge, he simply says, "That nasty-mouthed motherfucker's paycheck be in my pocket Sunday morning."

Reggie and Calvin drive across the bridge, out to the 68th Street exit from Grand Central Parkway and onto Ditmars Boulevard. Their conversation turns to an article on prostitution in midtown Manhattan that had appeared earlier that week in *The New York Times*. The article concerned a new police unit set up to bust what the police believe to be an "organized ring of pimps controlling midtown prostitution." The intent of the new investigation is to link the biggest pimps with Mafia figures and to prosecute them on conspiracy charges.

Calvin: "Chief pig Murphy says he's going to bring in the big players on conspiracy charges."

Reggie: "These cop geniuses with their theories! Shit! He can put three detectives' noses in my asshole twenty-four hours a day, and they'll pass away from the sweet smell before they catch me cozying up with some guinea *capo*."

Calvin: "Reggie, how many girls are you running now?"

Reggie: "That junkie bitch Debbie left me with only seven on the stroll. Not counting Ginger, who'll be back at work tonight. That's eight. Plus Ginger is supposed to be turning me out a tender new little girl friend this very morning."

Calvin: "Your game is together, man, and I wouldn't tell you what's not the truth. I don't know how you do it. When I had three girls workin' out of the club, I nearly lost my mind staying ahead of those sly bitches."

Reggie: "I know what you mean, man, I really do. I was up to twelve last summer, I made some name for myself, but I just didn't have time to relax. My pool game got pitiful, man, really sad. But I'm thinkin' about branching out. I'm going to Philly next month and see if I can't get down on that town. Now I've made a place here in the capital city of the Life, I'm going to lend out some of my talent to the provinces."

Reggie's reference to New York as "the capital of the Life" is quite accurate. The usual penalty in New York for prostitution is fifteen days—the lowest in the country. Besides the easy penalties, New York City is the largest, most cosmopolitan city on the East Coast and the most important tourist center. Thus, the ironic nickname "Fun City" signifies something more to most people than Mayor Lindsay might have intended. New York offers pimps and prostitutes the highest take and the least risk. For these reasons, there are more pimps and prostitutes in New York than anywhere else: 70 to 80 big-time pimps—all but one or two of whom are black— and their more than 600 active prostitutes. In that remarkable underground communications network known as the hustler's grapevine, New York is the main switchboard. Many hustlers from all over the country who have made it in Cleveland or Chicago or Boston come to New York when they think the time has come to move up.

Reggie, of course, is a hometown boy. Certainly, some of his success and much of his reputation derive from the fact that he knows and understands New York and Harlem and has many friends and contacts here that someone from out of town could never really duplicate. Conversely, he knows that his New York pedigree will precede him anywhere he goes. And in the sense that Reggie is not associated with any of the Italian-controlled syndicates that were mentioned in the *Times* article he is quite right in his indignant belittling of the police theory of pimping as part of organized crime. Reggie has no direct dealings with any of the Italian crime "families" or with any larger, formal syndicate of blacks. He is, however, part of a loose confederation of pimps all of whom know each other, respect each other's territorial claims in the city, rank each other within their profession and meet frequently to compare notes and discuss business arrangements. Not only do the New York pimps know each other, but through the hustlers' grapevine they know about the doings of players in other cities as well. Unlike other professional groups they do not have a national association but they do hold a yearly convention. Known as "The Pimp's Ball," the convention is largely a social occasion that draws pimps from all over the country to a preselected hotel in a different city each year. Each player brings his two top girls with him, and being chosen to go is a much-sought-after honor among prostitutes. There is the traditional convention dinner and at it there is the presentation of the "Pimp of the Year Award." In recent years a pimp's fashion show has been added. While the commonly accepted practice is to bring only one's two top girls, one year, when the convention was held in Atlantic City, a pimp from Texas arrived with six carloads of girls, all driven by chauffeurs in black leather uniforms.

The pimp's job, as is generally understood by those in the Life, is not only to make money. He is primarily responsible for spending and displaying the wealth that his women bring in, for he must maintain his image to remain successful. In Reggie's case, his friends note that he is not even a particularly good businessman. His major talent is pimping, which means having everything done for him. This includes having his family, usually his most trusted and capable "wife," handle all his business. Though Reggie flaunts his illegal profession publicly, he is so far away from the actual illegal acts performed by his whores as to be virtually untouchable by the police.

Reggie and Calvin have finally reached the narrow bridge that leads to Riker's Island. They pull off before they reach the wooden shed housing the two guards who screen the entrance to the island. Since they cannot go onto the island and Ginger is not in sight, they settle back for the wait.

Reggie: "You know, three years ago we wouldn't be the only young men sitting here waiting for a pross to walk."

Calvin: "That's because the women here are going through some evil changes. Look: there's just what I'm talking about."

The first person to come across the bridge is a black girl with short hair and mannish dress.

Reggie: "Goddam Lesbians. I don't give a shit what goes on inside that hole, but they're starting to bring it out. Next to dope, that's the thing I better not find out about."

Whether or not the mannishly dressed woman is a Lesbian as Reggie and Calvin think, she does represent a change in appearance and behavior that has been taking place among women on Riker's Island. Other factors in the change besides sexual attitudes may be an increase in feminist consciousness and simply growing militancy, particularly among black women. Whatever the cause, the change clearly threatens Reggie and the rest of his profession.

During the rest of their wait, Reggie muses about Lucy Greer, the deceased prostitute who turned him out into the Life. She was the child of a woman who was herself a prostitute, as well as an addict and Lesbian. Before Lucy became a prostitute, she had already been incarcerated as a wayward youth. With the cumulative experience of her background and the things she learned while still a teenager in jail, Lucy Greer knew that when she hit the street she would begin to practice prostitution. At this time, Reggie Martin was still a young man on the streets with no particular direction though he had so far withstood the ghetto hazards of dope and arrest. He was much like the kids he had been fooling around with earlier that morning: excited by and envious of the hustlers who prowled the ghetto in their expensive cars and fancy clothes, showing off flashy manners. His main desire in life was naturally to make as much money as possible in the fastest, easiest way.

Lucy Greer started turning tricks but had not chosen a pimp. Reggie was her childhood prince, and she began showering gifts and money upon him. Once she had turned him out, she taught him well. It was she who devised the scheme by which Reggie built up his first stable and which he was continuing today. Lucy had known many girls when she was incarcerated who were completely abandoned by their families and the outside world. She and Reggie began sending these girls money orders and letters at a time when no one else in the world was giving them anything. Since they were inside, they could not even cash the money orders, but they inevitably became attached to those who paid attention to them. Once outside, having nowhere else to go and knowing that they could depend on Reggie, they were eager to join his stable.

Reggie has become proficient at the traditional method of copping girls, attracting them with his flash and seducing them into becoming his whores. Whenever one of his wives is sent up, however, he encourages them to make contacts so that he can use the method devised by Lucy Greer. The dependence so fostered in abandoned and incarcerated girls is very great. Before meeting Reggie, they are completely lost. With him, their lives will contain many hazards, but they can look to him for emotional as well as financial security.

Then, at long last, Ginger Allen, Reggie's wife, comes over the bridge accompanied by Patricia Quinn, and Reggie turns to Calvin and says in mock anguish: "There goes my pool game again."

THOMAS IRWIN

There is little in either his appearance or in that of his establishment to suggest that Thomas Irwin amounts to much more or much less than most other small businessmen in Central Harlem. His combination dry cleaning and tailor shop is routinely drab, as though it were, like so many other black-owned businesses, rocking back and forth on the edge of bankruptcy. In the dusty window he has placed portraits of Martin Luther King and John F. Kennedy. Irwin genuinely admires those two men above all others and also hopes that their bad luck will somehow bring him good luck.

Irwin himself looks as conventional as his shop, and he thinks of himself as conventional, an ordinary black man trying to make a living. He favors dark-colored slacks and short-sleeve sport shirts in checks, always conservative although always expensive and well tailored. Irwin recognizes that at forty-five he is aging, growing old faster perhaps than need be. Although his short-cropped wavy hair has only a fleck or two of white in it, his stomach bulges and his doctor has warned him again and again about his high blood pressure.

But worry over the state of his health doesn't account for Irwin's nervousness and discomfort on this day. He has absent-mindedly checked his supply of cleaning fluid for the third time and he shuffles through the day's receipts repeatedly and without purpose. He glances up at the clock and notices that it's only 1:30—early, although it always seems late on a day like this. Uneasily, Irwin studies the woman who is sitting on the only chair in the store, her head nodding in a narcotic stupor. She is still a good-looking woman, a real fox, Irwin reflects.

Her name is Elizabeth Dukes. She is forty-one years old, a heroin addict and, more important, on a day like this at least, a member of a small gang of thieves or "boosters" who work for Irwin. The others are her husband, Cleveland Dukes, who is forty-four, and his partner, Timothy "Tippy" Jones, who is thirty-seven. Cleveland and Tippy are out on a job, boosting merchandise from fashionable stores on Fifth Avenue in midtown Manhattan, a posh world that although only 100 or so blocks away seems to Irwin like the far side of the moon.

Irwin is more than he seems to be. Intertwined in his legitimate business of cleaning and mending clothes is another enterprise, actually a series of overlapping enterprises, most of them illegal. Irwin buys and sells stolen goods. He is also a loan shark. And he operates a gambling house. As a result, far from being a marginal businessman teetering on the brink, he is actually a substantial entrepreneur with a personal worth of about half a million dollars.

Irwin, nonetheless, is troubled. It isn't the fear of discovery that bothers him. Many of his neighbors know who and what he is and respect him for it, respect him no less than his brother Robert, who is his partner in the cleaning business but not in crime. If his neighbors disapproved of Irwin they could take their business elsewhere. But they patronize his shop, as often for his contraband as for his legitimate services. The neighbors know that if they are looking for the best, whether it's whiskey or an Italian knit suit, Irwin's shop is the place to go. One of his best customers in fact is Reggie Martin, who buys clothes from Irwin for his own use as well as for resale in his boutique.

Irwin's reputation is as a seller of top-quality goods; the fact that they are stolen is incidental. He will sell a top brand-name suit for 40 percent less than Saks Fifth Avenue, and as his neighbors see it, in doing so he is correcting a social imbalance. Most goods, they reason, are sold at a premium price in Harlem. By making certain things available at a cheaper price, Irwin is helping to set things right.

Irwin is not only a merchant of quality goods but also the community banker. Some would call him a loan shark, although the viciousness implied in the term does not apply to Irwin. True, his rates are usurious. On a loan of $50, for example, he demands repayment of $62.50. But the fact is that it is Irwin and only Irwin who always has ready cash when anyone needs a few hundred or even a few thousand dollars because of a sickness in the family or for a trip back home to the South or for whatever reason.

If a borrower defaults on a loan, Irwin has little choice but to shrug it off. He is not an enforcer and has no associates who are enforcers. He has never sought any connection with any of the mobs that operate in Harlem—black or Italian—and has never had any connection forced upon him. But Irwin doesn't worry much about defaults. He knows that most people will pay him back, no matter how slowly, because some day they will need cash again, and where else can they go? Banks don't lend money to welfare recipients or to the sometimes-employed. It's not bad loans that are troubling Irwin on this day.

Several customers come in to leave clothes to be mended, and one of them, a stranger, asks if Irwin knows where there is a good liquor store in the neighborhood.

"What kind of liquor you looking for?" Irwin asks.

"I like the best," says the stranger.

"How's Johnny Walker Black Label?"

"Uh-huh."

"A friend brought me some," Irwin says, "but I'm always happy to share good fortune. Do you have $25?" The stranger counts out two tens and five singles and Irwin walks through the curtain that divides the back of the shop from the front and in a minute reappears with four fifths of whiskey. Irwin is pleased, not only with the sale itself but also because it breaks, momentarily at least, the tension of waiting. It occurs to Irwin that he is becoming a well-known figure throughout Central Harlem. He is not accepted on the highest level of Harlem society, of course—not, for example, in the company of the wealthy doctors who send their families to Oak Bluffs, Martha's Vineyard or Sag Harbor for the summer. But he is a well-regarded member of a newly established Harlem business club he joined two years ago.

And there is no question in Irwin's mind but that he is far above people like Elizabeth and Cleveland Dukes. He knows little about their world of drugs and desperation and doesn't want to know more, doesn't even want to know how it is that Elizabeth Dukes can make her contact and shoot herself up within half an hour after Irwin advances her a few dollars on a day like this. He does wonder sometimes, though, if it was she who got Cleveland hooked on drugs, the way Cleveland says she did. It could be, but it could be just the opposite, too. You can't tell with junkies, Irwin reflects, their heads are so messed up even they don't know themselves when they're lying. She's a good-looking woman, Elizabeth, but Irwin could never get himself involved with a junkie. He shakes his head.

Irwin has never been part of that world, not even as a youngster. True, he smoked marijuana once or twice as a teenager and in the Army he even sniffed the cocaine that one of his buddies had smuggled onto the post. But he hadn't enjoyed either. He didn't like the feeling of delirium, of floating beside himself. What he really liked was drinking a few fingers of Haig and Haig Pinch with the guys in the businessmen's club.

Nor had Irwin been brought up to understand crime, to live in it and with it and by it, without discomfort. He had never been a member of a street gang as a kid. His parents were very strict about that. They impressed upon him that they were bringing him up in a good, religious home and that they would not tolerate his running with a gang. Both of his parents were working people. His mother was a practical nurse and his father worked for the railroad. At least he did when there was work. Irwin was slightly ashamed of his father, although he had to admit that he himself wouldn't have been any more successful if he hadn't simply been lucky.

Irwin had quit school at the age of fifteen. He just couldn't get the hang of it, couldn't read well enough to make it through any book that might have interested him, and so he quit, lied about his age and joined the Army. He reopped once to stay in Germany for another three years, then came back to the States and looked for a job. When he couldn't find anything else, he followed his father into railroad work. But he soon saw himself trailing his father to a dead end, and so within a few months he quit and with the separation money saved from his Army discharge, he and his brother bought the tailor shop. They knew almost nothing about tailoring, but the Jewish tailor who had owned the shop was eager to get rid of it and he threw a few free lessons into the selling price.

Irwin and his brother learned enough to get by, and Irwin was pleased to learn that at least he had a good sense of quality. He learned to tell the difference between good tailoring and bad tailoring by such telltale signs as the finishing of the seams and the lining.

It was really his honesty that made him open the illegal side of the business, or so Irwin tells himself. Night after night junkies broke into the shop and stole the suits and dresses that the brothers were holding for their customers. The way Irwin saw it, if they didn't do right by their customers and replace their stolen clothes, the shop was going to go out of business.

That's when a friend introduced him to Philip Thomas, a man Irwin still thinks of as remarkable. Thomas was a heroin addict, and it took Irwin some time before he got over his distaste for Thomas and his habit. But from the first Thomas impressed Irwin with his professionalism. Thomas described himself as a booster, an operator who was situated on the scale of criminal capability somewhere between pilferer and hijacker. He wasn't up to hijacking a full truckload of, say, electric typewriters, truck and all. That took a big organization.

"But at the same time," he said, tapping Irwin on the arm to hold his attention, "I'm not a man to waste my time shoplifting or picking up a coat that somebody drops here or there. You understand?"

Thomas worked with two partners, Cleveland and Elizabeth Dukes, and together the three of them would hang around the delivery garages of the best stores on Fifth and Madison Avenues between 34th Street and 59th Street. When they spotted a truck carrying the kind of high-quality goods they wanted, perhaps leather handbags or expensive silk ties, they would make a note of the number of the master lock on the truck.

They had a friend, Richard "the Pick" Williams, a hardware man. Williams owned his own hardware store and on request from the gang he could supply any master lock key they wanted within fifteen minutes. After that it was simply a matter of locating the truck again and waiting for the driver to make a delivery. Then, while the driver was inside, they would pick up one of the mail carts that was always lying around the sidewalk, roll it up to the back of the truck, open the door and load up.

The first few times, Irwin bought from the gang only enough to replace what his customer had lost or to substitute for it. When he substituted, he always made sure that the substitute was worth more than the lost article. No customer ever complained. Few of them even asked where the replacement came from. It was so easy that Irwin soon began buying more than he needed to make up his losses and selling the extras.

He had a knack for selling and he thought that if he had been born white instead of black he could have made a legitimate fortune out of selling. He resented that sometimes, particularly when he became frightened about how involved he was getting in crime and how little he knew about being a criminal.

In fact, he had to take lessons from Thomas. Two or three Sundays a month he visited Thomas, and in "Sunday school," as Thomas liked to call it, Irwin learned how to operate a criminal organization. Thomas taught him how to bribe the police to keep them quiet, how much for the patrolmen and how much for the sergeant. And he taught him how to deal with the junkies who worked for him, including Thomas himself, so that he could make money off them twice, by lending them money for drugs and later collecting from them stolen goods equal to the value of the loan plus interest.

The success of the scheme awed Irwin as much as it pleased him.

He couldn't stop the money from pouring in. As soon as word circulated through the neighborhood that he was carrying quality goods at 40 percent less than they could be purchased downtown, there was a stream of customers filing through the shop all day long and so late into the evening that Irwin had trouble closing up almost every night. There was always someone at the door who wanted to look at a pair of shoes or a dress.

The money that came in far exceeded his losses through theft and far exceeded what he needed to live on, even though he lived well. On the advice of friends that he invest his money in property, he bought a big gray stone building across the street. The upper three floors he rented out to tenants and, at Thomas' suggestion, he turned the basement into an after-hours and gambling club and hired Calvin Meadows to run it for him. He had intended it only as a neighborhood hangout, a place where the local crowd could have a few drinks and play a little blackjack and Georgia skin. But before long most of the high rollers throughout Harlem had heard about Irwin's place and many of them showed up regularly. It was a new place and safe, because Irwin, who was already paying off the police to protect his trade in stolen goods, had taken the sensible precaution of raising the payoffs and extending the protection to the club.

But success frightened Irwin. His small enterprise was swelling into a network of businesses, legal and illegal, that was bigger than he could handle. "Cover yourself better," Thomas advised him. "Put some more shade on what you're doing." Irwin bought three more tailor shops to put more weight on the legitimate side of his operations and hired a bookkeeper who knew how to clean money, that is, how to make it look as though the profits were coming not out of loan sharking and gambling and selling stolen goods but out of the cleaning and mending business.

Sometimes, Irwin had trouble falling asleep, worried as he was at how big he was becoming, how the business was growing far beyond his ability to handle it. He was no "super bad dude" to be controlling a major criminal organization. He knew that his talent and his ambition were limited. All he wanted to do was make some easy money and not worry too much. He also wanted to keep the shop and talk with customers and sell to them. He was good at that part of it, and he enjoyed it.

Irwin was not only flattered but also relieved when several of the younger men in the neighborhood copied his scheme and bought a candy store to serve as a front for a "buying and selling" business. Irwin hoped it would take some of the pressure off him, and it had, at least a little. Still, he was living under enormous pressure, which on a day like this made him sweat much more than could be blamed on the heat of the steam iron and which sometimes made him feel sick to his stomach.

Philip Thomas had been arrested a few months before on a narcotics charge and was doing time. It wasn't just that Thomas had gone to jail owing him $800 or that he lost his adviser that bothered him. Thomas' arrest made him realize that he was vulnerable, that he could buy off the cops in his own precinct, but he couldn't be sure of buying them all off. What would happen, for example, if Cleveland Dukes or his new partner, Tippy Jones, were caught by the cops downtown? If the big-wheel storeowners put pressure on the cops, the cops would put it on Cleveland and Tippy, and they'd talk. Sooner or later a junkie will talk. Irwin looked up at the clock again. It was 2 P.M.

The way they planned the job for that day didn't differ much from the way they planned any of the other jobs the Dukes and Tippy performed four or five times a month. Irwin trusted them. They seemed more professional to him than any of the other gangs he ever did business with. The Dukes knew their way around Fifth Avenue, felt comfortable and sure of themselves as not all blacks did in midtown, even blacks who had nothing to hide except perhaps the color of their skin.

That morning Irwin, as he usually did in preparation for a job like this one, had gone to Hertz and rented a panel truck. He parked it in front of the tailor shop and left the keys in the dash. Cleveland and Tippy picked it up there and drove to a diner on the West Side of Manhattan. Elizabeth, in the meantime, took a subway to midtown and walked up Madison and down Fifth, methodically scouting all of the loadings and unloadings on the cross streets. As soon as she had a list of four or five promising trucks, she telephoned the diner. Once they had experimented with using walkie talkies but when they discovered, to their alarm, that their conversation could be picked up on other receivers, including police radios, they quickly retreated to the telephone.

Elizabeth had done her part and was back in the shop before noon. Now came the tedious and agonizing part, waiting for Cleveland and Tippy. Suppose they had been picked up? Their arrangement with Irwin was to tell the cops that they had stolen the panel truck along with the goods. Irwin, meanwhile, would do what he could to buy the cops off, and if that didn't work, at least Cleveland and Tippy would have some money waiting for them when they got out of jail.

The waiting. The waiting. It is now 2:30. Irwin thinks about his high blood pressure. He is only vaguely aware that half a dozen customers have come and gone within the past hour, a few leaving clothes, others picking up, another asking if Irwin knew where he could buy some leather luggage, Irwin said he didn't know of any place at the moment but suggested that the customer come back later.

Then at 10 minutes before 3, Irwin sees Cleveland's scrawny figure at the door. He barely weighs 120 pounds and his Levis and gray sweatshirt and his tattered basketball sneakers all hang so loosely that Irwin wonders why they don't fall off. But in the crowds swarming around the delivery garages of midtown he looks as though he belongs, more or less.

"Hey brother," says Cleveland. "We picked up something that fell off the back of a truck. You wanna look?"

Then Cleveland twirls around as though he is dancing and keeps twirling until he is in front of Elizabeth. He crouches down and gives her a light slap on the cheek. "You did good, mama," he says. "You did good." Elizabeth's head just bobs and releases a moaning sound that suggests contentment.

Sitting in the driver's seat is Tippy, who is unlike Cleveland in almost every respect, except for the similarity in their clothes. Tippy is thickly built. His manner is reserved, sullen. Irwin suspects, and quite accurately, that Tippy, even though he is a junkie, looks down on him. Tippy is, after all, Jamaican and Irwin the son of a Mississippi sharecropper-turned-railwayman. Tippy also has read widely in black radical literature, always has some paperback by Malcolm X or Eldridge Cleaver stuck in his belt, and despises Irwin's bourgeois manners and ambitions. Irwin nods at Tippy, who doesn't bother to nod back.

Irwin peers into the back of the truck and sees two mounds of raincoats, apparently top quality. "Okay," he says, "let's look at them inside." In the back of the store the three men hang the raincoats up on long racks suspended from the ceiling. They are London Fogs, Irwin notes with satisfaction as he counts them, carefully examining each one to make sure that it isn't torn or soiled. He counts eighty-two coats, all in excellent condition. "Good, good, good," Irwin says to no one in particular. He is certain he can sell them and guesses that $30 is about the right selling price.

He reaches into his pocket and pulls out a roll of bills, from which he counts out ten $100s. He likes this part of the job, being able to impress Cleveland and Tippy with his ability to flash a large amount of money. He gives six bills to Cleveland for Elizabeth and himself and four to Tippy, who will have to pay the hardware man out of his share.

Now it is Cleveland's turn to put on a show. He sticks a cigarette in his mouth and lights a match, but doesn't light the cigarette. He is impatient to start talking. He shakes the match and pulls the cigarette out of his mouth and begins his explanation. Then he stops and puts the cigarette back in again. And pulls it out again. It always takes Cleveland at least a dozen matches and five minutes to light a cigarette.

Cleveland explains that Elizabeth had tipped them off that a truck with which they were familiar was making a delivery at a well-known men's store on Madison. They double-parked at the end of the block and waited until the driver went inside the delivery entrance. From experience they knew that it took the driver about eight minutes to make his delivery, and so as soon as he was out of sight they pulled up alongside. Through the windows in the rear doors they could see two long rows of raincoats, and with a master key they opened up.

"We grabbed every one of them mothers except the last two in the rows," explains Cleveland. "That way when that dude driver come back, he gonna peek in and see them last two coats and think he still got a truck full."

Cleveland laughs so hard that he almost falls down. Irwin laughs too, partly out of appreciation for Cleveland's technique and partly out of relief that the job is over. Tippy smiles privately, as though he is enjoying a joke on Cleveland and Irwin as well as the driver. They talk for a few minutes about the possibility of another job the following week, but it is left uncertain and Tippy and Cleveland, supporting Elizabeth, walk out the door.

That evening a woman brings in a pile of her husband's clothes for cleaning, and among them is a raincoat. It is an old coat, badly frayed, and Irwin rubs the frayed cuff disapprovingly and then speaks to the woman. "Mrs. Walters," he says, "I've got something I want to show you. Now if you don't have the money right now, it's okay. You know that. But you just step right back here and let me show you something."

JAMES MITCHELL

Robert Lewis, known on Lenox and the adjoining streets north of 125th as Bobby Hassan, is coming down out of Harlem in a taxi. He gets out at 96th and Central Park West, even though he still has a few blocks to walk, so as to give himself a little time to think about things, figure things out, what he is going to say exactly.

He doesn't like having to come down here. It doesn't feel good. Not the nearly deserted street, 96th, not the white folks walking their dogs, not the staid old brick apartment buildings with their awnings out front and their Irish doormen looking out just for the likes of him. He doesn't like any of it. It definitely is "out of town," and even worse are the big new white-face concrete co-ops over on Columbus, which is exactly where he is headed, down to 93rd, to Roko's, the bar on the ground floor of one of the biggest and flashiest co-ops of all, where maybe a certain class of folks goes these days, but not Bobby Hassan, definitely not, not if he can help it. He likes it uptown just fine.

Except how else is he going to do what at last he figured he had to do, or at least what he figured at least he had to try to do: take the shot, make the truly *big* hustle. Or at least the only one he could think of for the moment. For the daily bullshit, the last months especially, since he'd got back on the shit himself again—he'd been off it, but he'd come back, and so the last months had really been the worst—it just wasn't worth it any more, the same thing, every day, going out, having to find the stuff, having to have the money, the $150 or whatever it was, it wasn't that much. But still when you had to have it every day, and some days then you couldn't find your connection—you could look all around, up and down Lenox and in every place, and everyone knew he just wasn't there—and then you had to have your back-up man, and what if he wasn't there either— some days he wouldn't be, if your main man was on vacation too— and then what did you tell the customers, half the time you could lose your customers that way, and how about yourself, of course you kept a little for yourself, but what if it was a few days and you were broke by then, and you really needed the shit yourself. No, it was enough of this bullshit for Bobby Hassan. He'd been doing it eight years and enough was enough. Especially now he had an idea, a way to score good, or at least a real find maybe.

The maybe being James (Jimmy Brown) Mitchell, the man Bobby Hassan will be looking for in Roko's, and likewise the man whose possibilities occupy all Bobby's thoughts as he turns down Columbus and heads for 93rd. Get on Jimmy Brown's payroll, slide in with him, and easy street from then on, right, Bobby? Who could blame a dude for wanting a little organization in his life, getting up a little later, knowing where the stuff's coming from and where it's going, real regular, real good pay, no sweat, and think of the shit for himself—if, let's say, let's just say, he can't quite kick it for a little while. For Bobby Hassan told himself that 'course he wouldn't mind kickin' it, gettin' clean, but a dude's gotta be realistic, you can't always do what you wanna do exactly. And so working for Jimmy Brown, if he needs it, he's got it, right? And not to mention, Jimmy Brown's got all those real legit operations now, those ice cream parlors, laundermats, boutiques, and so forth, et cetera, to put the shade on, so maybe he, Bobby, will get into a little of that someday, get out of the bullshit for good. Maybe, that is . . . But anyhow the point is that Bobby Hassan doesn't like coming down here, but if that's the way things are, okay, so Jimmy Brown, he grew up in Harlem his whole life, he's got all his friends in Harlem, all his business, all his success is Harlem, but so now he figures he wants to come down here, be too respectable for Harlem, get in these big fancy whitey places with all the other big boys, the ballplayers and the TV announcers and those folks with families on all the commercials looking just like whitey himself, well then, if that's how it is with Jimmy Brown, if this is where Bobby Hassan's got to come down to find him, then okay who is he, Bobby, to argue?

The Roko was indeed a place unlike Harlem. Black faces, yes. Everywhere black faces, crowding the bar, filling in all the low tables, up on the bandstand too. Letting the handful of whites know who this place is for. But then look at the place itself. Low and square, clean lines, abstract expressionism on the walls. And the air conditioning built in, ceiling vents, cooling. And corporation-style carpets on the floor. A place, you could say, like the lobby upstairs, like all the apartments, too, that if somebody says they're expecting you the silent televised elevators take you on your way to. No, not the style that Bobby Hassan is used to. Nor in the clothing on these gents and ladies either, for on the trip downtown hasn't a little bit of color been lost and a little bit of expensive, careful tailoring been gained? Nor even in the music, for the girl is good, and she sure knows she is black, but isn't she a shade softer than she would be uptown, as the laughter at the bar is softer, as the carpet is softer? . . . Bobby Hassan is nervous. He doesn't belong here, his coat is too tight, he has too little money, and all of them, he figures, have to know it. But he nudges in to the bar, orders a whiskey and waits, trying to get cool. For over in a far corner across the room, at a table flanked by the only two unoccupied ones in the whole place, is the man he's come to see. Long face, mustache, medium sideburns. Eyes set apart, very quick. Lighter than average complexion, what your white folks would call "coffee." Bright white shirt, thick collar, thick knit tie. A suit that Bobby can't really tell about, except that it is fine. And so is the dude hustler wearing it, James Jimmy Brown Mitchell, because he is connected. He owns boutiques and bars, but he sells his dope through a big family of pushers who never come near those places.

For his part, Jimmy Brown doesn't even notice that Bobby Hassan has come into the place. There could be any number of reasons for this: he has his mind on the girls or the music; or the crowd is simply too thick to keep track of, even for a guy like Jimmy, who likes to keep track of it; or the coke he'd blown just a minute before coming in has left him feeling just a shade too good to notice; or he has no use for Bobby and actually prefers not to notice him; or indeed he doesn't even remember Bobby very well, except when (cheap junkie pusher, who needs him?) he presents himself—annoyingly—as seems to be a pattern, every several months or so. But the real reason probably is that when Bobby came in, Jimmy Brown was sitting talking, getting something settled with a class dude and some young white chick. The Roko is a place where not only can Jimmy relax but if need be enjoy a business dinner or a nice business after-dinner drink.

Which was exactly what he was doing when Bobby Hassan walked in. The man he is with is Reggie Martin, man of his from way back at school and of course 143rd Street, and more recently his silent business partner with a piece of one of Jimmy's boutiques. The girl is Patricia Quinn, who had that afternoon chosen Reggie to be her pimp. At the table, Jimmy Brown is straightening Reggie out as to exactly how you run a le-git-i-mate business in this day and age, concerning which, understandably, Jimmy has had little prior experience.

Essentially the discussion started when Reggie inquired as to why the books showed that amounts of $325, $725 and $110 and considerable amounts of clothing, shoes and the like, had been donated to the Seventh Avenue Boys Club.

"Man, I'm trying to explain to you, Reggie, the name of the game is tax deductions. Right, man? I mean, sure, we're giving it all away, but we're writing it all off, right? You got no sense of accountancy, man!"

"The fact is, we're still losing something, that's right. Is it not, Mister Business Expert?"

"Well, what if that's right, so what, so what are you one of them hustlers get a little and don't give a dime back to nobody? I mean, what's this shit, Reggie? What it cost us ain't worth nothing and it really gives some of them kids a break . . ." Then, sipping his drink, pleased with himself for speaking so righteously, "Hey, man, you know we both got certain enterprises there ain't nothin' to take tax deductions from, right? So what's this shit?"

"Well," Reggie, thoughtful now, "I guess I don't give a shit, I mean sure, kid, who the hell cares, the money. But, Jimmy, you do gotta tell me stuff like this. Okay, man? Is that right?"

"Sure, Reggie. That's right." But still feeling quite good about himself, he adds: "But, man, what were you gonna say, I mean, those kids, coming up, you want 'em to come up as hard as we had it, I mean, I know it ain't much, but a few of those kids, you know it can really do some good, get some books over there, you ever been in that place, a kid can go in there and read books, read Malcolm, all that shit, Man, it's good for a kid. I'm not giving you any bullshit, man, I mean, the way I figure it, we got some responsibilities, if we got some dust, right?"

To which Reggie Martin is considering replying, weighing the pros and cons of it, Jimmy being his old friend versus Jimmy being kind of a touchy guy—and also old friend or no, Reggie not wanting to put Jimmy down when they are business partners now and all, and what if he, Jimmy, would be pissed and remember, but anyhow Reggie is considering saying that maybe if Jimmy really wants to do some good he should get out of pushing that shit around, stick to coke or something, or what's wrong with girls, Reggie could set him out with some girls, but of course not Lucy Greer, who was dead from too much shit, as he, Jimmy, might want to take half a second and remember; but Reggie is saved from his inclination by the appearance, suddenly, in front of their table, of an obvious street dude, red jacket, red pants, black hat and slick shoes—however, not an expensive street dude, just your ordinary Seventh-Lenox type, and in fact, kind of rundown and slouchy, this one.

Bobby Hassan is cool now, if not inside then at least on the surface. Not a spark of recognition comes from the class dude in front of him, but to Bobby that's all just fine. "Salaam, Jimmy Brown. I'm standing at the bar, I see you over here, I say to myself I better come over say how d'you do."

"Hello." Jimmy extends neither a hand nor a smile.

Bobby remains standing.

"Pleased to meet you," Bobby says to Reggie, who extends a hand as Jimmy now makes a perfunctory gesture of introduction. Reggie looks over to Patricia, saying, "Go over and see what's going down over at the bar for a while, Patty."

Bobby looks doubtful a moment. "Hey, man, look," he addresses Jimmy. "Now I see you, I got something I could use to talk to you about." He asks, then, nodding in Reggie's direction, "That okay?"

"Anything you say to me, you say to him too."

"Okay, man." And he looks around once nervously.

"But I don't need no more color TVs, so if that's what you got in your pants . . ."

Bobby laughs uncomfortably, for Jimmy had obviously not meant the remark to be funny. Out with it then, Bobby tells himself, and out it comes, in little more than a whisper: "I hear you looking to score big, real big. The Cubans, I hear you're thinking 'bout that Latin shit. Or also I heard you're talking about out of town. Vietnam, Detroit, places. Now look, man, you know I'm from Detroit . . ."

Jimmy nods.

"I mean, I'm from Detroit, that's why I am where I am only,

right? Like I could go back, be a big man, you know, know everybody, shit like that. But I like it here, so I stay, so that's it, right?"

"Yeh, well?" Jimmy Brown is already growing impatient.

Bobby Hassan swallows rather heavily.

"Man, you think I could sit down?"

"Well, lookit, man, what is it you're talking about, hey, what is it
now?"

So Bobby remains standing.

"I see a deal, man. I want to do you something good. You know,
I been thinking about it. I like your thing. That way you operate,
having a group and everything like that. You know what I got's not
bad, but I wouldn't mind, you know, branching out a little, hooking
up with somebody, you know what I mean, man, something like that.
But never mind, what I'm saying is, let me hit you with this man. I
got a friend. I grew up, I did time with, reform school, the Life,
with this dude, and he grew up, when I came here, he became, like
Marzette's number-three, number-four dude. I'm not shitting about
that . . ."

What is here intended to impress Jimmy Brown is the name of the
black man Henry Marzette, the one-time narcotics cop turned pusher,
who ran the biggest narcotics ring in Detroit until his death in 1972
and who at the time of his death was reputed to be on the verge of
establishing an Asian connection for heroin independent of the
Italian syndicate. However, Jimmy Brown betrayed no special interest in hearing Marzette's name mentioned, and Hassan is obliged to
keep right on going:

". . . and so anyhow I was thinking about getting in touch, going
out there or something. Like I never had the dust myself, right, but
what I been thinking was maybe I could get there, see him and
everything, and I mean I don't have to tell you, everybody knows
what Marzette has going, with that Hong-Kong man, that China-man,
whoever the fuck he was, right? No brother never done better than
that Marzette, right man?

"Well, so here's what I'm thinking . . ."

At that point the waitress comes by, college girl, white, long brown hair, clean smile, asking if everybody is satisfied. Courvoisier and White Label are the orders for Reggie and Jimmy respectively, but when Jimmy rather grudgingly offers Bobby Hassan a drink, Bobby feels that he'd damn well better decline.

"Yeh, well go on."

And indeed, Bobby feels like he is running out of time now. "Okay. So I figure. You just could pay me on a regular basis. You know, man? Just put me on, nothing special. Just like all the rest of your boys, not that I need it or anything, you realize, but part of the deal, you get? And I call up my friend, go out there, get into things, and maybe we got dynamite . . . You get me, man? Then maybe we talk from there.

"Like, man, remember, we were in the same fix once you and me, remember, Jimmy, how I scored that time?" Bobby Hassan laughs now, recalling maybe his one moment of glory in the field of pushing, back in the drug panic of 1965, when he'd first met Jimmy Brown, who was then a hustler pretty much like himself, although considerably younger and already with the crucial local connections and the big-league savvy. "I bet even you were stuck, ain't that right, man? Bet it, shit, I *remember* it. There's Jimmy Brown, out in the streets not knowing where to look, that's what they told me, man, that's just what they told me about you, when remember, I told you I had this friend, and you weren't goin' to believe me, or something like that, and I went over and scored. Man, wow! How I scored. The way stuff was then, I could of retired right then, ain't that right, man? Had me a *good* time for a while." For a few moments the good times memories rolling around in his brain make Bobby feel a little light-headed. The drug panic of 1965 had been a new experience for Bobby—nothing like it had ever happened in Detroit. He never did find out what caused it but for several weeks there were no drugs to be bought, not at any price. Junkies were all over the street pleading for drugs, stopping anybody they saw, asking, pleading for any kind of drugs, anything. At night they would sleep in hallways, waiting to make a connection, all of them moaning. If some pusher came down the street they would swarm all over him, it was like a mob scene.

Then, as quickly as it had happened, it stopped, the stuff came back and started moving on the street again. Bobby had learned some bitter lessons then about being an outsider. He had arrived from Detroit a few months earlier and now he found that he couldn't get any stuff in his own neighborhood. He started going all over town, into Spanish Harlem, down to the Lower East Side, anywhere—but nobody knew him. Going into blocks that you didn't know and where people didn't know you was dangerous. Once, in Spanish Harlem, he was stopped by two Puerto Ricans who beat him when he put up a struggle instead of giving them his money. Then he made contact with a guy he knew, a guy who had been born in New York and spoke enough Spanish that he could deal in the language. Now he was able to get a good stash of dope and for a while he was selling like crazy all over Central Harlem. Then when the drug panic was over, he was an outsider again, no connections, never quite able to get connected and make the big hustle. But Jimmy Brown's raised eyebrows are right there encouraging him to come back to the world, to Roko's and July 1971. And so sober now, with finality, Bobby Hassan says:

"Well, I'm telling you this again, man. I got this friend. I'm coming to you first, because I like the way you do. I could do good with you . . . But are we together, man? I got plenty to offer. I don't wanna have to go to some other dude . . . So you put me on?"

But now he has to wait. He's exhausted all his ploys. He's told Jimmy Brown every hustle he can think of.

Yet all Jimmy Brown does now is put his two hands over his mouth, like he is praying in some kind of special way. Although really all it does is hide what he is thinking and show off his hand-worked gold cuff links. Bobby Hassan keeps waiting. The eyes above the hands look cold . . . and it seems like Jimmy simply isn't going to say anything at all, like maybe he hasn't even been listening, he's been half-sleeping or thinking about a girl or something. Letting the coke feel real fine.

Then his hands fall from his mouth and he speaks: "Well lookit, Bobby, that's it, isn't it, your name, Bobby? Lookit, me and Reggie here, we got some things we gotta have some discussions about. So, uh, nice seeing you, right, man? . . ."

Thus the end of the line for Bobby Hassan on this particular hustle. No mistaking that it is time to leave. He edges away from the table, nodding good-by to Reggie. And to Jimmy: "But you'll let me know, right, man, you'll be thinking, right? It's real good, man. I'm holding it for you."

"Yeh, I'll let you know," says Jimmy Brown, his lip curling with considerably exaggerated contempt.

And Bobby Hassan is gone, back to the bar first, where he thinks he'll have a drink, get back in control of things a little, show that it is all okay, no feelings hurt, et cetera. But then the bar is so crowded, and not with his kind of folks at all, no sir, not all those dudes who look like they could be taking home twenty thou from General Motors. So out the door he goes. Maybe next to the Turf Club, uptown . . . However the first yellow cab he flags doesn't care to go to 137th and Lexington, not one bit, nor does the second. Lucky for Bobby there are gypsies cruising Columbus, and he finally gets one of them to take him up there.

Meanwhile, back at the table in the corner at Roko's, Jimmy and Reggie are putting the final touches on their freshly departed acquaintance. Jimmy, annoyed that the dude has taken up so much of his good humor, says, "Fucking junkie, always schemes, always pushing something, bullshit, get rich quick. One day he's gonna cross me on something, really get in the way, and I swear I'm gonna waste him."

Reggie says, "Fucking junkie. Who needs him? . . . But you know, what about what he was saying, that dude in Detroit? Man, you think? . . ."

Jimmy says, "If the dude's big, he can't have shit to do with that boy."

Reggie says, "Fucking junkie."

And that's the end of it. They start talking about a cop up in the 33rd precinct who'd been making a fortune by selling the stuff he'd confiscated from pushers on his beat. An interesting story, a dude to stay clear of, but nothing very unusual, they both agreed.

The Central Harlem Network

These scenes of part of the life of Central Harlem on a fairly typical day in July 1971 are drawn from the reports of the two field assistants who observed and interviewed in Central Harlem during that same time. They are only events that I have selected because they describe the kinds of crime activity we are interested in looking at and because they are illustrative of the points I want to make about how such activities fit together into an emerging pattern of organization among black crime activists. Much else happened in Central Harlem that day, just as in any other community. But the scenes I depict here are true; they did happen and they are happening every day. All of the characters, events and settings described are real. This realism, given in the words of the subjects themselves, in itself should convey some feeling for the immediacy and wholeness of life in black organized crime groups. But, since I will be presenting a number of such sketches, it should be possible to do a great deal more than simply describe what is happening. With the obvious exception of the meeting in Roko's between Reggie and Jimmy, the three short episodes are seemingly unrelated. Each describes a discrete set of events in three operations that seem to share little besides the fact that all of the people involved are black and most of them come from the same twenty-five-block area of Central Harlem. Neither do they seem to be very large-scale operations, involving hundreds of operatives in multimillion-dollar schemes, as is true in Italian-American crime families. Actually, as we shall shortly see, there are a number of connections among the people involved in these three episodes and they do form a definable "network" that reaches out to include hundreds of people—boosters, drug pushers, fences, gamblers, loan sharks, pimps, police, politicians and prostitutes, as well as thousands of customers—and that has a combined income in excess of $1 million each year. But we should be able to learn much more than size and probable income from looking at how these three operations join together to form a crime network and then comparing it with other networks that we shall examine later. Consider, for example, what we might generalize—on a very tentative basis—from these three brief segments of daily life and how they are related. First, what do they tell us about the people involved and how they relate to each other?

Essentially, they tell three interwoven stories that describe some of the organized crime activities that take place in Harlem. The first episode describes prostitution as a form of black enterprise that caters to the needs and vices of the white world outside Harlem. The amounts of money involved seem small when compared to the amounts involved in the numbers or in narcotics, but they are still substantial: our informant estimated that Reggie Martin probably makes about $150,000 per year through pimping. The number of people involved in the operation also seems quite small, although Reggie's stable of eight women is quite large compared to most. Martin also seems to be an independent operator, not linked to any larger syndicate, black or white, although he does maintain contacts with other pimps. The whole operation, in keeping with the fact that it involves women and the use of their bodies, seems to depend for its success or failure more on the personal feelings its members harbor for each other than we would probably find true in other organized crime activities such as narcotics or gambling. This is evidenced by favors, love, security and the personal relationship Martin maintains with each of his "wives." Certainly, however, there is also fear, hatred and even physical abuse at times. A major part of Reggie's success— and he is considered a very successful pimp—is the fact that none of his women is hooked on hard drugs.

The second episode tells the story of a small but legitimate black businessman who almost inadvertently discovered the profits that could accrue to him from dealing in contraband. As a result, he went on to develop a complex of criminal operations: the sale of stolen clothing, loan sharking, gambling and an after-hours bar, giving him a net worth of $500,000. None of Thomas Irwin's criminal activities is likely to offend even the most high-minded of the residents of his Harlem neighborhood. In fact, each and every one of Irwin's activities seems to provide a valued public service, and Irwin is respected and emulated in his neighborhood. He has nothing to do with narcotics; violence never seems to come even close to touching him or his business. So tentative and uncertain is Irwin's commitment to illicit activity that he has frequently been concerned with the problem of gaining too much criminal notoriety. By way of contrast, the thieves who supply Irwin with clothing are not nearly so ingenuous about the criminality of their lives as Thomas Irwin (with the support of his neighbors) seems to be. This is perhaps because they live so much closer to fear and violence and capture and because in their criminal activities so much more depends on alertness and skill. Note, however, that each of the thieves is a drug addict, a habit that keeps them dependent on Irwin.

The last episode concerns two hustlers, both of whom are involved in the drug trade, but there the similarity ends. James Mitchell, because he grew up in Harlem, because he has life-long friends there, has a certain pedigree, a certain reputation that gives him acceptance and the right connections. These connections are not just in crime circles but in the community as well. Jimmy has made it big in the hustling life and is now branching out into legitimate businesses. He maintains a distance between his drug trafficking and his boutiques. Our informant estimates that his combined income from both the legal and the illegal activities is in excess of $200,000 a year.

Bobby Hassan is a low-level hustler, a drug pusher who lives from day to day and actually operates on the fringes of organized crime. Some of the difference between Bobby and Mitchell may well result from personal characteristics, drive and ability, but in large measure they stem from the fact that while Jimmy is connected, known, and respected, Bobby is not. Bobby is an addict and inevitably this must raise serious questions among crime associates as to his reliability. But he also suffers from being an outsider, a migrant from Detroit who does not have the life-long associations that are the cornerstone of Mitchell's success. His greatest moment in New York was during a drug panic when, through friendship with another black who did know New York, he was able to obtain a quantity of drugs and began to establish a reputation on the street. When the drug panic passed, however, his connections fell apart and he had no pedigree to fall back on. Today he still remembers his one big score and dreams the hustler's dream of putting it all together again.

What we know from each of these episodes, however, is still very general. We know something about who is involved and how they operate but not enough about how they relate to each other to make any judgments about their behavior as a group. If we look a little more carefully at the episodes we can begin to find some similarities among them that might allow us to make some tentative guesses about how each group is organized and how its members relate to each other over time. This permits us to make some beginning assumptions about where to look for the rules that govern these relationships and eventually to build a model of what black organized crime groups really look like.

There is enough information in each of the episodes to illustrate how this might be done. The first episode, because it deals with a small number of people with a well-patterned set of relationships, is a good place to begin. Reggie Martin, the pimp, is the leader in this group. His relationship with each of his wives is roughly the same. Certainly he has closer relationships with some than with others and the quality of the interaction he has with each may differ from time to time but he is always the leader.

Martin's relations with his prostitutes generally can be put at this: his women stick close to him because they believe that he will lead them to wealth. Martin has all the physical attributes, style and manner that attract women, but in addition to that, his unwillingness to involve himself in any activities that might jeopardize his prostitution business and his ability to maintain a reputation as a man who supplies safe, healthy and unhooked women makes him seem to prostitutes a reliable choice, that is, a pimp who will make them prosperous. Martin's women have never testified against him in court, with the result that he has never gone to jail.

His relationship with Lucy Greer, however, was somewhat different. Reggie was Lucy's childhood "prince." It was she who, when she got out of jail, led him into the pimping life. She showered gifts on him, and she loved him. And when she went into prostitution she made him her pimp, she in fact made him a *good* pimp. Our informant here tells us that the best pimps are those who are made pimps by prostitutes, rather than vice versa, since when the former happens there is much that the prostitute will likely be able to teach the new pimp about how to treat women. It was Lucy Greer who conceived the scheme of sending money orders to the lonely girls who were Lucy Greer's friends when she was incarcerated and who remained in jail after she got out. It was these girls, shunned by their families and their men, who came to Reginald Martin and Lucy Greer when they got out of jail and who eventually served to make up Martin's stable.

This abstract of the relationships within the episode makes it a little easier to talk about the relationships. It also gives us some sense of how the group is structured, but it would be almost impossible to use such descriptive material as a basis for comparing varieties of organized crime groups to see what is common and what is different in their social structure. What would be helpful would be some form of blueprint, some map that could display the relationships visually in much the same way that a kinship chart allows anthropologists to describe the gestalt of family relationships. One of the reasons why kinship charts have been used so successfully by anthropologists, however, is that they are representations, a shorthand, of an already defined group called a family. We know, generally, who is in it and who is not. When I studied the Lupollos, for example, I knew who was in the family and who was not because the traditional Italian-American organized crime family was already a commonly accepted pattern of organization. Our problem in trying to chart relationships among black and Hispanic organized crime activists who are in interaction is that we did not even know if they were or were not a group and we had no idea what such a group might or might not look like. All we knew was that one individual interacted with another who in turn interacted with others. What we needed was something that had the utility and simplicity of a kinship chart but would allow us to indicate who was related to whom without really understanding, as yet, the nature of the relationships or whether they did or did not represent some structured type of group. Then, by comparing the charts of the various patterns of social relationships we were observing we might be able to identify some common pattern of organization that would tell us what the equivalent of the Italian-American organized crime family is or will be among blacks and Hispanics.

There is such a device in anthropology and, although it is not as well developed and accepted as kinship charting, it has some utility for our problem. The concept of a *network* or web of relationships is of fairly respectable antiquity in anthropology but it was not until J. A. Barnes wrote a paper in 1954 in which he formally defined the term that "network" began to be a significant anthropological tool. Barnes' original vision of a network is still the best description:

Each person is, as it were, in touch with a number of other people, some of whom are directly in touch with each other and some of whom are not . . . I find it convenient to talk of a social field of this kind as a *network*. The image I have is of a net of points, some of which are joined by lines. The points of the image are people . . . and the lines indicate which people interact with each other.[1]

Applying this notion of a social field to Reggie Martin's case we can represent the network of relationships we have seen by a diagram, a map, in which each of the people involved with him is represented by a point and in which lines are drawn between points to indicate when two people are in one way or another interacting with one another. Thus, we know that Reggie was in interaction with Lucy Greer and so we can draw a line between the two of them to represent this relationship. Reggie also interacts directly with each of his prostitutes so that if we draw a line from him to each of them this begins to form a net. We also know that Lucy Greer was in interaction with each of the prostitutes because she recruited many of

---

[1] J. A. Barnes, "Class and Committees in a Norwegian Island Parish," *Human Relations,* 7 (No. 1, 1954), 38–39.

them and, as Reggie's number-one wife, she was responsible for handling some of Reggie's relationships with them. So we can draw a line from Lucy to each of the prostitutes. So far everything I have described is fairly standard practice in network charting. There are some other things we know (or don't know), however, that I thought were important to display in charts, so I elaborated the technique somewhat. We know that Lucy's relationship with Reggie was closer than his relationship with any of his other wives. This can be shown by making the line between Reggie and Lucy darker than the others. What we don't know, however, is what interaction if any there is among the various prostitutes, a fact we can display by using a dotted line to indicate a suspected or assumed but unconfirmed relationship.

Reggie's stable of girls, however, is not really an organized crime network in the sense that I shall be using the term to describe the patterns of organization we observed and charted among black and Hispanic organized crime activists. One reason why it is not is that we already know a great deal about its purpose, how it got started and who its leader is: Reggie is the originator and the leader and its purpose is prostitution. Reggie's ring is what is known in network analysis as an *action set,* a net of social relationships that has an originator who makes the decision for the members to work together for a common goal. Using network charting here doesn't tell us anything we don't already know unless we are interested in how Reggie's action set can be viewed as a *partial network*—a segment or extract of some larger network with which it shares some common goals and membership. This immediately suggests the second reason why I do not present Reggie's operation as a network. My real interest in Reggie and his stable is as part of a wider network of crime activists and how his operation is linked to those of Thomas Irwin and James Mitchell, since we know that he has some contact with them. It is only by understanding how separate operations such as these are linked that some beginning idea of how black and Hispanic crime activists are organized and how that organization relates to the community and to society can emerge.

In the second episode there is a greater complexity of relationships and also one character—Calvin Meadows—who ties the Martin and Irwin action sets together. The characters in this episode are Thomas Irwin, the legitimate businessman who has gradually fallen deeper and deeper into crime; his original three thieves, Philip Thomas, Elizabeth Dukes and her husband, Cleveland Dukes; Tippy Jones, who replaced Philip Thomas when he went off to jail; Calvin Meadows, who manages Irwin's after-hours bar, from which we know he steers customers to Reggie Martin's girls; and Richard Williams, the hardware store man who doubles as a clandestine master key maker. There is one additional character who should be added at this point. The field assistant who described this operation gained entry to the network because, prior to going to prison, he was schooled in the art of boosting by Cleveland Dukes. So our informant should be included as part of the network also. So far, the two action sets are still only a partial network because we know that Reggie, at least, maintains some contact with James Mitchell.

The third action set is again a fairly simple one involving only James Mitchell, the leader of an organized group of drug pushers; Bobby Hassan, an unconnected and largely unsuccessful small-time hustler, and Reggie Martin, whom we already know from the first episode. Now, taking each of the three episodes and the characters who are part of them, we can begin to look at how each of these seemingly separate operations fit together. Reggie Martin and James Mitchell are business partners in a boutique that Mitchell started and Reggie bought into seeking to put some of his money from prostitution into a legitimate field of investment. Reggie has known James Mitchell ever since childhood when both grew up on 143rd Street in Harlem but, as far as we were able to find out, the boutique is their first joint venture. The friendship between Reggie and Mitchell brought them together but it is their partnership in the boutique that links Reggie's prostitution activity to Mitchell's drug ring. There seems to be no functional relationship between the two; in fact, as we have seen, Reggie is antagonistic toward heroin and refuses to allow his girls to use or deal in it, but the profits from the two operations are commingled in the seemingly legitimate boutique business. Actually, there is an informal business relationship between Reggie's pimping and Mitchell's drug pushing. Because they do know each other and are linked together in some activities, Reggie's girls know who Mitchell is and steer their customers who want drugs to one of Mitchell's pushers and Mitchell in turn sends customers to Reggie's girls. There is no formal relationship between the two rings but, as we shall see over and over again in later networks, it is the informal connection between two people in two different sets of operations, often developed in childhood gangs or in prison, that ties two sets of operations together. These relationships, which are described in street language as "having my man" in some other area of criminal action, develop informally out of friendships or even chance meetings but eventually are formalized and become the basis for the growth of small independent action sets into larger networks.

While the friendship between Reggie and Mitchell is the most obvious one connecting two of the episodes together, there are others. Reggie Martin's friend and companion on his drive to Riker's Island, Calvin Meadows, is also the manager of Thomas Irwin's after-hours club, and we know that Reggie and his girls steer customers there for after-hours drinking and gambling just as Calvin sends customers to Reggie's girls. We also know from interviews that actually took place after the events described here that Mitchell, as well as Reggie, on occasion buys stolen clothes from Thomas Irwin to sell in their boutique. We do not know how Mitchell came into contact with Irwin, if Reggie Martin because he knows Calvin Meadows mentioned Irwin's operation to Mitchell or if there is some other form of contact. Remember, however, that the three leaders of these three operations —Reggie Martin, James Mitchell and Thomas Irwin—all live in the same Harlem area, and just as neighbors in any community establish mutually advantageous business relationships that grow out of social contacts, this happens in crime as well.

Finally, the field assistant who reported the operations of Martin and of Mitchell also knows Bobby Hassan. It was the other field assistant in Central Harlem, however, who knew of Thomas Irwin's operations because of his former working relationship with Cleveland

Dukes. Adding all of the relationships we know about in all three of the operations we described earlier, we end up with the full network chart shown below.

The process just described is the way we identified each of the organized crime networks. Once we had identified a network, we used a variety of fairly standard anthropological techniques—observing and recording behavior through participant observation, tape-recording interviews, keeping records of daily activities in the neighborhoods, drawing charts or maps of who was in interaction with whom under what circumstances, collecting a few life histories of crime activists and intensive reporting and analysis of some critical or recurring event or happening in the neighborhood. From all of this we hoped to get reliable information on:

· Who interacts with whom under what circumstances in organized crime in the ghetto and what is the frequency and intensity of the contact?

· What is the nature of the social relationships established by this interaction in terms of mutual rights and obligations, patterns of dominance and submission (or who leads and who follows under different circumstances) and other factors that define and explain the quality and purpose of the relationship?

· What are the codes of rules that regularize and regulate these relationships and how are they learned and enforced?

· How do organized crime activists in ghetto areas organize themselves into groups and how do they describe these groups and their relationship to the community and to society?

Over an eighteen-month period we observed who was in interaction with whom and under what circumstances. Then, by painstakingly going over the field notes of the assistants, we identified sets of people who seemed to work together with some frequency. Through constant analysis of the field reports, we gradually built these small nets of relationships into larger ones until we felt that we had identified a functioning network of crime activists. We did not go into the field with some preconceived notion of what a network would look like and then manage to find it; rather, we went out and constructed

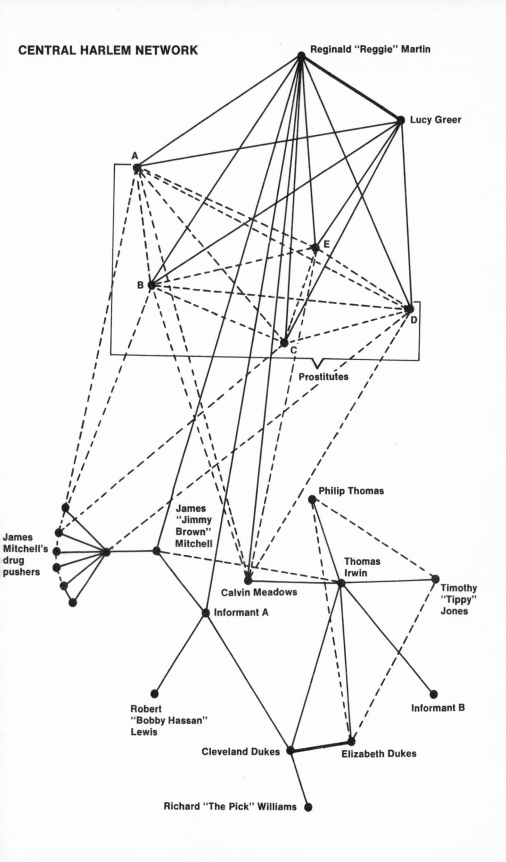

CENTRAL HARLEM NETWORK

Reginald "Reggie" Martin

Lucy Greer

A

E

B

D

C

Prostitutes

Philip Thomas

James
"Jimmy
Brown"
Mitchell

Thomas
Irwin

James
Mitchell's
drug
pushers

Calvin Meadows

Timothy
"Tippy"
Jones

Informant A

Robert
"Bobby Hassan"
Lewis

Informant B

Cleveland Dukes

Elizabeth Dukes

Richard "The Pick" Williams

the network from the bits and pieces of information we gathered. Each network chart presented (*see* Appendix B) is the visual repro- duction of months of observing, recording and plotting of relation- ships, checking them out in later observations, gradually connecting sets of relationships as we learned that Reggie Martin, who is in prostitution, shares friendship and some business connections with James Mitchell, who is in drugs, and then trying to find out who else both of them work with.

Network charting used alone, however, seems to do little more than allow us a device to display and examine a set of social relation- ships as a totality and to begin to look for some patterns by compar- ing charts. The charts do not, for example, tell us very much about the vertical (hierarchical) patterns of crime organizaiton because they do not show the nature of the relationship between two people, only that a relationship does, in fact, exist. Yet we know, even from the three short episodes we saw earlier, that even at this level among blacks, crime organizations are not cooperatively organized but are instead a hierarchy of crime operatives. At the bottom are the con- sumers: drug users, numbers players, buyers of contraband and the Johns who patronize prostitutes. On the next level are the dealers, the retailers who sell the dope, collect the gamblers' money, sell the stolen goods or give their bodies in trade. Above these dealers are the suppliers or wholesalers, the organizers of organized crime. These are the men (and women) who procure the drug supplies, plan the sales and organize the numbers operations and the theft of goods. In most cases these operatives are unknown to the consumer level and may even have put someone as a buffer between themselves and the dealers. And, in my definition of organized crime, the public which demands the illegal goods and services and the corrupt officials who protect the operations for profit must be included in any analysis of organized crime as a social system. None of this could show up in a network chart. The informal patterns diagrammed in network charts are important, however. It is these informal—lateral—patterns that condition the "real life" nature of organized crime procedures. And they determine in many ways the "crime chances" of individuals potentially active in illegal operations.

Informal patterns in crime have to do with communications, face-to-face relations, access to crime opportunities and the possibilities of turning chance circumstances and situations into encounters with profit making in crime. All in all, the life patterns of individuals are in part determined by the networks of communications that exist in crime activities in the various racial-ethnic communities. A youngster on 125th Street in Harlem will encounter crime activities and operatives many times more than a youngster in a suburban town or even in other sections of the city.

The three episodes I have described earlier do not, of course, form any adequate basis for making any but the most tentative generalizations about black organized crime networks. But in order to begin the process of framing questions, let me speculate on a few such questions that could be raised even at this point. First, taking just one of the episodes, Thomas Irwin and his boosters, what points emerge here that might be interesting to look at comparatively in other networks?

1. A successful black organized crime activist may be respected and even emulated by his neighbors, provided he isn't involved in something messy like narcotics, and he offers some form of community service.
2. An activity or set of activities that can be formally defined as illegal can, with community acceptance if not support, actually be run along lines very similar to those of legitimate small businesses.
3. If he is involved in socially acceptable and noncompetitive activities, a successful leader of a black crime network need not resort to violence.
4. Once a black man slips into one area of criminal activity, he can expand quickly into related areas.
5. A crime activist who is addicted to drugs does not seem to rise above the lowest levels of an organization.

The next step, of course, was to see if any of these generalizations emerge often enough in the various networks to warrant incorporation into the theoretical model we were building. As we look at the other networks, we see that these five do. For now, consider just the last of these: *Drug users do not go very far up the ladder in organized crime hierarchies.* In two of the episodes this point emerges with clarity; Bobby Hassan and Thomas Irwin's thieves are all users and each remains at a low level. To organize, deal and sell illegal merchandise or to hustle in the big leagues requires a degree of expertise of its own and few drug users can sustain the discipline necessary to these tasks. For this reason addicts are an especially impotent group of people and their frequent arrest by the police increases their impotence, a fact that surfaces in many of the networks we will look at later. Neither can they command the level of trust necessary in the cooperative activities of organized crime.

There are many other tentative assumptions we might make from these episodes, but to understand them fully requires more experience with the networks that follow. These networks were developed from our field experience in precisely the same way as the one we have just analyzed. In each case we began by looking for patterns of relationship and once we had extended those patterns to cover as many sets of relationships as we could, we closed the net and began intensive observation and interviewing of those crime activists and their associates within the net. Taken together these networks describe the totality of organized crime networks we discovered. There is much to see within them. They speak of gambling, prostitution, violence and corruption. They cover a range of activities from gangland killings to the semilegal gypsy cab industry. But of equal importance is the relationships they show between those in the net—the gamblers, pimps and drug pushers—and those outside—their customers and their protectors. We see organized crime as a community ethos with many of the crime activists obtaining some degree of respect in their neighborhoods but we also see that some of the services these crime activists provide now reach outside the ghetto and find support there as well.

In the next chapter we see a very different level of organization, in a quite different type of community. One of the field assistants lived in Paterson, New Jersey, and through him we were able to identify and follow one large network there, which is especially interesting since, because of its size and complexity, it gives a good picture of a black organized crime network that is much more fully developed than the one in Central Harlem and that maintains an important connection to the Italian crime syndicate. The network in Paterson also presents a dramatic example of the conflict and violence that can accompany ethnic succession in organized crime.

2

PATERSON, NEW JERSEY

✠

EVEN IN the New Jersey Meadowland the dusk was beautiful on that cold, icily clear day in late November. From where the two policemen were squatting they could have looked over the top of the swamp grass and seen the Manhattan skyline twenty miles away, glittering pink and gray in the last rays of the twilight sun.

But the two officers were preoccupied. They were studying a body that lay face down in the half-frozen mud. "Jesus, they just threw him here like an old mattress spring," said Brian Mulcahy, the older of the officers. "Bring me a stick."

Near the carcass of a pickup truck that had rusted to a point just short of oblivion, officer Nelson Engroff found a branch. Together the officers rolled the body over on its back.

"Man, look at the job they did on him," said Engroff. "They cut it off."

After eighteen years of highway work Mulcahy had grown accustomed to head-on collisions, roll-overs, multiple fatalities, the worst that cars and roads can do to men, women and children, but murders —and particularly this kind of murder—still made him nervous. His voice was edgy when he called in on the patrol car radio.

"We've got a homicide."

"Go ahead." The voice from the radio shack was bored and a little impatient.

"The deceased is a Negro male about forty years old. Looks like he was shot repeatedly at close range. . . . The deceased subject's sexual organ has been severed from his body . . ."

"A mob job?" The voice on the radio had become more interested.

"I guess so. You know who I think this is? I think it's the nigger from down in Pat . . ."

"This is an open transmission." The voice was irritated again.

"I think it's that colored from down in Paterson who was muscling the Turk. I can't remember his name."

"Wait a minute," said the voice. "Let me ask around here . . ." The voice was silent for a few minutes and then crackled back on: "Willie C. Squires."

"Yeah, that's the one I'm thinking of."

Engroff had returned to the patrol car and was rubbing warmth into his hands. "Wow, they really stopped him from screwing around."

"That's what the newspapers call a 'gangland style' killing," Mulcahy said. "Glamorous, huh?"

"Oh, yeah. You bet. You know who he was?"

"I think that was Willie C. Squires, the biggest nigger hustler in north Jersey. He used to work for the Turk down in Paterson. Then the way I understand it he split off from the Turk and tried to muscle the Turk out. Now there's no way in the world you can do that, because when you push the Turk, you push Velia and when you push Velia, you push the organization. Any nigger who's crazy enough to do that is going to get what Willie got."

Engroff didn't bring the subject up again until their shift was almost over. "You know," he said, "I don't know if I go along with you. There are a lot of crazy, rebel blacks running around now. They'll burn down Newark, tear up Asbury Park, anything. I'm not sure there are enough Turks around to keep them in line."

JOE THE TURK

Although everyone called him the Turk, Joseph Hajar wasn't really a Turk at all. He was a Syrian, or at least his parents were Syrian. Hajar himself had been born on Atlantic Avenue in Brooklyn. As an explosive teenager, he used to blow up every time someone would call him the Turk. It was like calling a Sicilian "Frenchie" or an Irishman "Limey."

"I'm a better Catholic than any of you goddamn guineas," Hajar would rage. Then he would put his head down and drive his short but powerful body into whoever or whatever was closest to him and try to tear his tormentors apart. In those days it took five or six strong guys to hold him down. When he was quieted down they'd laugh and pat him on the head and call him the Turk all over again just to see him turn into a fireball.

But after a while Hajar got used to the nickname. Not only did he get used to it, he began to find it useful. It fit him. He was a quick, furious, ruthless fighter, and being called the Turk added to his reputation. A Syrian was just a rug merchant, but a Turk was a fearsome fighter. Just hearing his nickname took a little of the fight out of his opponents. And so by the common consent of his allies, his enemies and Hajar himself, he became the Turk.

The Turk was still a strong man. As he sat on the barstool he studied his heavy forearms resting on the bar, and he twisted his wrists to flex the muscles. He was fifty, but he hadn't lost any muscle. He was just as strong physically as he had been twenty years earlier. He wasn't going to let anybody say he wasn't.

But knowing that didn't seem to help much any more. He was depressed and vaguely nervous on this day. Ever since he had pulled himself out of bed at 2 P.M., he had been chain-smoking Chesterfield Kings and reading through all the newspapers—all the New York papers, all the New Jersey papers—just as he had been doing every day for almost a week. It was almost 5 P.M. and he still didn't know much more.

It was eighteen months after the body of Willie Squires had been found in the swamp. The police had come. The Turk had told them he didn't know anything about it, which he still swore to everyone was the truth. It must have been the Galente gang that killed him, the Turk had insisted. He knew that not many people believed him, certainly not Willie's brother, that wild man "Bro." But there was something else on the Turk's mind this day. It was just one week after the murder of Tommy Velia, head of the Bergen County syndicate and the Turk's protector.

And the Turk didn't know who had done it. Was it part of the war between the Gallos and the Colombos? Was it Cosimo Galente who had ordered it? Was it a bunch of crazy blacks like Bro Squires, trying to get even for Willie? The Turk didn't know any more than he read in the stupid newspapers. Some guys in a panel truck shot Tommy Velia down on Utica Avenue in Brooklyn early one morning. Period. That was all he knew. The Turk looked out the window as though he half-expected to see a shotgun pointed into the bar ready to blast his head off. But all he saw was what he always saw, one of the empty streets on Paterson's Temple Hill. He stared for a minute at the house directly across the street, a crumbling frame house covered with tarpaper disguised to look like yellow brick. What a crummy shit hole this black neighborhood is, the Turk thought.

"Did Elsie call?" Without looking up from the *Paterson Evening News* the Turk spoke to the bartender, Tommy Washington. The Turk thought that Washington was probably the one person left in the world he could speak to without having to look into his eyes to see if he was lying or not. Tommy was black but the two of them had too much in common to let race get in the way of a long trust. They both were proud of their physical strength, and they both had wanted to be prizefighters early in their lives. That was a bond. Tommy was not even six feet tall, but he was almost as wide as he was high and was probably the strongest man in Paterson. On slow nights the hookers used to make book on how many times he could lift a beer keg over his head.

"Uh-uh, she didn't call," said Tommy.

The Turk was furious but he kept it to himself. That goddam black whore. He had made her his mistress. He had done more than that for her. He had made her his number-one assistant. Black women are smart, he always said. Black men are dumb. Forget the men. It's the women who count. But Elsie Payne had changed a lot lately. She was getting too independent. There was no longer any respect in her voice when she called him the Turk. She said it like it was a joke. For all the Turk knew, she was plotting against him with Bro Squires.

The Turk was getting tired of it all. How many years had he been in Paterson? He counted them: thirty-five. Ever since his parents had thrown him out of Atlantic Avenue. He still missed that old Syrian and Lebanese neighborhood, missed the Arabic music in the air, missed the import shops with their rugs showing pictures of Damascus. Of course, he understood now that it was mostly Puerto Rican. Jesus, he thought, just like Paterson. Those spics will drive people out of every place in this country.

The Turk remembered how on steamy summer days like this one they used to run barefoot up and down Atlantic Avenue, stopping off at Alwan's to beg for an apricot ice. Then they used to steal jars of olives and after eating the olives they'd throw the jars at the watchmen on the Brooklyn docks.

They were wild kids. When they got older they broke into the trucks along the docks and ran off with whatever they could. Once they found a case of bourbon, and what they didn't drink they threw, dizzily drunk, at passing cars and buses. Some nights they would sneak across the Brooklyn Bridge into "New York," which is what everyone in Brooklyn used to call Manhattan. Only Manhattan was "New York." They'd go look for Chinese to beat up. Then they would run all the way back across the bridge, half-laughing in delirium and half-screaming in terror that the cops or the Chinks were going to get them.

Hajar's parents found it impossible to control him, and so when an aunt and an uncle moved to Paterson to work in one of the textile mills, Hajar was packed off with them. Hajar's parents hoped that "the country" would cure him, but cure him or kill him they were at least glad to get rid of him.

Hajar hated Paterson at first, hated the Irish and the Italians and the Slovaks who called him the Turk. But he learned to get along on his reckless brutality. No one pushed the Turk around for too long. And then when he was nineteen he got a job pumping gas in a service station, and that's when he stopped being just a wild street fighter and occasional thief. That's when he made his first contact with organized crime.

Hajar had been at the station only a couple of weeks when he caught on to what the owner, Mike Daddario, was up to. It was during World War II and gas was rationed, but somehow Daddario was stealing ration cards and reselling them to customers. The Turk didn't say anything. Instead, he started stealing money from the cash register from time to time, a five here, a ten there. It wasn't long before the owner got suspicious and confronted him, but the Turk just laughed and told him that if he tried to turn him in or even fire him, he would go to the feds.

From then on they were partners. And the Turk soon learned that the phony ration cards were just a small part of Daddario's illegal operation. It was also an important waystation for a gang of car thieves. They brought the stolen cars into the station, filed down the engine numbers, repainted them and sold them as far away as Pennsylvania. The Turk learned the trade quickly, and within no time at all he was part of the gang. It was a mixed bunch, some Irish, some Slovaks and some Italians, and it was through the gang that the Turk first heard about an up-and-coming operator, Tommy Velia.

Before the car thieves had a chance to expand their activities into other areas, however, several members, including the Turk himself, were caught and sent to prison. The three-year prison term interrupted the Turk's career, but in a very important way it advanced it as well. Because he refused to squeal on members of the gang who weren't caught, he earned a reputation for tough silence that matched his reputation as a ferocious street fighter and brawler. Just as important, in prison he had met "Ponzi" Ponzillo, who later became Velia's "man" in Paterson.

The Turk came out of prison full of confidence, although not quite sure whether he was going straight or into the rackets. The only useful thing his uncle had ever told him was this: "We Syrians know how to make it. You go into any town in this country and you look in the phone book and you see if they got a Jew, a Greek and a Syrian. If they do, you know there's a living that can be made in that town. If you don't see any of them, that town is hopeless. Get out."

The Turk decided to go into business for himself and since Paterson passed his uncle's test, the Turk decided to stay in Paterson. He tried a number of things, door-to-door selling, freelance automobile repairing. He made a bare living, but the Turk wanted more. Then he heard about a chance to buy a tavern in a section of the city on the other side of the Passaic River called Temple Hill. It was an old Slovak neighborhood that since the war had been fast turning into a Negro neighborhood. The Slovak who owned the bar wanted out, and he was willing to give the Turk the place for a couple of thousand dollars.

The Turk took it. It didn't bother him that it was a colored neighborhood. Puerto Ricans he didn't like, but colored never bothered him. In fact, as soon as he bought the place he saw that there were opportunities in the changing neighborhood that the previous owner had overlooked. The Turk set up a little numbers operation. There was nothing wrong with that. All the colored played the numbers, the Turk knew, and no one in the community was going to object.

The numbers was a black savings bank. These people never saved any money anyhow. So they'd play a few bucks on the numbers every week. They were bound to hit a few times in their lives and when they did they could pay off some debts or buy a new sofa or quit a lousy job and go out and get drunk for a few months. They needed it.

It's a simple game. All the customer has to do is pick a number from 1 to 999. Then he gives his number plus his money to a runner, the lowest man in the numbers hierarchy. Sometimes the runner goes to the customer, such as a runner who makes the rounds in a factory. Other runners let the customers come to them. The Turk started out as a runner but he knew from the beginning that he wanted to go higher, up where the Italians were.

The runner hands the money over to a controller. Each controller has a dozen or so runners reporting to him. In eight months Hajar was the first non-Italian controller in Paterson. The controller disciplines the runners, keeps the accounts tabulated and passes the money up to the big man, the banker. And soon the Turk was the big man, taking in the money and paying off the winners.

The winning number has to be unpredictable, of course, and a number that people trust in, one that can't be easily fixed, such as some day-in and day-out number that appears in the daily paper. In the Turk's operation it was the last three digits of the total amount wagered at a nearby race track. If the total amount bet that day was $3,428,348, the winning number would be 348. The chances of a customer hitting that number are 1 in 999, but the payoff in Paterson at that time was $741 on the dollar, higher than it was in New York but still leaving a margin of $258 out of every thousand. That $258 is split up among the runners, the controllers and the banker.

And then there's a fourth party that has to be cut in, the organization. That's where Ponzi came in. Everybody needs the organization —the banker, the controllers, the runners, even the customers. Here's why. Only a big organization can handle the "layoffs," that is, can pay up when the bank gets hit very hard. Suppose a lot of people play the same number one day. For example, when Willie Mays hit his 599th home run, a lot of black people played "600" the next day, figuring Willie was going to make it and so were they. If that number had come up, the banker would have been wiped out, and not only that, a lot of customers would have gone without their payoffs. The whole system would have collapsed.

The Turk explained to people why they needed the organization and everybody agreed that the Turk was right. There was another reason they needed the organization. Only the organization had the money and the muscle to keep the cops and politicians from breaking up the game and shaking down the players and the operators. Ponzi controlled the cops and politicians in Paterson, and because he was part of the Velia organization he could fix things at the county and even the state level.

Except for the organization and the Turk himself, everybody in the operation was black. It had to be that way. It didn't make sense any other way. It wouldn't have made sense to have some white guy running around collecting numbers in a black shop. He'd arouse suspicion and get himself shaken down by some wise guy. More important, having blacks run the operation kept the community quiet. It assured the community that at least not all of the profits were going into white hands.

Even the Turk was surprised at how well things went. In time, he was taking in $15,000 a day on the numbers alone, and he didn't let the profits lie around. Get that money out on the street, the Velia organization told him. Keep it working. The Turk kept the money circulating, loaned out at Shylock rates ($50 borrowed on Sunday had to be paid back as $60 on Monday). But the Turk told himself that it wasn't so high an interest rate, considering that these people had no collateral and a lot of them no jobs and bad credit references. Let them try to get it from the bank.

In the back of the tavern he opened a room where the sporting crowd could shoot craps and play Georgia skin. (In Georgia skin, the cards are dealt face up around the table. If a player gets a matched pair he's out.) As "house man" the Turk got a cut from every pot and loaned out money at the $60 for $50 rates. The players wanted women and so the Turk got them women. They were a better class than the street hookers, too. No VD. The Turk was very insistent that they be clean. At least he was at first. He fixed up a few rooms over the bar, where the girls could take their customers. He charged $2 for each room, and the girls got to keep whatever price they could command above that.

The Turk's power on Temple Hill was unquestioned. None of Ponzi's men were going to try to push him off. They were happy to stay down in the Italian neighborhood on the other side of the Passaic River down on Market and Cianci, where they could hang out around the Sons of Italy Hall and the Italian Sports Center. They were happy to take their cut from the Turk's action. Let the Turk live with the *tutzones* up on the hill.

Certainly, no one in the Turk's own operation ever challenged his authority. Back in those days the Turk was a figure of awesome power, who was keeping not only the Italians but also the politicians and the police from robbing and terrorizing them. The Turk liked to make the people of the hill believe that his power was limitless, and one day he had a brainstorm.

He was out driving with Albert Montgomery. Al was one of the Turk's controllers and also supervisor of the loan shark operation. And in addition, he ran a legitimate dry cleaning store. As they were driving up on the hill, the Turk told Al that he had forgotten something and had to stop off at the mayor's office. He parked right in front of City Hall and told Al to wait in the car for him.

The Turk jumped out of the car and rushed inside City Hall. But once he was out of sight of Al, he simply strolled around, looking at portraits of former mayors and waiting for the first important-looking public figure he could find. He hit the jackpot. A police captain was leaving the building, and as he did, the Turk caught up with him and walked alongside.

Al was growing more and more uncomfortable parked in front of City Hall. Not too many blacks were seen on the streets of downtown Paterson in those days and passers-by were looking in at Al, wondering who he was to be parked in front of City Hall. Al looked up and saw the Turk walking side by side with the captain.

As soon as the Turk was certain that Al was looking, he turned to the captain and said, "Hi, captain, what do you think the Yankees' pennant chances are?" From where he was, Al couldn't hear the question. All he could see was the police captain turn toward the Turk and engage him in deep conversation for a few minutes.

"You sure are something," Al said when the Turk got back into the car, "talking turkey right out in the open like that."

"No, Al, you got it all wrong," said the Turk. "That's the safest place to talk. Any of these jerks walking by would think we were talking about the ball game or something. Only you and me know better."

As the Turk knew it would, the story made the rounds on the hill very quickly and added to his already awesome reputation. The Turk himself made sure that Ponzi heard the story—the right version. The Turk was sure that Ponzi told Velia and the two of them probably never laughed so hard in all their lives.

Those were great days in the 1950s. He was riding so high that by the end of the decade he owned three bars on the hill and two in the lower Main Street area. He was making several hundred thousand dollars a year from numbers, loan sharking, gambling, prostitution and even some legitimate money on the drinks he sold in the bars. He owned three Golden Gloves fighters, and he was proud that an interest in prizefighting was one that he shared with Velia. Velia, in fact, was better known to the public as "Tommy Egan," the hot-headed fight manager.

"Hey," said the Turk tossing aside the *Evening News,* "remember that time Velia jumped into the ring and took a swing at the referee?"

"Yeah, I remember," said Tommy the bartender. He didn't stop washing glasses. "That was long ago. Long ago."

The Turk still wasn't sure just when or just why things started to go wrong. But in the early 1960s he started noticing that there was a different attitude in the young kids, not just the punks who were hanging out on Fifth Street and Temple, but some of the young guys who were coming up through his own operation. Some of those kids were real wise-ass niggers. He'd talk to some of them and they wouldn't even answer him, or if they did, they'd be looking at one of their buddies and smirking.

Even Elsie had changed. She didn't talk about it when it first started but even the Turk could see something was wrong. One morning when they were lying in bed reading the papers the Turk said to her, "You know something? You're worth five of any of the dumb-ass guys I got in this place." Then he moved to grip her arm to show her that he really meant it. But she pulled her arm away. The Turk couldn't believe it. He stared at her. And she stared at the ceiling. Finally she said, "Why don't you fuck off." And the Turk could tell that she wasn't kidding.

That goddam bitch. The Turk still burned when he thought about how she had humiliated him. He was flattering her and she had kicked him where it hurts. He could never forget that and maybe she couldn't either, because after that, although she was still important in the operation and although they still slept together from time to time, they were both very cold with one another. There was no more kidding about anything. He didn't pay her for it as he had when he first started sleeping with her, but even the sex was strictly business.

Nothing had changed with most of the colored guys he had brought up with him since the early 1950s. It better not, the Turk thought, as he looked at Tommy Washington. I made all those bastards rich. Without me they'd be down there in the Lackawanna train station cleaning out toilets. But they were okay. Tommy and Al Montgomery and "Horse" Jackson. In fact it was Horse who first pointed out to the Turk that a lot of the young kids were getting restless.

It was right after the Watts riot and Horse told the Turk that a lot of the young bucks on the hill not only sympathized with the rioters, they were already talking about what they were going to burn and what they were going to steal when the riot times came to Paterson.

The Turk was shocked. "You get the word out, Horse, that if somebody tries throwing a Molotov cocktail in here," the Turk said, "I'll pick it up and shove it down his black throat and then I'll bust his head with a brick."

And it was Horse who first told him about Willie C. Squires. Back in the late 1950s Willie was nothing more than a runner, working out of a dump grocery store halfway down the hill. He was a smart kid and he worked his way up in the operation. But Horse, who supervised the numbers, showed the Turk that Willie C. was holding out on some of his accounts. It was a dumb trick, but one that every runner and every controller thought about pulling every now and then. And if they just did it every now and then by doctoring some of the slips they could get away with it. But Willie C. was getting greedy.

The Turk couldn't remember why he didn't have Tommy Washington bust Willie's ass open right then and there. Maybe he had something else on his mind, or maybe he remembered his own youth and how he slipped fives and tens out of Daddario's cash register. Anyhow, he told Horse to let Willie C. off with a warning.

The Turk couldn't believe it when months later Horse told him that Willie C. was at it again. He's crazy, the Turk thought, and for the first time he got a little scared. Any nigger who would rob the Turk twice had to be out of his head. But again the Turk didn't strike, this time because a bigger event intervened.

Newark, just a few miles away, erupted in a ghetto riot that made the Turk realize that he might have to live up to his promise to demolish anybody who so much as touched one of his properties. For one reason or another Paterson didn't blow up, although there was some minor damage done. None of it was directed at the Turk.

When things quieted down, the Turk talked to Ponzi about what to do about Willie Squires. Ponzi advised him to be cautious. No point in killing some nigger and have the whole town blow up and lose a lot of good money. Just toss him out of the operation. The Turk went along with Ponzi and tossed Willie C. as well as his brother, Franklin—"Bro" they called him—who was even crazier than Willie C., out of his organization.

Other things were beginning to worry the Turk. The Italian neighborhood in Paterson had been getting smaller all the time as more and more whites moved out to Rutherford and other suburbs. After the Newark riot more whites got scared and more left for the suburbs. Puerto Ricans were starting to move in. Right across the street from the Italian Sports Center there was a crumbling apartment building, and the Puerto Ricans moved into it. Those spics even had the balls to draw a Puerto Rican flag on the outside of their building, like they were defying the red, white and green flag of the Italian Sports Center. When the spics move in, that's it, thought the Turk. Blacks are dumb and sometimes crazy, but spics just tear a neighborhood apart.

At the same time, the black neighborhood was spreading down the hill and across the river and along lower Main Street. Black faces were common all over Paterson. There were even some blacks on the police force. The Turk's power downtown no longer seemed as great as it once had. Old Al Montgomery might still fall for that phony talk with the cop, but probably nobody else would.

In the middle of the 1960s the Turk started to peddle drugs. Why the hell not? Almost all of the hookers who worked his place were on drugs anyhow. They were going to get the juice somewhere. Why not from him? If he let somebody else muscle in and start supplying his hookers with drugs, soon they'd be taking a cut on the rooms. Anyhow, Velia, who controlled the drugs coming in by ship on Manhattan's West Side, was looking for "sales outlets," and Ponzi told the Turk he was expected to do his part.

Up until then, most of the community on Temple Hill had at least tolerated the Turk's activities and even the most respectable participated in at least some of them. In the Sunday spirituals on the local black radio station some of the ministers would roll off hymn numbers to play the next day, tips straight from heaven. Most of the Turk's activities fit more or less neatly into the local economy, loan sharking, gambling, even prostitution. After all, men actually came from outside the community to visit the Turk's hookers. It was one of the few ways in which outside money found its way up to the hill.

But drugs were different. Drugs didn't fit in at all. They were not just disruptive. They were tearing the community apart. Kids were stealing money from their mothers, beating up old people, selling the family TV, doing anything to get drugs. And the people blamed it all on the Turk. Someone once saw a fourteen-year old boy working as a lookout in one of the Turk's places, standing guard while another kid, an older one, was buying drugs.

That story made the rounds on the hill as fast as any of the stories about the Turk's fearsome powers back in the old days, and it had just the opposite effect. The Turk became the villain, the exploiter of black youth, the ruination of the community, Satan himself.

The Turk was isolated. Those mothers, he thought. What do they want, some hippies in here selling drugs to their kids? I didn't make them junkies. They did it themselves. They get some hippies in here cutting and selling all kinds of crap and they're going to see their kids dropping dead right and left.

Willie C. had been peddling drugs, and his brother still was. The

Turk felt he wasn't doing anything worse than that "Bro," but they were making him sound like Mr. Big. That goddam Squires. After the Turk threw Willie and Bro out of his operation, the two of them went into business on their own. They started luring guys, particularly young guys, out of the Turk's operation with all kinds of crap about black power and also a bigger cut of the numbers take. The Squires raised the take for runners from 20 percent to 25 percent. Then, they somehow got hooked up with the Galente gang in Brooklyn, which was trying to find sales outlets for its drugs, just as Velia was.

The Squires were knocking over the Turk's runners. They grabbed $35,000 one week. The Turk cursed himself for not having wiped out that smart-ass nigger years ago. Then, it got too late. After a time, to go after Squires openly was to risk open warfare. And the Turk wasn't ready for that. Or maybe he was no longer up to it. The Turk looked at his arms again.

A few years ago he could have eliminated the Squires bunch just by setting Willie up for a bust. But he couldn't even do that any more. The feds were getting serious about cleaning up the cops and the politicians. Up in Hudson County they were even tossing them in jail. A cop or an assistant district attorney who would gladly have taken a bribe to set up Willie C. Squires was scared today. The Turk couldn't even guarantee his men any more that as long as they stayed loyal to him they wouldn't spend a night in jail.

Still, he swore he didn't kill Willie Squires. If he had done it he would have killed that bastard of a brother of his, too. That one is worse. He really didn't know who had killed Willie Squires. He thought that probably somebody in the Galente gang did it, that probably he started to fuck around with them just as he had with him.

And he didn't know who killed Velia either.

"Tommy," said the Turk, "I'm going over to Elsie's place."

It burned the hell out of him to have to go look for her. But what could he do? The controllers were dropping the money at her house. It was safer that way. It was easier to protect her place from that

Squires mob than one of his bars. At the top of Temple Street he looked down at the muddy Passaic River and at the abandoned textile mills that formed a grim wall on the far side of it.

This dump has had it, the Turk said to himself. It's all spics over there now. I'll bet you don't even find any Greeks or Jews in the phone book.

FRANKLIN "BRO" SQUIRES

"Take it nice and easy down the hill," Bro Squires said. "We want to make sure that all of our friends see us."

Bro Squires hadn't felt so good in a long time and he wanted to make sure that everybody on Temple Hill saw how good he felt and how good he looked sitting in the back seat of his black Continental. He hoped the Turk was looking at him from one of those windows. Not that the Turk counted for much any more, but it would be pleasant to know that the Turk had seen Bro and therefore his life had been made just a little more miserable.

It surprised Bro a little to reflect that this was the first time the Turk's name had crossed his mind in more than a week. There was a time, a time that lasted for almost twenty-five years, when a day didn't go by that Bro didn't think about the Turk. But the Turk's power was broken now. No doubt about that. The news of Tommy Velia's death had sent Bro higher than a noseful of cocaine. Who killed Velia was as much a mystery to him as it was to the Turk, but as far as Bro was concerned there was no doubt about what it meant. The power of the white man was dead, not just on the hill but all over Paterson. The black man was going to be running things from now on. And that meant that Bro Squires was going to be running things.

It angered Bro that he still had to do business with the Galente family, at least until he worked out another supply route for heroin. But it was going to be business on Bro's terms. And if the Galentes thought they were going to do business with Calvin Horton, they better forget it. One of these days that jive motherfucker was going to be cut up so bad there wouldn't be enough of him to mail back to Jamaica.

The Continental slowly nosed its way down the steep incline of Temple Street. It looked out of place among the rubble of the dreary ghetto, and that was just the way Bro wanted it to look. He wanted the people of the hill, particularly the young, to see what the black man could achieve if he put his mind to it the way Bro had. Bro smiled at the curious and admiring residents of the hill who gathered around the car. Runny Brown, who was sitting next to the driver, Roy Howards, kept a gun under his seat; the memory of Willie C.'s death had made all of them more cautious.

Roy and Runny had been with Bro much of the time for the past eighteen months, ever since Willie C. was kidnapped and murdered. They stayed with Bro to protect him both from a similar plot and also, they had to admit, from himself. Bro went wild with rage when he heard what happened to Willie C. He wanted to go gunning after the Turk and Ponzi, even Velia and every other white face in north Jersey. Roy and Runny managed to hold him down. Then, in the weeks that followed Bro slid into a deep depression in which he never left his room, never saw anybody.

Finally, he rose out of that to a mood of sullen cunning. During his brooding depression he had figured out that it was probably the Galente family rather than Ponzi and the Turk who had murdered Willie C. Delmo Jenkins had mentioned once that the Galentes thought that Willie C. was a wild man, smart and tough but unpredictable and unreliable. They would have preferred doing business with Bro. What enraged Bro as much as anything else was that the Galentes still wanted to do business with him, even after they had murdered his brother. Did they think he was too stupid to figure it out? Or did they just figure that black people are such animals that things like brotherhood don't count? But Bro controlled his fury. He needed the Galente organization for a while. After that, there'd be time to straighten some things out.

Willie C. and Bro had been more than brothers. They were everything in the world to one another, like two lonely street brawlers standing back to back and fighting off a hostile crowd. Their father was a drunk, disposed to violence, who only came home to borrow or steal, but since he never paid anything back the borrowing was the same as the stealing. Their mother had other men. Some were generous and would even play ball with Willie C. and Bro from time to time. Others were plain mean and would kick them out of the house. All of them were unpredictable.

The only thing certain in their world was the brotherhood of Willie C. and Bro. Willie C. was four years older, and whenever they'd go anywhere the bigger kids would say, here comes Willie C. and his brother, which over the years was shortened to Willie C. and Bro, so that most people on the hill had to think hard to remember that Bro Squires' real name was Franklin.

It didn't bother Bro a bit that he had no real name of his own. Being Willie C.'s brother was something that any kid his age would have given up mother, father and everything else for. Even before he was a teenager, Willie C. was a legend on the hill—the most exciting, daring, reckless, adventurous kid who ever lived. Willie C. had a genius for wildness.

On a day like this one, for example, Willie C. and Bro when they were kids would run barefoot down the broiling asphalt of Temple Hill. Bro had done that so many times that even with the air conditioning whirring and the tinted windows rolled up, Bro knew all the sounds and smells that were stirring outside. Except for the new project at the bottom of the hill, the neighborhood hadn't changed very much. Tired, sweaty, beaten old men were still puffing up the hill, coming from their kitchen jobs in downtown Paterson. Mothers and babies were still yelling at one another in dark rooms. The broken bottles and rusted cans that lay in the overgrown lots might have been the same ones that Willie C. and Bro had thrown there years before.

At the bottom of the hill was the Passaic River. Just swimming in the muddy but swift current was dangerous enough. Kids had been drowned in it. But that wasn't daring enough for Willie C. He used to climb up on the roof of the abandoned mill on the far side of the river and, without even looking, jump into the water.

Sometimes they used to have rock fights with the white kids on the other side of the river. Bro remembered one day watching a flat stone he had just thrown arch up into the heavy summer air and then slice down on the other side of the river. It caught some white kid in the side of the face. Bro remembered seeing the kid jump about a foot off the ground and then start screaming. Bro thought he could see blood gushing out from his eye.

"You nigger bastards," one of the other white kids had screamed. "We're gonna come over there now and kill you sons-a-bitches."

Bro was scared. He was pretty sure they'd do just what they promised. His stomach knotted and he wanted to cry. But he didn't run. He just picked up rocks as fast as he could and threw them furiously across the river, and rocks were thrown back, until both sides had exhausted themselves. When he thought about it later, Bro realized that he really got a kick out of watching that stone smack the white kid in the face.

By the time Willie C. was sixteen he was already working for the Turk as a numbers runner and, of course, that meant that Bro went along too. He knew more about the numbers than most kids his age knew about baseball standings. And so hustling just kind of became part of his life. It was no big deal. A lot of kids did it.

Neither Willie C. nor Bro had any contact with the Turk himself, of course. They just heard about the Turk from their controller, like he was some great white god who lived on top of the hill. The controller was always saying the Turk likes this but doesn't like that. The Turk is a wonderful man but don't try crossing him. And then there were always stories floating around that so-and-so was bumped off because he was messing with the Turk. It got so that it seemed that nobody ever died on the hill without the Turk being behind it.

Willie C. and Bro were smart enough to realize that many of those tales were circulated by the Turk himself to keep people afraid of him. But somehow it never worked on Willie C. and Bro. They were never awed by the Turk the way they were supposed to be. Part of the reason was that Willie and Bro had already seen that there was a big world outside Paterson and that although the Turk may have been a big man on the hill, he was nothing anywhere else.

When Willie C. was eleven and Bro only seven they hopped their first freight train to Jersey City. They came back again and again to roam the yards, smash switches, steal whatever scrap seemed worth taking and throw rocks or rusty bolts or whatever else they could get their hands on at the watchmen who pursued them. Soon they were stowing away on the ferries that crossed the Hudson to Manhattan and by the time they were teenagers they were regularly venturing into Harlem.

It was on one of those trips that Willie C. and Bro first ran into Delmo and Sonny Jenkins. Like the Squires, the Jenkins were brothers about four years apart in age, and although they were almost twenty years older than the Squires brothers, they took an interest in Willie C. and Bro, perhaps because they had the same kind of close relationship.

The Jenkins showed the Squires a style of hustling that was far more sophisticated than anything that was going on in Paterson at the time. One of the favorites was the nut hustle, or Murphy game, as it is sometimes called.

Sonny and Delmo would stake out opposite sides of Columbus Avenue looking for dudes who wanted action but were obviously nervous about it. If Delmo spotted one first, then Sonny would quickly hop a cab back to their hotel room and wait. Meantime, Delmo would be telling the dude about this club where they had any kind of girl he wanted, black, white, Puerto Rican. Whatever he wanted. The only catch is you have to be a member of the club. So Delmo and the dude work out a plan. Delmo will take him to the club and the dude will tell them he lost his membership card.

Now this dude is all excited. He figures he's really going to be getting some great stuff in this private club, so he and Delmo hop in a cab and go to the hotel where Sonny is waiting. Sonny pretends that he's the manager and asks the dude for his club card. The dude says he lost it. Sonny says, "Forget it. Members only." Then Delmo starts pleading with Sonny to let the dude stay, but Sonny keeps saying no. They didn't want to make it seem easy for the dude because he might get suspicious. They wanted to make it seem like they really had some great action at this place and also that Delmo was really working his butt off for this dude. The dude thinks that Delmo is the best friend he ever had.

Finally Sonny gives in and he says okay, he'll get the dude a temporary card. He steps outside the room and pretends that he's going upstairs to get a temporary card. There's nothing upstairs at all except the roof and so Sonny just waits outside the room a few minutes. Meantime, Delmo is giving the dude some advice. He tells the dude that they've had some trouble with the girls stealing. After all, a girl who will lay for a buck will steal a buck. He asks the dude how much money he has and the dude says he's got $200.

When Sonny comes back with the temporary membership card Delmo asks the dude if he wants to put his money in the safe, and the dude says okay. So Sonny takes the money and carefully notes the denominations of the bills and the serial numbers and gives the list to the dude so he'll think his money is being taken real good care of. Sonny walks out with the money and Delmo pours the dude a drink. There's no reason for the dude to be suspicious. He's got the list of bills in his pocket and Delmo's there drinking with him.

When they finish the drink Delmo says it's time for the dude to go pick out a girl. Once they're out in the hall, Delmo says, "Wait—you want your money, don't you?" Now the dude is confused, but the way Delmo asks the question he says sure. So Delmo takes the little list of bills from the dude and he runs up the stairs ahead of the dude. And he just keeps going, up on the roof, across two other roofs to where Sonny is waiting. They spent maybe $10 on the whole deal for hotel room and cabs and whisky and they took in $200. Not bad. And they could work that same hustle two or three times in an afternoon.

Delmo and Sonny taught them other things too, like how to buy a gun. Now you may know that this dealer has a piece for sale, but even if you've got a big street rep you can't just walk up and say, "Hey, man, I want to buy that piece." He'd look at you like you were crazy. He's not going to sell it to you that way because for all he knows you might be a cop. You've got to go to the middle man and tell him what you want.

Then, Mr. Middle he'll go and buy that piece from the dealer for $30 and sell it to you for $50. But that's no hustle. That's the way it has to be done. If you as the buyer turn out to be a cop, Mr. Middle has to take the bust without getting the dealer in trouble. He stakes his rep on his silence. That's what he gets his $20 for. There's no other way of doing it.

By the mid-1960s Willie C. had become a controller in the Turk's numbers organization, but at the same time his independent contacts with the Jenkins and other operators in Harlem had made him feel so confident that he wasn't any more afraid of defying the Turk than he was of defying some railroad cop. He started in small ways at first. He began lending money out on the street, a move that put him in direct competition with the Turk's loan shark operation.

Then Willie C. did something that should have guaranteed his immediate execution. He started holding out on some of the numbers money. It was easy enough to do. When the runners would bring the money in to him, Willie C. would pick out a couple of numbers that were being played heavily and hold that money and those slips aside. The odds were good that the numbers wouldn't hit, but the odds were also extremely good that the Turk would immediately notice the fall-off in the play coming through Willie C. and figure out what was going on. Willie C.'s caper was not just dangerous. It was suicidal. Even Bro had tried to talk Willie C. out of it. The Turk would have to send his goons after them and so for weeks Willie and Bro went armed, ready for a shootout. But it never came. The Turk didn't send his goons. He sent Horse Jackson, and Bro could still remember Horse, sweaty and scared, rubbing his head and wringing his hands and telling Willie C. and Bro that they were crazy niggers to be messing with the Turk, that the Turk must like them, otherwise they would have been killed for sure, but that they shouldn't stretch their luck.

Horse's visit made a big impression on Bro. It proved to him what he suspected all along. The Turk was just as much bullshit as those white kids yelling and screaming on the other side of the river, threatening to come over and kill the niggers. After that Bro was never really afraid of the Turk again.

But the event that really changed Bro's outlook was the Newark riot. Along with everybody else, Bro had been somewhat aware of the black power movement through the 1960s. He knew who Stokely Carmichael was and although he wasn't a great reader he got through Malcolm's autobiography. The Watts riot of 1965 excited him, but Watts was a long way from Paterson. Then, in 1968, Newark exploded. Newark was only a few miles away and what could happen in Newark could happen in Paterson, too. Black people were going to control the cities of America. The white man was finished in Paterson, and that included the Turk.

Even the Turk must have known that. Otherwise why didn't he come to kill Willie C. and Bro after Willie C. kept stealing money from the numbers? All the Turk had done was to throw them out of his operation, which showed that he had no power in his hand at all.

Under the circumstances Willie C. and Bro did what they had planned to do all along. They set up their own numbers in competition with the Turk. It wasn't that difficult. The key was getting the runners. The customers didn't know much about controllers and bankers. They only knew runners. So if Willie and Bro could bring the runners into their organization the customers would follow. The Squires made the runners a straight business offer. The Turk was paying them 20 percent of the profit. The Squires would give them 25 percent.

Of course, for that extra 5 percent the runners were taking some risk, the danger that the Turk or the cops, who worked for the Turk and so it was the same thing, would break their knee caps or even kill them. Every runner on the hill knew the story of the tavern owner who tried to set up his own numbers game. He was run over by a truck. When his bartender tried to keep the game going, he was hit by a car.

The runners had some reason to be scared all right, and so Bro came up with a plan that offered them extra security and also the sense of being part of a powerful brotherhood. It was a black power idea. Willie C. had never been enthusiastic about black power. It was his one blind spot, Bro thought. He had brains and guts, but he had no sense of black politics. He was convinced that black power wouldn't work because although real brothers like Willie C. and Bro and Delmo and Sonny would trust one another completely, as soon as you brought a third guy in, someone who wasn't related by blood, you were going to need a Jew to come hold the money.

But Bro was convinced that an organization based on black power methods could work. What he had in mind was a kind of paramilitary organization. He got the idea from the movie *The Battle of Algiers*. Bro was fascinated by that movie. He sat through it three times and took particular pleasure in the scene in which the Arab women blew up the restaurant full of Frenchies. But what really intrigued him was the way the Arab guerrillas had organized themselves. They had divided into small units of three or four men so that no guerrilla knew more than two or three others and therefore couldn't betray more than a few other guerrillas no matter how badly the French military tortured them.

Bro talked Willie C. into setting up their operation in the same way. And it worked. Within a year they had built up an organization of about sixty men working in fifteen separate units. There was one unit that did nothing but stick up the Turk's own runners. They'd stake a runner out for a few days, making sure that they knew all of his movements, and then when they were sure they had a good chance of getting away with it, they'd stick him up. They made $35,000 that way in one week.

Willie C. himself took personal charge of another raid on the Turk. The Turk had a bookie operation in downtown Paterson. Willie C. figured out a way of intercepting the race results that were being wired in from out-of-state tracks and delaying the results long enough for the Squires to play the winners. He hoped to hit the Turk badly enough to put him out of business, but the Turk's men got wise before they could pull it off.

That, according to Delmo Jenkins anyhow, was the reason that the Galente family decided to kill Willie C. They figured if he'd pull a caper like that on the Turk, he might pull it on them too. The Galentes wanted to make it clear to the Squires organization that they hadn't gone as soft as Velia and the Turk.

Bro quietly cursed Delmo and Sonny for the hundredth time for getting them involved with the Galentes. He knew it was an honest mistake. They had been his friends for too long for him to question their loyalty. Still, if it hadn't been for the Galente arrangement Willie C. would still be alive.

The deal with the Galentes had seemed like a good one at first. After some debate the Squires organization had decided a couple of years back to sell drugs, anything the customers wanted, from hash to heroin, ups, downs, the works. Roy Howards had argued against it, partly on moral grounds but mostly because he believed the community wouldn't stand for it. The people would isolate the Squires just as they had isolated the Turk. But Willie C. personally had overruled Roy. He argued that there was too much money in drugs not to go after it. Anyhow, they couldn't leave the drug trade to the Turk. That would leave him too much money and too much power.

And so Sonny and Delmo called on their contacts in the Galente organization. The Galentes were looking for retailers for the shipments they were bringing into the country and they didn't seem at all bothered that by dealing with the Squires they would be bucking Velia and the old Genovese organization. For all Bro knew there was a contract out on Velia even then. The arrangement worked smoothly enough. The Galentes could always be relied upon to deliver. Bro heard rumors that they had some key people in customs and even the Coast Guard on their payroll, but he didn't know that for sure. The Galentes told him almost nothing about their operation. And Bro told them no more than he had to about his.

The community resistance that Roy feared hadn't developed. Maybe it was because the people on the hill found it easier to believe that Bro's dealers were simply the unfortunate victims of drugs themselves, peddling only to support their own habits. It was the big Italian families who were profiting. Bro didn't know how the people on the hill would have reacted if they had known that Bro had laid down strict orders that everybody in his organization was to stay off drugs. (Bro himself sniffed cocaine from time to time. But he never touched heroin, not even to skin pop.) Bro didn't know how the hill people would react, and he wasn't about to test it.

Most of the people on the hill were at least neutral toward the Squires and some of the younger people were enthusiastic. Bro attributed some of this to his own community relations program. Bro made it a point to talk long and openly to anyone who would listen about how important it was to have black people run everything in the community, even the so-called "illegal" activities, like numbers and card playing. He carefully avoided mentioning drugs. Bro pointed out that one night a week at each of his five card rooms the house cut of the take would be donated to some good community cause, like buying books for the young folks or sponsoring chess tournaments so that the young kids could grow up with their heads together and wouldn't have to go into hustling the way the older generation did. In that way so-called "evil" acts could be turned into good. Even a hooker was doing good by turning tricks if she gave up some of that money to help educate some young black boy. The only kind of whoring that was wrong was to sleep with some white pig and not get paid for it.

"Hey, Roy," Bro ended the silence in the car. "What was that hassle you used to give the Turk's whore, that Elsie Payne?"

Roy thought a minute. "Oh yeah. Whenever I'd see her I'd look her straight in the eye and I'd deepen my voice and I'd say, 'Sister, you are an offense to all black people. Your body and soul stink from lying with the rotten flesh of the pig who has murdered your black brothers. Your putrid body reeks in the nostrils of the black race.'"

"And what did she say?"

"She'd look me right in the eye and say, 'Eat my black pussy!'"

They laughed.

The car had already crossed the Passaic River and had passed the chipped and faded signs that said, "Welcome to Lower Main Street, the Heart of Downtown Paterson." Bro was pleased that as far as they had driven into downtown and Paterson, he had seen no more than a handful of white faces. Someday, he told himself, he wasn't going to have to look at any white faces.

The Turk was no longer a threat. The Galente family? Bro knew he wasn't ready to take them on yet. For one thing he still needed their drugs. But someday. They thought Willie C. was a trouble-maker. They ain't seen nothin yet. But Bro had a couple of other things to work out first. That smartass Jamaican Calvin Horton, for one. Bro cursed himself for hiring him to begin with, Horton with all his soccer league and British finery and jive, looking down on Missis-sippi Delta folk like Willie C. and Bro, Horton thought he could split off and form his own organization. He was going to be cut down and quick.

Bro had something else on his mind too. It wasn't all worked out yet, but Bro couldn't see any reason why he couldn't pull it off: an alliance with the Puerto Ricans. Anybody could see that the Italians were finished in Paterson. For every Italian bakery in the old neigh-borhood around Cianci Street there was a Puerto Rican grocery and a furniture store. What better way to expand than by finding some Puerto Rican allies? And what better way to set up an independent Latin American drug route to get around the Galentes?

Bro was very pleased with himself. He not only felt good for the first time in eighteen months, he was sure that the feeling was going to last.

The Paterson, New Jersey, Network

There are, within this network, a number of interesting linkages and some important tentative conclusions we might make about ethnic succession in organized crime and emerging patterns of organization among black crime activists. Actually, the Paterson network is an example of a large network, once entirely controlled by the local Italian syndicate but now broken into two competing networks whose contacts are based largely on conflict. Networks, like any other col-lective of people, split and divide. In organized crime this can be a violent process, as was the case here. It is interesting to note that this also seems to be happening in Bro Squires' new organization as members such as Calvin Horton seek to break off and form their own groups. The first part of the network tells the story of a white crime activist who came to Paterson and by using black employees and allying himself with the local Italian syndicate managed to build up a powerful crime empire in the black area "up the hill," legitimated in the community by his black employees and protected in the city by his organized crime connections. Joseph "Joe the Turk" Hajar's career is interesting insofar as he has been involved in a wide variety of criminal ventures—stolen cars, gambling, prostitution, the numbers and narcotics—and also insofar as he is a rare example of a non-Italian who managed, through a connection he made in prison, to gain the protection of the local Italian syndicate. In a sense, Hajar is a criminal entrepreneur, acting as a middleman between the syndicate suppliers of illegal gambling and drugs and the local black customers in Paterson. His prostitution activities, however, tend to draw customers into the black area so that to some extent he appears to be bringing some money in, but this amount certainly does not compensate for the large amounts of money he siphons out of the black community for himself, the local syndicate and the police and politicians who protect him. His black employees, at least in the gambling and prostitution ends of his illicit enterprise, bear much the same relationship to him as would employees in any of a variety of legitimate businesses: they receive a commission for their work and, eventually, a growing share of the profits. The fact that Hajar is connected to the local syndicate lends a stability to his business activities but this is true only so long as there is community acceptance of his business enterprises and so long as that syndicate maintains the governmental connections that permit his illegal operations to continue largely unmolested.

The second part of the network, the operations started by Willie C. Squires and taken over after his death by his brother Franklin, describes a fledgling dynasty. There is some interesting evidence in this portion of the network that even if kinship among blacks is not an important linkage in the formation of criminal organizations (as it is among Italians), nevertheless it is at least possible for kinship to serve as an important determinant in bringing together individuals into an interrelationship that adds some strength to developing criminal networks. Not only did Bro Squires take over his brother's operations after his death, the presence in the network of Delmo and Sonny Jenkins, also consanguineous brothers, both of whom are successful men who work for Bro Squires, adds some support to this assumption.

Another interesting linkage in the network is Elsie Payne, the black woman who is both mistress and close associate to Hajar. The role of women in Italian organized crime families is minimal and there are no known examples of women reaching any position of authority in such syndicates. Such does not, however, seem to be the case among black crime activists, and Elsie Payne's rise to criminal success is not uncommon in such groups. There are other examples in our networks and historically women such as Madame St. Clair, of whom we shall read later, have held high positions.

There is also the interesting set of links between both portions of the network and Italian organized crime families. Hajar has always been connected, through Angelo "Ponzi" Ponzillo, with the local Italian syndicate. When Willie C. and Bro Squires split off from Hajar to form their own organization they made contacts, through the Jenkins brothers, who were originally from New York, with a Brooklyn-based Italian crime family in order to obtain narcotics. Thus both portions of the network—Hajar's established organization and the Squires' emergent one—reach up to an Italian-controlled organization for supplies and, at least in Hajar's case, for protection as well. In Hajar's operation this arrangement is the basis of his success and without it he will not survive. Bro Squires, however, sees it as a temporary expediency and seems impatient to build up enough strength and connections of his own so that he can become independent of it. It is interesting to speculate on what seems to be an unusual case of two Italian crime families apparently backing different factions in the same territory. Traditionally, territorial rights have been respected by the Italians. There are a number of possible reasons for what appears to be an unusual circumstance in Paterson. First, it is really not that unusual; there have been territorial competitions among Italian crime families in the past, particularly when new markets are being opened up. In the 1960s, both the local Velia family and the Brooklyn-based Galente family were seeking new territories for the burgeoning narcotics trade. Toward the end of the 1960s and increasingly in the early 1970s, northern New Jersey also became one of the most active areas in the country for intensive surveillance and eventual prosecution of Italian-American organized crime figures and the politicians who were associated with them. The Bergen County syndicate suffered heavy casualties, and they were in disarray and their territorial hegemony was rapidly disappearing. Finally, Hajar's own position as a non-Italian made him vulnerable for, as anyone in Paterson will tell you, the Italian mobsters will protect "their own" but non-Italian allies do not fall in that category.

We also learn something about hierarchical arrangements in organized crime, at least in Paterson, and this combined with what we shall learn from other networks will allow us to draw some conclusions later. Both the Hajar and the Squires operations are characterized by strong leadership of a single individual with a number of lieutenants under him. In Hajar's case there are also at least two levels above him: Ponzillo, who is the Paterson leader for the Bergen County syndicate, and above him Thomas Velia, who heads that syndicate, or did until his death. In the Squires operation we have no evidence of any higher lines of authority although it is connected to the Galente family. That arrangement does not seem to carry any direct organizational affiliation with it and the connection seems to be a straight business one with Bro Squires purchasing drugs from the Galentes. If the Galentes provide other services such as protection or enforcement, our field assistant was unaware of it and later interviews in Paterson (1973) did not indicate any formal organizational relationships either.

There is also something to be learned about how organized crime activists operate in concert in Delmo and Sonny Jenkins' lesson to the Squires brothers on how to purchase a gun. Even if a crime activist knows who is dealing in guns, he cannot go to him directly and ask to purchase one, since he is likely to get a know-nothing response:

"What are you talking about, man?" But if you know someone who knows the gun dealer, you can approach your friend. He could "cut you in" to the dealer by sending you directly to him but usually he will not because he loses his exclusive connection with the dealer and so loses one source of profit. He can, and probably will, however, become "Mr. Middle" and obtain the gun for you and add on his own profit to his purchase price. Each person who is part of this deal knows what is happening; the gun dealer knows that Mr. Middle will resell it at a profit and you know that your price will be higher than if you could go directly to the dealer. But selling to a limited number of people is added protection for the supplier and Mr. Middle's connections are part of his stock in trade and you have your gun. Crime activists hold to the same principle that illuminates legitimate business enterprise: "There is profit in knowledge" and so who you know becomes a business asset.

What the history of this network shows most dramatically, however, is the process of ethnic succession at work. It also indicates how an ideology, in this case black militancy, can serve as an organizational imperative for a crime network. Paterson is a fairly small city and social processes there are somewhat easier to observe and plot than in a city the size of New York. The emergence of the Squires brothers' illegal power coincided in time with the more legitimate demands of other blacks for independence and some control over their own destiny in areas such as politics and education. Bro's vision of his thrust for power as essentially a revolutionary movement, even to the extent of modeling his organization after what he had learned from the film *The Battle of Algiers,* suggests that black militancy in crime draws at least some of its value orientation from the same sources as more legitimate protests among blacks.

Bro's report of how he contributes some of his illicit earnings to better the lot of ghetto youngsters is reminiscent of James Mitchell's description of his social service activities, which he told Reggie Martin about in the earlier Central Harlem network. There is no doubt that such philanthropic activities do take place. In Paterson, for example, a group of numbers writers and hustlers recently contributed $250 each for buses to send a local boys' drill team to a convention in Philadelphia and then chipped in something extra to pay for their lunches. We found other examples in a number of networks of organized crime activists who were sometimes available with good will and short-term cash when a mother needed milk for her baby, when a family was behind in the rent, when a son ended up in jail. There is ample evidence that the numbers have been a great neighborhood employer. This in part explains a phenomenon encountered in this network that will appear again and again in later ones; drug peddling is condemned by the same community in which gambling and loan sharking are condoned. Law enforcement officials and organized crime specialists link all of these crimes, maintaining that they are controlled by the same individuals. But the public, particularly those who patronize organized crime, make no such link. Blacks who play the numbers condemn narcotics traffic because they consider it a form of white enslavement of blacks; they consider gambling a minor vice providing entertainment and hope while hurting none save the tax collector. Malcolm X, however, never one to traffic in illusions, speaks in his autobiography of another view of the role of numbers in the ghetto economy and of how the lack of more legitimate routes of mobility concentrated wealth and power in the hands of those who chose the illegal avenues that were available:

Back when I was growing up, the "successful" Negroes were such as waiters and bootblacks. To be a janitor at some downtown store was to be highly respected. The real "elite," the "big shots," the "voices of the race," were the waiters at the Lansing Country Club and the shoeshine boys at the State Capitol. The only Negroes who really had any money were the ones in the numbers racket, or who ran the gambling houses, or who in some way lived parasitically off the poorest ones, who were the masses.[1]

Although it may seem strange to debate the value of an activity

[1] Malcolm X and Alex Haley, *The Autobiography of Malcolm X* (New York: Grove Press, 1964; paperbound edition), p. 14.

that is patently illegal, the conflict between community or even societal views of activities such as gambling and legal definitions of criminal behavior will come up frequently as we examine the various networks. It is a question at the heart of the problem of organized crime in American society and one that we shall come back to later.

In a comparison between this network and the one in Central Harlem the most obvious difference would seem to be one of degree of development, with Central Harlem loosely organized and Paterson tightly structured. There is, however, another difference and it helps to explain the differential patterns of organization. In Central Harlem, Reggie Martin, Thomas Irwin and James Mitchell all seem to have escaped control by the Italian syndicate, a fact Reggie boasts about during his drive to Rikers Island with Calvin Meadows. In Paterson, however, the Italians still seem to maintain some control over Bro Squires' operations because, unlike Harlem, they still represent the only sure access to political and police protection. In Paterson the process of ethnic succession is just beginning and so the black crime organization there still resembles that of its Italian predecessors out of which it is emerging and to which it still owes some grudging fealty. In Harlem, the blacks are already free from the Italians and there they are just now beginning to develop their own forms of organization, the characteristics of which are emergent from their own community ethos. Thus, the two patterns of organization we have seen are to some extent the result of the dialectic between society and the ethnic community in America. In the next section I want to look at both of these sources: at the history of the black urban experience to establish their exploitation by both crime and politics and at two more black networks in an attempt to identify the social bonding mechanisms in the black community that will serve to organize them in crime as kinship did for the Italians.

PART TWO

✠

THE ROOTS OF
ETHNIC SUCCESSION

3

POLITICS AND ORGANIZED CRIME IN THE GHETTO

⌘

IN THIS chapter we shall look first at the historical background of the current social, economic and political forces at the root of organized crime in ghetto culture. Next, two networks—one involving a childhood gang that grew into an organized crime network and the other, life in prison—will be presented. Both can be examined as early or prototypical networks in which a kind of ethnic bonding takes place at the community level (for many blacks the prison setting *is* the first community experience) and that become a foundation for later criminally organized activities.

The social history of American urban ghettos documents how ghetto dwellers were forced to seek escape from underclass status into the dominant society through the interrelated and interdependent routes of crime and politics. The corrupt political structures of major American cities and organized crime have always enjoyed a symbiotic relationship in which success in one is dependent on the right connections in the other. In this relationship, the aspiring ethnic, blocked from legitimate access to wealth and power, is permitted to produce and provide those illicit goods and services that society publicly con-

demns but privately demands—gambling, stolen goods, illegal alcohol, sex and drugs—but not without paying tribute to the political
establishment. The gangsters and the racketeers paid heavily into the
coffers of political machines and in return received immunity from
prosecution. The ghetto became a safe haven in which crime syndicates could grow and prosper. Two factors—immigrant slum dwellers' alienation from the political process and society's characteristic
attitude that so long as "they" do it to each other, crime in the ghetto
is not an American problem—kept the police indifferent and absent
and added to that prosperity. The immigrant and his children found
organized crime a quick means of escaping the poverty and powerlessness of the slums. The successful gangster like the successful
politician was seen as a model who demonstrated to the masses of
lower-class co-ethnics that anyone could achieve success and power in
the greater society. And if they did this while defying the police and
other oppressors, so much the better. Then, when political power
came to the group, partly as a result of these same illegal activities,
access to legitimate opportunities became enlarged and assimilation
was facilitated. The tradition became one of up and out.

Since the end of World War II, with the rapid influx of black
people from the South and from the West Indies and Spanish-
speaking persons from Puerto Rico and other areas of Latin America
(especially, since the 1959 revolution, from Cuba), organized crime
activities in the cities have now come to involve these new groups.
As a result, some new features have been added to organized crime in
America, many of which seem related to the largely unfulfilled quest
for social equality by recently emerging social-ethnic groups and the
turn toward get-rich-quick schemes (such as numbers) and escape
mechanisms (such as hard drugs) among recent, unsatisfied ethnic-
racial groups. Consumer demand for drugs and numbers playing, for
example, coupled with official prohibition of such traffic, has led to
the creation of a new and lucrative market resembling the situation
created by liquor prohibition in the early part of the century. Since
black and Spanish-speaking people are among the largest users of the
illegal drugs and players of numbers, it should not be difficult to guess

that they will be and indeed are fast becoming the next wave of ethnics to exert community control over organized crime in the ghetto. But their involvement in organized crime also has an interesting social history.

The Great Policy Players

"The Negroes of [New York] City are great policy players," Edward Martin wrote in his *Secrets of the Great City*. Moreover, "In every district where they live you will find dingy little lottery offices, patronized mostly by them. . . . A Negro must play his policy even if bread is lacking at home." [1] If one ignores the condescension here,

[1] Edward Winslow Martin, *Secrets of the Great City* (Philadelphia: National Publishing Company, 1868), p. 517. "Policy" (the numbers) is, very simply, a lottery. In the black and Hispanic slums of New York, Chicago and other cities it operates daily or twice daily. Anyone who wishes to play finds his neighborhood runner, who in the ghetto will be literally as easy to find as the neighborhood barber or newsboy. In the typical game, the player bets on any three-digit number, from 000 to 999. He is betting that the number he chooses will turn up as *the* number for the day. The number for the day is in most cases derived from racetrack betting pools: in New York City, for example, there is the "New York number," computed from the total parimutuel handles of the third, fifth and seventh races held at a given track, and also the "Brooklyn number," the last three digits of the total parimutuel handle for the day. The important point is that today, the source of the number will be a relatively public, random and normally unmanipulative one. However, the number in Chicago is still arrived at as it was in New York before the turn of the century: by lottery drawings. In a typical drawing seventy-eight consecutively numbered black-and-white balls are placed in a drum, a "wheel," and rotated, and then a certain number of balls are drawn out. Normally, a winning bettor is one who has chosen three numbers correctly out of those drawn. A winning number, for example, might be the three figures 4–11–17. In New York, the odds against winning will obviously be 1 in 999. The payoff, however, will be at only 540 to 1.

Examining where the rest of a typical $1 bet goes discloses the organizational structure of the game. As mentioned, the player places his bet with a runner. Each runner takes bets and pays off winners over a fairly small territory. He reports his bets, as will several other runners, perhaps from the same neighborhood, to a single collector, who in turn takes all the betting slips he has collected to a central bank, or district office, which is managed by a controller. The runners, collectors and controller will share in approximately 25¢ of every $1 bet, plus 10 percent of all winning hits: thus a total of 35¢ on the dollar. The banker, at the very top of the hierarchy, is left with 11¢ on the dollar, or perhaps, after various incidental expenses, chiefly payoffs to police, 10¢ on the dollar. However, this can be 10 percent of a truly vast number of dollars each day.

The game was essentially the same forty or fifty years ago. However, then the bets were chiefly in nickels and dimes and, as we shall see, this was the chief reason one can begin to see the formation of a pattern: from the earliest days of their life in America's big cities, blacks played policy. Why? Obviously because lotteries, the playing of long shots, provide both entertainment and a hope of escape from grinding poverty. One can see the same kind of pattern in nation after nation: for the proletariat there are always provided sweepstakes, lotteries, games of chance.

In any case, policy gambling was partly legal in New York until 1901, and whites controlled it. Until that time, policy bets were taken at lottery exchanges, where results of lottery drawings held twice daily in Southern cities were announced. At the end of the nineteenth century, there were about 400 policy shops in New York, frequented chiefly by "Negroes, sailors, and foreigners." [2] In 1901, these lotteries became illegal, but clandestine games continued.

World War I and its aftermath brought a vast migration of blacks to New York, as it did to other cities. Harlem took shape as a true community, a mecca for black Americans everywhere, and perhaps, for what it's worth, as the nightlife capital of the nation. In the "tea pads," "reefer dens," and "King Kong joints," and amid the amazing collection of pimps, prostitutes, zootsuiters, gamblers and petty hustlers that went along with them, a free-flowing life style developed. And in the community, aside from all its nightlife, the first great stirrings of black pride and black accomplishment were developing. It perhaps seemed only natural that blacks should operate policy for themselves. However, the fact that white gangsters were not particularly interested in the numbers, that they considered it "the nickels and dimes game of the poor," [3] surely didn't hurt.

Madame Stephanie St. Clair, a migrant from the West Indies whose likeness has more than once found its way into the black

---

why in New York blacks came to run policy. It was considered by most whites to be peanuts, when in fact its immense popularity and therefore immense volume assured that it was always highly lucrative.

[2] James D. McCabe, *New York by Sunlight and Gaslight* (Philadelphia: Hubbard Brothers, 1881), pp. 550–552.

[3] Fred J. Cook, "The Black Mafia Moves into the Numbers Racket," *The New York Times Magazine* (April 4, 1971), p. 27.

movies, became the Policy Queen of Harlem in the 1920s and early 1930s. As Woolworth's made millions, so did she: out of pennies and nickels and dimes. And she wasn't the only one. There were also Wilfred Brender and Casper Holstein, who according to a long-time resident of Harlem provided funds to build Harlem's first Elks Lodge. By 1925 there were thirty black policy banks in Harlem, several of them large enough to collect bets in an area of twenty city blocks and across three or four avenues.

Puerto Ricans living in New York's first *Colonia España,* situated around Columbia Street and Atlantic Avenue in Brooklyn, developed a policy game based on the Italian lotteries operating in the area and played it throughout the 1920s. The leading Spanish-speaking policy bankers of the period were Henry Miro, the Puerto Rican "King of the Numbers"; Alex Pompey, a tall, distinguished Cuban from Tampa, Florida; and "Cubano Loco," a Cuban who cut an elegant figure in Harlem, appearing in the summertime in a custom-tailored white suit and an Ecuadorian Panama hat.

A former Harlem numbers runner describes the Spanish-speaking policy bankers: "Affluence made them happy to be alive." Coming as stowaways from Puerto Rico on the old Red Star shipping line, many of them spent their youth in poverty. When they came to New York, many of them found employment scraping ships on the city docks. Then they discovered *la bolita* [4] (the numbers game).

For those who became numbers operators, good times arrived. "They'd hop into two, three cars, drive down to La Conga, on 51st," an ex-runner, once a Miro employee, recalled. One of the cars was a LaSalle, the property of Henry Miro. The Spanish-speaking policy bankers often met at the Central Grill on Lenox Avenue, sometimes to talk business, more often to drink and chat with the girls.

[4] When Spanish-speaking persons speak of *la bolita,* they are usually referring to the New York number. There is a policy operation, however, in which a two-digit figure, rather than the normal three-digit figure, is played; sometimes this game is called *la bolita.* Some law enforcement specialists believe *la bolita* is a *Spanish* numbers game that originated in Cuba or Puerto Rico. This is not the case. In the 1920s and 1930s, when Puerto Ricans and Cubans often traveled between the United States and the islands, the New York numbers game was transplanted to Cuba and Puerto Rico, where it acquired the name *la bolita.*

It was as early as 1885 that "Policy Sam" Young migrated to Chicago from New Orleans, bringing with him Chicago's first policy wheel.[5] By 1903, Chicago policy had become a $5 million a year business. And from the beginning black gamblers ran the game in Chicago's South Side "vice" district, where the Negro population of the city was concentrated.[6] Among other early black Policy Kings were John "Mushmouth" Johnson, who operated a South Side saloon and gambling house that was a meeting place for railroad men, waiters, porters and professional gamblers—Chinese, black and white; and Dan Jackson, head of a gambling and vice syndicate operating in Chicago's black Second Ward.[7]

[5] "Wheel," the drum from which lottery numbers are drawn. In current usage, "wheel" more often refers to a policy bank or district collection office—Francis A. J. Ianni, *A Family Business: Kinship and Social Control in Organized Crime* (New York: Russell Sage–Basic Books, 1972), pp. 193–194.

[6] In 1871, Chicago's downtown red-light district was burned out in the Chicago fire. The prostitutes and gamblers who made up Chicago's underworld then moved to the near South Side, in the heart of the black settlement. There, at the 22nd Street "Levee," in the First Ward, prostitution and gambling flourished openly until 1912, when reformers succeeded in having the red-light district officially closed. Prostitution and gambling continued in the First and Second Wards but less publicly. These South Side wards became known as a segregated black "vice" district. Because the area remained a center for gambling and prostitution down to the 1930s and because blacks continued to move into the area and could not move out (Chicago real estate brokers and tenants' associations combined to block housing integration as early as 1910), Chicago blacks became associated in the minds of white citizens with the vices that existed in the neighborhoods where they lived. Many blacks patronized gambling joints and houses of prostitution; there were also many black prostitutes, pimps and gamblers. Among the people who availed themselves of the illegal goods and services the district had to offer, however, the majority were white—St. Clair Drake and Horace Cayton, *Black Metropolis* (New York: Harcourt, Brace & World, 1945), Vol. 1, p. 47; and John Landesco, *Organized Crime in Chicago* (Chicago: University of Chicago Press, 1929), pp. 31–38.

[7] Drake and Cayton speak rather contemptuously of Chicago's black "demimonde and underworld," alleging that Chicago blacks never got more than the petty "cuts" from gambling and vice—Drake and Cayton, *op. cit.,* p. 111. They further claim Chicago's black community never had a "highly organized gang world . . . dealing in alcohol, dope, robbery, murder and women." In drawing these conclusions, they neglect the career of Dan Jackson. Jackson, a college graduate, came to Chicago from Pittsburgh in 1892. He opened several undertaking parlors and, at the same time, opened a string of gambling joints—one located in one of his funeral homes. He became "head of a great syndicate controlling vice, bootlegging, cabarets, and such gambling games as craps, poker and policy." In 1927, during the third administration of Republican Mayor William Hale Thompson, Jackson was named Republican Second Ward committeeman. Soon after, Illinois Governor Small appointed Jackson to the Illinois Commerce Commission. Jackson's policy wheel was the Tia Juana, one of the largest wheels in Chicago—Harold Foote Gosnell, *Negro Politicians* (Chicago: University of Chicago Press, 1935), pp. 130–133.

Chicago policy drawings were held three times a day at "wheels" located in cigar stores, beer joints and other neighborhood meeting places on the South Side. The drawings were public and sometimes witnessed by several hundred people, among them a large contingent of policy writers who, when they heard the results, ran out to pay their winning customers. Chicago wheels had exotic names. Some of the more well known were the Maine-Idaho-Ohio, the East-West-North-South, the Tia Juana, the Iowa-Wisconsin-Birmingham-Memphis and Royal Palm, the Black-White Streamline, the Calcutta-Green Dragon, and the Old Reliable.[8] By 1930, income from the game had reached $1 million monthly. Every day 350,000 bets were placed.

Before 1930, there existed among Chicago policy operators "unregulated rivalry, fights and bloodshed."[9] This warfare ceased, however, when the major operators allied themselves into a "policy syndicate." Although the syndicate was not a tightly controlled, hierarchical organization but merely an informal alliance, its formation allowed policy operations to continue without major violence down to the 1950s, when white racketeers took over the game.

A major reason for the success of Chicago blacks in controlling policy for so long was their political connection with William Hale "Big Bill the Builder" Thompson, Republican mayor of Chicago twice from 1915 to 1923 and from 1927 to 1931. Here we see a prime example of entry into organized crime and entry into urban politics going hand in hand. Kickbacks from the policy bankers to Thomp-

[8] The game of policy has quite an arcana, aside from exotic names. Since the nineteenth century, policy players have consulted "dream books" to determine the numbers they should play for the day. These numerological tomes, which are sold in small shops in the black community and in *botanicas* in Spanish-speaking areas, list a number for every symbol that may appear in a dream. There are, for example, numbers for falling from a building, numbers for people's names and numbers for the various forms of copulation. In the Spanish community, spiritualists sometimes advise on the numbers people should play. There are magic substances, such as Holy Oriental Oil and Lady Luck Room Spray, said to enhance the player's chance of winning, available at shops and *botanicas*. Where luck is not enough, an event of the day may help determine the winning number. Among numbers heavily bet in the past are Willie Mays' batting average and the day of the Pope's visit to Yankee Stadium.

[9] Lewis A. H. Caldwell, *The Policy King* (Chicago: New Vistas Publishing House, 1945), p. II.

son's political machine were estimated at $500,000 a year in the early 1930s. Although this was only one source of income for the Thompson machine, and by no means the largest, it was an important one.[10] And Thompson had other political reasons for protecting the policy racket.

By 1930 the black population of Chicago was 180,000—8.7 percent of the total city population, and the second largest urban concentration of blacks in the world. Almost all Chicago blacks were policy players. Almost all Chicago blacks also were voters, and they turned out in force on Republican primary day. Big Bill Thompson, "the second Abraham Lincoln," took an interest in the black Republican vote.

Chicago blacks were organized politically long before blacks in other parts of the nation. Commenting on the achievements of blacks in politics in Chicago in the years 1900–1935, Gosnell avows:

The Negroes in Chicago have achieved relatively more in politics during this period than have the Negroes in other cities of the United States. They have been more aggressive along political lines than have the Negroes in Detroit, they have been more adventuresome than the Negroes in Cincinnati, and they have been more united than have the Negroes in St. Louis.[11]

"Bathhouse" John Coughlin and Michael "Hinky Dink" Kenna, alderman in Chicago's First Ward during the early years of the century, were among the first to organize Chicago's black voters.[12]

---

[10] Thompson was mayor of Chicago during the heyday of the big-time mobsters —the Torrio-Capone syndicate on the South Side and the North Side's O'Banion-Moran mob. Gambling, prostitution and bootlegging flourished—all with protection from the Thompson political machine. In 1927, gambling protection kickbacks from Capone, Moran and others were estimated at over $500,000 a month. During the five years of Thompson's third term, there were 227 gangland slayings in Chicago. Landesco, *op. cit.,* pp. 80–81; aiso Virgil Peterson, *The Barbarians in Our Midst,* 1952, excerpted in Gus Tyler (ed.), *Organized Crime in America* (Ann Arbor: University of Michigan Press, 1962), p. 167.

[11] Gosnell, *op. cit.,* p. 11.

[12] "Bathhouse John" and "Hinky Dink" were closely allied with saloonkeepers, brothelkeepers and other criminal elements in the First Ward. It was under their political leadership that the First and Second Chicago "River" Wards (they bordered on the Chicago River) became notorious nationwide for corrupt election practices.

The gambler Bob Motts, who until his death in 1911 ran a saloon, cabaret and gaming house in the Second Ward, was one of the first blacks to promote black participation in politics. Gosnell says of Motts:

He was not only a good "pay off" for the police and the politicians, but he was also active in organizing the Negro voters. He would pay political workers five dollars to register people and to get them out to vote. Even before woman suffrage, wives were also enlisted in the process of "ringing doorbells and seeing faces." In return for his political activities, he demanded jobs for Negroes. Through his efforts some forty women were placed in the Recorder's office. He was also instrumental in securing the election of Edward Green (a Negro) to the state legislature in 1904.[13]

Mayor Thompson began cultivating the black vote as early as 1900, when he was a candidate for alderman of the Second Ward. Appearing at political meetings in the black district wearing his famous ten-gallon hat, Thompson presented himself as the jovial, genial friend, as well as forthright, upstanding champion, of the black. Cracking jokes and shaking hands, he extolled the virtues of negritude, while at the same time damning his opponents as "meddlers" and "Southern crackers." Mayor Thompson, a man who once said, "If your opponent calls you a liar, call him a thief," entertained the voters on numerous occasions with impromptu speeches laced with illustrations drawn from the prizefighting ring, the cattle range, the saloon, the Bible and everyday experiences of city life. He was widely popular among blacks.

During his first two terms of office, 1915–1923, Thompson appointed a black floor leader of the City Council, three black corporation counsels and so many blacks to lower-level positions that one of his Republican factional opponents called the City Hall "Uncle Tom's Cabin." Moreover, the black policy banker Dan Jackson was named Second Ward committeeman. This approach paid off for Thompson. In his first mayoral race, 1915, and in the third, 1927, black votes meant the difference between victory and defeat.

[13] Gosnell, *op. cit.,* p. 128.

Thompson seemed to feel that if his supporters wanted to play the numbers, there was no good reason to stop them from doing so. In 1928 Police Commissioner William Russell, just before assuming office, discussed the policy game with Chicago reporters. The Thompson appointee said:

Mayor Thompson was elected on the "open town" [14] platform. I assume the people knew what they wanted when they voted for him. I haven't any orders from downtown to interfere in the policy racket and until I do get such orders you can bet I'm going to keep my hands off.[15]

Chicago's black policy bankers and gambling kings performed another service for the Thompson machine above and beyond sharing with Thompson a large part of their profits. When election time rolled around they, like white racketeers, turned their army of underworld employees to the services of the political machine. At election time, what is known in Chicago as the "Big Fix" occurred:

When word is passed down from the gangster chiefs, all the beer runners, the proprietors of speakeasies, book-makers, burglars, pimps, fences and their like were whipped into line.[16]

These underworld employees had a threefold job: to register voters, to get them to the polls and to serve as election judges.

In Chicago, policy was so closely linked with police corruption that in 1938, well after Thompson's terms of office, when black policy runners went out on strike, police were sent to policy stations to protect numbers players from picket line violence.[17]

---

[14] Thompson's third election, 1927, was run on a "wide open town" platform. That, Thompson explained, meant nonenforcement of prohibition. But gangsters considered the statement a "laissez-faire for vice"—Ralph J. Bunche, "The Thompson-Negro Alliance," *Opportunity*, VII (March 1929), p. 80. Before Thompson's third election, Al Capone centered his gambling, prostitution and bootlegging operations in the outlying town of Cicero, Illinois. After Thompson's bid was successful, Capone moved his gambling rackets back into the city.

[15] Ovid Demaris, *Captive City* (New York: Lyle Stuart, 1969), p. 110.

[16] Gosnell, *op. cit.,* p. 115.

[17] Albert Votaw, "Chicago: 'Corrupt and Contented'?" *The New Republic* (August 25, 1952), p. 12.

By the time black control of the numbers in Chicago ended, in the early 1950s, a handful of Chicago blacks had been made millionaires many times over by the game. Edward A. Jones, black "policy king" of Chicago from the 1920s down to the early 1950s, was estimated to be making in excess of $8 million annually by 1950.[18] Moreover, Chicago police have calculated that the Maine-Idaho-Ohio, only one of Jones' wheels, earned $4.5 million for him between July 1949 and June 1950.[19]

What happened to the black numbers bankers? To put it briefly: whites with superior manpower and organization muscled in. In Chicago, as we have seen, this did not occur until after World War II. White crime leaders Sam "Momo" Giancana and Tony Accardo then finally staged a takeover. Theodore Roe, who was Edward A. Jones' lieutenant and "the last independent entrepreneur in Chicago's $30 million a year policy racket," was executed in traditional gangland style in 1952.[20]

But the story of Dutch Schultz's takeover of the Harlem numbers in the 1930s is a little more colorful, if perhaps apocryphal. It is said that a Harlem numbers banker, in order to cover a large "hit," borrowed $8,000 from Schultz and repaid the full amount in two weeks (or, alternatively, that he borrowed $40,000 and paid it back in three weeks). Surprised by such a rapid repayment of so large a loan, Schultz, who at the time was the biggest Jewish gangster in New York, investigated the banker's source of income and thereby discovered how much money was really being made in the numbers. Thereafter he moved in fast, striking with muscle and attempted murder. Madame St. Clair was at one point forced to hide in a coal cellar, buried under a pile of coal, until Schultz's gangsters, all set to gun her down, gave up the search and went away. Unaccustomed to violence and ill-prepared to fight for control of the game, black and Spanish-speaking bankers were driven from the highest echelons of the numbers by 1935.

[18] *St. Louis Post Dispatch,* December 12, 1950.
[19] Demaris, *op. cit.,* p. 45.
[20] A June 1951 kidnap attempt was unsuccessful. A year later, Roe was shot. *Ibid.* p. 47.

"Dutch Schultz organized the numbers racket," asserts Sergeant Cook of the Intelligence Division, New York City Police Department. Long-time Harlem residents agree. Paying Tammany Hall for protection, through West Side leader Jimmy Hines,[21] Schultz was able to consolidate the fragmented numbers business, bringing to it his fine organizational skills and making of it a highly structured operation, far more profitable than it had ever been.

Before Schultz there were no big layoff bankers in the numbers— that is, if an unusually large number of bettors won at any given numbers bank on a given day and the banker was having trouble raising funds to pay off winning bettors, there was no one to whom he could go for a loan. Schultz became a layoff banker and had blacks and Puerto Ricans working under him as controllers.

If black numbers bankers were kings, Schultz was absolute monarch of policy. In the Schultz era, "You worked for Schultz or you didn't work at all," says a numbers runner who was employed in Harlem at the time. After Schultz's death, in 1935, control of the numbers racket passed into the hands of Italian racketeers operating in East Harlem. There, until very recently, it remained. The first Italian policy boss was "Trigger Mike" Coppola of the Vito Genovese crime family. When Coppola was implicated in the murder of Joseph R. Scottoriggio, a notorious incident of the late 1940s, he retired to Florida and left the racket in the hands of his lieutenant, "Fat Tony" Salerno. " 'Fat Tony' has controlled the numbers as long as I can remember," relates a veteran Harlem police official. And only now are things beginning to change again.

This is not to say that in the intervening periods there have been *no* blacks in organized crime. This has simply not been the case. For instance, the most celebrated black gangster of all, Ellsworth Raymond "Bumpy" Johnson, famed now as a model for the increasingly popular "Shaft" movies, flourished for more than twenty of these years, from the 1940s through the mid-1960s. Bumpy Johnson was

[21] Joseph L. Albini, *The American Mafia* (New York: Appleton-Century-Crofts, 1971), p. 209. Hines had many friends in the rackets. Not one to conceal his associations, he shared a room with Frank Costello at Chicago's Drake Hotel during the 1932 Democratic Convention. Demaris, *op. cit.,* p. 125.

an extraordinary man. Suave, well-spoken, always well-dressed, he was an avid reader and more-than-competent chess player as well. Fellow prisoners at Dannemora, the New York State Penitentiary where Johnson once did time on a drug charge, were accustomed to calling him "The Professor." Yet Johnson worked essentially as a middleman for the Italian syndicate. When a black wanted to buy a franchise to establish a numbers bank, he went to Bumpy Johnson, who arranged it for a fee. When a black drug dealer wanted to buy a large quantity of drugs, Johnson arranged the sale. Italian racketeers knew him as a "persuader," one who could settle underworld quarrels before disputes erupted into violence, and violence into the publicity they naturally wished to avoid. As such, Johnson was assigned a place that for a black in those days was considered high in the ruling circles of organized crime. When he was not in jail (where he spent twenty-six years of his life), millions of dollars in syndicate funds passed through his hands. Yet Bumpy Johnson was never entirely free of the Italian mob above him.

Harlem folklore holds that the Forty Thieves, a black gang that emerged in Harlem in the late 1930s to compete with East Harlem mobsters for a share of the numbers business, was able to operate for a while without making payoffs to the Italians. But evidence on the question is inconclusive, and one can only speculate. The Forty Thieves began as an extortion ring operating from 140th Street and Seventh Avenue in Harlem. In the late 1930s they began to establish themselves as "single-action" policy bankers, and by 1939 some of the members of the Forty Thieves had accumulated enough capital to start whole figure policy operations. However, to start policy banks without paying a large percentage of the profits to Mike Coppola and his group would presumably have required the Forty Thieves to resist the Italian mob.

Long-time residents of Harlem assert that bankers among the Forty Thieves were allowed to operate numbers banks without paying off the East Harlem syndicate. The Forty Thieves, every one of them extremely tough, were known never to have backed away from a fight. Italian racketeers, according to residents of Harlem, were not eager to do battle for control of the illegal activities they were involved in and thus allowed the Forty Thieves to set up independent numbers territories in Harlem.

This story may or may not be true. That white racketeers would have been unwilling to engage in a struggle for control of illegal activities seems a specious claim, on the face of it, since supposed *mafiosi* have spent a fair amount of their time killing each other off in territorial disputes. But the late-nineteenth-century Italian "Black Hand" extortionists often left their intended victims alone when the immigrants who had received the threats announced that they would not pay and were prepared to put up a fight. And some police officials say that today one of the chief reasons blacks have been able to advance to the higher levels of gambling and narcotics operations is that now the blacks are willing to fight for control of the rackets. Just as the Forty Thieves employed "hit men" to protect their operations, so it is said that black numbers bankers are now hiring their own "enforcers" to assure that the profits from their policy banks will remain in their own hands.

As this history indicates, we seem to know a good deal about the involvement of blacks in organized crime. The knowledge, however, is illusory: we actually know very little. What we do know about are the dramatic events—the kinds of crime activities that made the papers, the killings, the political scandals and corruption—but we don't know very much about the day-to-day life of the people who are part of that drama. And we know far more about the lives and deaths of the crime activists who were involved in the past than we do about those who presently are moving to take over and control the organized crime activities they have inherited or seized from their white predecessors. Neither does this history tell us much about how various black and Hispanic crime activities are related to each other, who leads and who follows and how all of this fits into the life of the community.

There are, however, some interesting clues in this history that suggest some of the things we should be looking at in the networks that follow—in trying to understand the current stage of development and to predict the probable future directions of black organized crime groups. The first of these is the lack of any inherent pattern of organization within these groups in the past that might suggest how they may organize as they move to greater control in organized crime. When blacks did control the numbers, it was the very lack of any overall pattern of organization that allowed them to survive. While numbers games and *la bolita* were widespread throughout the black and Spanish-speaking areas of the inner city they were scattered and independent operations, not tied together by any overall syndicate or organization. It was this dispersed quality that allowed the numbers to remain in their control for some time. What organization there was or came to be was externally imposed. First the corrupt political machines discovered them and demanded tribute in terms of graft and votes in exchange for protection. Then, when the numbers games became large and profitable enough to come to the attention of the Italian syndicate in Chicago and Jewish gangsters in New York, they moved in and made them part of their organizations. Our study validated this historical observation of the lack of any inherent organizational pattern in black organized crime. We found that while there are characteristic patterns of organization within the various networks we observed, there is no overall pattern that ties the networks together. These patterns of behavioral organization grow out of the kinds of natural social relationships that link crime activists to each other in networks. Thus, we found that childhood gangs are an important recruitment device for organized crime networks; youngsters who grow up together on the street in such gangs do continue to operate as a group as they grow into adulthood. As they grow older, these youngsters acquire a street reputation for competence in crime and silence in the face of police investigation and are recruited— sometimes as a gang—into organized crime by older crime activists. A second pattern of organization grows out of prison experience; men who have been together in prison continue their association after release. Finally, there are a number of similar patterns that center around an entrepreneurial form of organization, a group of men and women working together for mutual profit in some criminal operation just as they might in a legitimate small business. There are, as we shall see, also some other important organizing principles; kinship, for example, seems to be important among Hispanic networks but much less so among blacks. Among blacks, however, the presence of women even in positions of some authority is as distinctive and important a feature of black criminal organization today as we have seen it to be historically. But again, each of these patterns exists only in the individual action sets and networks themselves and do not link networks together into larger syndicates. We do, however, have enough information from our analyses of the various networks to make some predictions in a later section about what we think might well serve as an organizing principle to bring these presently unrelated networks together into a black Mafia.

Another feature of this history that is important to remember as we look at both black and Hispanic networks in the ghetto is the relationship between organized criminal groups and the communities of which they are a part. It is in the streets of the ghetto that black and Hispanic crime activists come to know each other and to form networks. As a result, these networks are an intimate part of the community and, while some of their activities are external—pimping and hijacking, for example—most of their operations are directed toward other ghetto dwellers. Many of these goods and services, however, are valued by ghetto dwellers and the crime activists who provide them are looked upon as providing important resources to the neighborhood. Thus, like Chairman Mao's classical description of successful urban guerrillas, black and Hispanic organized crime activists are like fish in a protective sea of supportive co-ethnics. This tension between the ethnic community and the criminal justice system, with the larger society defining some acts as illegal that the ethnic community does not, accounts in part for the persistence of organized crime in the United States. To some extent this distinction represents a hypocrisy to the ghetto resident, who see the race track, bingo and even the stock market as hardly different from the numbers game except that the first three are for affluent whites while the numbers is for blacks. The moral disparity that this attitude reflects is not lost on minority groups and it should not be lost on us. Many of the people I describe in the various crime networks we followed are not condemned by most of their neighbors, because they are viewed either as victims of the same system that keeps the ghetto poor and powerless or as folk heroes. Kids who grow up on the streets learn early in their lives that while they are cut off from other routes to social and occupational mobility, organized crime is an available avenue out of the ghetto.

Finally, there is the role of the established power structure itself. If community support for organized crime is one reason why it persists, official corruption is an equally important factor. While much of the evidence presented here shows police indifference and even collusion in some of the criminal activities involved, the evidence should be tempered by the realization that most of our observations were at the street level, where the police are usually the only visible representatives of the power structure. Price gouging by merchants, dilapidated housing giving profits to absentee landlords, kickbacks demanded by inspectors and the ever-increasing evidence of corruption in the judiciary, in city hall and in the federal government as well are equally obvious to the people of the slums. These are lessons in which the ghetto resident has been schooled and they should not be lost on us.

Each of these features, which grow out of this history and are vestigial characteristics of organized crime today, is to be found in the networks I describe. There they appear as part of the record, described as they occur and related to how each network functions. Taken as a totality, however, they become valuable evidence for assessing the present and future role of blacks and Hispanics in organized crime.

The War Dragons: Growing Up in Organized Crime

When we studied the Lupollos, one of the questions we asked was "How do new members get recruited into organized crime families?"

We found that kinship was an important determinant in recruitment and was critical in moving to positions of leadership. Old Giuseppe, the patriarch of the Lupollo family, carefully screened his kin, near and distant, and selected those who would join the family business. Others he would steer into professions or legitimate business. This same recruitment pattern is characteristic of other Italian-American organized crime syndicates (which is why they are called families) and of the Mafia in Sicily as well. There was, however, also a method for getting "new blood" into the family. Even today, throughout the various Italian-American enclaves in the city, established organized crime figures watch the street behavior of youngsters, scouting for new recruits in much the same way athletic teams do. When a youth shows promise he quickly comes to their attention and he is given some small tasks to do, some of which are legal but some of which are not. As he improves his criminal competence and as his loyalty and close-mouthedness become established, he is given increasing responsibility and moves ahead in the organization.

When we asked this same question concerning recruitment into black and Hispanic organized crime networks, we found that kinship does not play an important role among blacks but that, as we shall see later, it does among both Puerto Ricans and Cubans, especially among the latter. The street, however, is an important recruiting ground for all three groups. Black and Hispanic organized crime activists follow the street "reps" of youngsters just as carefully as the Italians did and use the same process of gradual involvement to draw youngsters into the network. One of the best places to look for new recruits has always been in the neighborhood gangs, the street associations of ghetto youngsters. Within these groups, ghetto youth find and internalize the patterns of mutual trust and dependence that are sometimes the only social structure they know.

One of the networks we observed developed out of just such a childhood gang. One of the black field assistants was a member of this gang—the War Dragons—while he was growing up in the vicinity of Grand and Green Avenues in Brooklyn. He followed the crime careers of his fellow gang members and we were able to interview some of them and to trace their careers back to their early experiences as members of the War Dragons.

The Setting: A fifteen-square-block area near Grand and Green Avenues in the Bedford-Stuyvesant section of Brooklyn. "Bed-Stuy" is Brooklyn's Harlem, and like Harlem, organized crime there is moving from the hands of the Italians who long controlled it into the hands of new and emerging black networks. The transfer, however, is not as rapid in Bed-Stuy as it is in Harlem, and in the 1950s, when these events took place, the Italians were still in control and blacks were just beginning to move up in organized crime in that area.

The Characters: There were seven members of the War Dragons, a street gang in Bedford-Stuyvesant, all black males:

Harold "Manchu" Robinson, born in 1932.

Timothy Minton, born in 1936.

Theodore "Teddy" Stevens, born in 1934.

John Ellis, born in 1933, killed in an attempted bank robbery in 1971.

William "Tiny" Smith, born in 1935.

Ray Ballantine, born in 1933.

John "Sugar" Johnson, born in 1936, now serving a prison sentence.

All seven of these men grew up in the area described above. In 1951, when they committed their first significant crime together, all but Ray Ballantine were living at home with relatives. Only Harold Robinson, however, lived in a home with a father present. In November 1951, after a fire in a neighborhood bar, these seven young men vandalized and burglarized the damaged premises, making off with eighty-five cases of whiskey from the basement of the bar. This was the start of their joint criminal career. In the following fifteen years, Robinson, Minton, Stevens, Ellis, Smith, Ballantine and Johnson were to come into contact with everyone involved in crime in their neighborhood.

Michael Herlihy is a white male who in 1951 was a police lieutenant in the neighborhood precinct. He was also at the time the coach of the neighborhood Police Athletic League basketball team, of which Robinson, Minton, Stevens, Ellis, Smith, Ballantine and Johnson were all members.

George Gordon is a black male born in 1924 who lived on Grand Avenue and was a local fence, shylock and numbers operator in 1951.

Cynthia Brown is a black female born around 1925 who in 1951 lived with George Gordon and worked as a prostitute out of a bar he owned on Grand Avenue, which was known locally as "the whorehouse."

Winston Phillips is a black male who in 1951 was the bartender at "the whorehouse" on Grand Avenue.

Dorothy Ellis, John Ellis' mother, is a black female who in 1951 made her living as a numbers operator.

Timothy Minton was one of our black field assistants and he tells here how he joined the War Dragons and of the first major theft, how the gang "fenced" the loot and how gang members were recruited into organized crime. Then Harold "Manchu" Robinson, the leader of the Dragons, describes his own recruitment into organized crime. Finally, Manchu and Ray Ballantine, another Dragon, tell of what happened to their childhood friends. Here, then, are their own words.

TIMOTHY MINTON

Being new in the neighborhood nobody told me anything about a basketball team starting up. But the signs were everywhere. All the kids were still dealing with me cautious and sometimes mean—they hadn't really accepted me yet. Hell, I was still being pushed around and being shook down for money in the school cafeteria, but I don't like being shoved around though I know they're mostly testing. Still I pushed back and there was a hassle and I usually lost but now some guys are giving little smiles and nods and I only get hit for money a couple of times a week.

You know just before we moved I had a dream that, well, you wouldn't believe. Eating at some table filled with ribs, chicken, beer, wine and soda and there was my mother real happy and dressed in a new blouse and skirt and all my brothers and sisters were keeping quiet and my father was passing the food and everyone was patient, and not yelling "hey, hey, me." Crazy but even though it was a dream, shit, I only knew it was my father because my mother said once in a while "listen to your father, your father will give you the slaw . . ." The next day we moved. And I was a new kid in an old neighborhood, but it's no different in Bedford-Stuyvesant than where we were last time and the times before that. The smells are the same —the winos in the hallways, the cop car cruising around daring you to do something in front of them, the men stumbling out of bars from nine in the morning on . . . and all the kids and men leaning against the corners mostly doing nothing. I been there before in four other neighborhoods. So it wasn't new. Inside of another two or three weeks no one will be pushing me around and I'll be with some guys and the truant officer will be looking for me. Nothing is new for me . . . for us . . . But you know I was a kid and then there was this sign, something I hadn't seen before.

SIGN UP NOW
P.A.L. BASKETBALL LEAGUE
LIEUTENANT MICHAEL HERLIHY, COACH,
PRACTICE 6 P.M.

Sure I heard of the PAL but I had never joined it or wanted to, smart to stay away from any cop. But this was basketball and I wanted to play. I wasn't strong or very big but I was fast and had quick movements . . . basketball was my thing. In that sport you could trick the big guys and make them fools with their dumb muscles. I could flex my hips like a regular hooker and the guy guarding me goes for my great fake and I'm by him making the easy lay-up. I was good at head fakes too and I was no gunner. I don't mind passing the ball to someone who's a better shooter or in a better spot to make the shot. I love the game because I'm in control, it's

like being in a club and having the leader listen to you because he
knows that you can't fight for shit but you have good ideas how not
to lose a rumble. And you know I almost went out for the high school
team but the coach is also a social studies teacher and he's a prick
and I know I would miss practice and he cut guys who don't show up
just once even if they have a note. So fuck it. This is a better chance
—I can play with the guys around here and they'll stop giving me
nasty looks when I feed them a good pass or they see my one-handed
jump. Maybe this cop, this lieutenant is one in a million, shit, you
never, never know.

So there it was, six o'clock, and I was right there down at the playground, ready.

"Hey, hey, it's little Tim, last, but least, right, Timothy right . . ."

Tiny was a wise-ass but it didn't pay to answer him back or shove
him when he shoved. You ignored him, he was the least important
member of the War Dragons. To beat him up or make him look bad
with cracks was no big deal, better to look around as if you heard
something but couldn't see it—he was just a punk. So I didn't answer.

The leader of the War Dragons, "Manchu" smiled at me. "You
looking to play ball?"

"Sure," I said, "that's my game."

"No kidding," Ray, Manchu's sidekick, joined in, "no kidding you
a big rebounder, hey."

"If I gotta get 'em I'll get 'em."

There were three other War Dragon club members there and
everybody laughed except Tiny, who mumbled, "Timothy is a high
scorer tonight because the other team didn't show. Right, Tim?"

Nobody paid him any mind.

I asked nobody but hoped somebody would answer, "When is the
lieutenant going to show?"

Manchu smiled. "Herlihy will show once he gets the Davega man
to give him a free basketball or he rips one off."

I looked around the school yard, some kids were playing stick ball
at the other end. Then I looked at the empty basketball court and
wished I had brought my ball. Funny nobody here brought a ball,

two of the Dragons weren't even wearing sneakers. Crazy, but then a cop car pulled up at the school yard entrance and a small fat guy with red hair, a beer barrel belly and a dirty T-shirt and clean gym shorts walked over to us. Hot damn, he wasn't carrying a basketball either . . .

He ordered us to sit in a semicircle and warned us to shut up and listen.

"Basketball," he said, "is life. If you fuck it up you're going to fuck everything else up. You can learn plenty by not losing control if you mess up a shot. If your man scores off'a you, you don't belt him. Hey, Harold, you listening?"

"I sure am," Manchu mocked, "I sure, sure am."

"Okay, because you're the kid around here so damn free with his fists, you learn discipline you learn to set up plays and be happy if anybody on your squad scores. You can learn a lot from Nat Holman believe me and Clair Bee—they're winners because they don't bullshit. They tell their kids what they expect and they expect them to produce. No losing tempers, no punching, no sassing the referees. So what if they make a bad call, you just keep playing the right way and you'll come out okay."

"When do we play, when do we start playing?" Ray wanted to know.

"When I tell you that's when. I purposely didn't bring a damn ball because there's other things besides just playing. You gotta open your thick heads and understand words and orders. You don't fight to get a shot, you wait till you're a step ahead of your man. One thing, you guys are fast, ask the storekeepers around here, so we'll fast break. You won't drink or smoke and so we'll run all the way and the other team will be flapping their tongues by the end of the game."

"My ass is sore," Manchu volunteered.

"Your mouth is going to be also, if you don't watch out. But I'm finished, tonight. Tomorrow, I'll bring a ball and we start practicing and you all be on time. Hey you," he pointed to me, "wait a minute."

The rest walked away fast, he grabbed my arm, not rough, but not light as a feather either.

"You new here?"

I nodded.

"What's your name?"

I told him.

"You like basketball, huh."

"Yeah, I like it a lot."

"Okay, you're on the team, I'll be watching you carefully so don't dog it."

"Just bring the ball."

He really grabbed my arm and said, "Just bring the ball, *Lieutenant Herlihy.*"

I repeated the sentence like he wanted it.

Then he smiled real friendly. "You got a nice look about you, we're going to hit it off."

Terrific, now I had a fat cop for a friend.

The next night Herlihy gave us the ball and we played three on three until about seven. Poor Tiny never got a chance to play once I started making my moves and making my shots. Once I faked Manchu right out of his jock when he came back down then I went up like a bird and dropped one in from fifteen feet. And he slapped my back, "You can play, Timmy man, you can play." Even Tiny once he overheard Manchu's praise, starting suck-assing me . . . Herlihy was smoking a big cigar telling us about medals we get for playing and bigger medals and certificates we can win for winning and good sportsmanship. He's a nut for the good sportsmanship award, that's more important than winning he says and I can't believe it.

Walking home I asked Manchu, "Does he mean that shit?"

"Which exact shit."

"About the good sportsmanship?"

"Herlihy means everything he says, he's the big man in the precinct house and in the streets here. Timmy, you should always look at that man like he's hot stuff. Because he's one mean bastard. Okay?"

"Sure, I was just asking."

"And I was explaining, see ya, kid . . ."

About a week later Ray invited me to join the War Dragons and from then on no more shifty looks, everybody is on my side. And my mother is starting to complain about how I'm never home. Boy is she right. I mean be home for what?

A few days later I'm walking to the schoolyard for practice when I hear a voice . . .

"Hey, Tim, hey Tim."

It's Herlihy in his coaching outfit driving a patrol car. We had done a little job last night walking out with six toasters and one TV so I give him a funny look.

"Just a talk boy. I don't care about toasters."

"What do you mean toasters, lieutenant?" I ask, as I get in. He punched me very softly on the chest. "I was just kidding, why would a nice kid like you with a high IQ be interested in stolen goods. I just hope you kids got a fair price from the fence. You did use Gordon, didn't you?"

"What is an IQ?" I asked.

He laughed. "An IQ means you could get high marks if you weren't into other things."

He parked in front of the schoolyard and I started to get out. I don't like riding in a cop car even if it's taking me where I want to go. "Hold on, kid, I'm not finished."

He knew the damn answer but he asked, "How long you lived here now?" So I told him again.

And he said, "By now you know the score, probably you knew it a couple of weeks ago with your high IQ. But listen to what I'm saying, you're damn lucky I'm choosing you. There's plenty of crap games going on here."

"I don't . . ."

"Cut it, I know there are games, the stationhouse knows it, and the people here know we know it. If it's just gambling, no fighting or cutting we stand back and let it happen okay."

I smiled.

"You're the new pick-up boy. You go around to every game in this area and you get two dollars every hour it's happening. Really nothing to it—they expect you and there won't be any hassle. You just reach out and they put the money in. And you give it to me and I take it to the stationhouse. Then me, you, the guys shooting crap and all the cops around here are happy. We're all one happy family, if that's all that's happening is shooting crap. We take a risk you know, if some one else outside the precinct spots it, we'll catch hell. Any questions?"

So I answered, "No, I have no questions. When do I start?"

"Tomorrow morning, Timothy, and you give me the money before practice tomorrow night and after practice you look around some more for new games going on. Okay?"

"Are *we* going to play any games?" I asked softly.

"Sure we are, I've got a couple lined up."

It got so Herlihy only showed up at the schoolyard to get his pad money and we fooled around with the basketball. It was the same shit though. Since nobody cared we didn't really practice and then when we really played a few games, we lost by plenty. We lost our control and our poise. We threw the fucking ball away too many times. Me too, I got called for walking so much, I threw the ball in the air and got a technical. We lost all four games but it didn't matter. Herlihy only showed up for one of the games and then he didn't stay the whole time. Of course, we didn't win any medals and we forfeited the last game by not showing up at all . . . we were into other things by then and even I wasn't missing playing ball too much.

Nobody looked up really when the fire engines rounded our corner. You could see the smoke in the middle of the block. It looked like it was coming from the Golden Bar and someone yelled out, "Hey, free whiskey." Boy, that wise guy turned out to be some prophet.

We had nothing else to do so we watched the firemen hard at work. As fires go it wasn't much. The real fire had been on the third floor and it was working down when someone pulled the alarm. It was boring to watch and it was over soon. You know sometimes late at night when the ladders point straight up to the sky and there are guys hanging all over the place hacking away at windows and ceilings and hosing down the works it looks like a circus but this, a fire in the morning, was really nothing. That's how wrong I was.

Manchu signaled me to head for Marty's, a candy store, and wait there; that was our meeting place and when we had money we took over a booth, ordered stuff and fooled around. Marty was a little nervous, but we didn't raise much hell compared to other clubs. The Dragons were very polite. Only when some punks tried our turf were we not so polite, we were just like the *Daily News* headlines, "Toughs Mix It Up."

According to Manchu the fire had forced all the families upstairs to get out, the fire department had closed down the bar for repairs. Manchu said the bar wasn't bad off but the Jew collected all he could for fire and water damage.

"You mean it wasn't no Jewish lightning."

"Nah, not any neighborhood lightning either. Who around here wants to burn down a bar?"

"Hey right."

Manchu said softly, "If it ain't been axed to death, I hear there's plenty of whiskey in that basement."

Teddy said, "Are you sure?"

Manchu shrugged his shoulders. "I know that damn Jew, he's got plenty of whiskey down there and no firemen stayed down there long. There was no fire there. I think we ought to find out about the whiskey."

Somebody whistled. Nobody said anything for a minute. My hands were sweating and my heart was beating like a big drum. And we hadn't done anything yet.

Manchu said, "We hit tonight."

See, we had a pickup truck waiting right outside and Teddy busted the lock on the cellar door and we each had a flashlight, Manchu led us, I was last one down. The street was quiet—there wasn't even one car around. I'd been excited all day but now, now I was cool and very calm. Manchu kept licking his lips again and again, Tiny was whistling but nobody told him to keep quiet, we were all pretty much in a straight line walking down the steps into this big cellar. I had a great feeling of like family for the six guys ahead of me, I would rather be with them than anyone else and I'd rather be here in that wet basement than anywhere else in Bedford-Stuyvesant.

"Boy," Ray said, "this ain't like shoplifting, nobody is watching you at all."

"I hope not."

"Don't be stupid, we got time."

"C'mon, let's find it, keep those flashlights going . . ."

Ray was right, before this we only broke into the back of trucks and some raggedy-ass stores but down here you felt calm like you had time to watch everything and get all the goods. You're not really rushed, see, it was a funny feeling like we were in power, it felt a little like this when you steal a car but then you have to ditch the car and the feeling goes with it. But now we were together and this was no rumble with another club but we all stuck together looking for that whiskey. You could still smell smoke and there was water dripping somewhere but I could have slept there, it was a very comfortable feeling and place. I bet the others felt the same way but I never asked.

Then Manchu began laughing, his flash dancing around like a drunk spotlight. "Look, look what big daddy has found."

Then Ray was laughing and jumping so high he could have stuffed a ball down the highest rim. Tiny was still whistling and clapping his hands. John, Sugar and Teddy were grinning like fools and had even turned off their flashes. Finally I saw what made everyone so damn happy.

"Keep on the lights, stupid," Manchu said, still grinning. Like it was buried treasure there were cases and cases of whiskey piled on each other neat as hell, case after case, damn!

"How many?"

"Close to a hundred."

"See, school comes in handy, you can count whiskey."

"Never needed no school to count that."

"Shit, you could drink down here forever."

Manchu added, "This is it."

For some reason I wasn't joking around. Shit, I was all business. I asked Manchu, "Do we take it all?"

"Yeah, Tim, every damn case, leave the loose bottles. Just the cases. C'mon before Herlihy looks down and wants a cut."

"He's not getting one?"

"We'll give him a good sportsmanship award."

"C'mon let's go."

"Who we going to sell the cases?"

We were passing the cases down the line to each other it was real assembly line, every one smiling and sweating and happy as hell. Even when we stomped the Iron Lords last summer nobody was this happy or loose. Man it was terrific.

Manchu finally answered when the last cases were going up the cellar stairs and into our truck.

"George will buy this load, we'll find George."

"Wow, George."

"Sure," Manchu smiled, "This is the kind of operation he'll be interested in. We'll drive by the whorehouse. Hey, Tim, you get out, see if he's in there."

"Don't stop off and see Cynthia, George won't like that," Sugar teased.

"When it's working hours George knows what she does."

"Little Tim is scared of catching something . . ."

"Fuck you, Tiny, we all know why they call you Tiny . . ."

Manchu said, "Shut the cellar door—we don't want anybody bothering that Jew man's merchandise."

"Yeah right . . ."

Manchu said to me, "Tell George we got something for him right away."

I nodded. Manchu patted my head. "After we get paid, you can live in the whorehouse for a week or three."

"How much will we get, you think?"

"We'll know soon. George will pay off before it gets light."

"Oh man, money to burn, to burn, to burn . . ."

George the fence was the busiest and biggest man around, maybe Lieutenant Herlihy was more powerful but George was one of us. I mean he was a guy from the streets who had made it very big. All of us, especially Manchu, looked up to him. Though he was a fence this was the first time we ever dealt with him since this was our first real heavy bit of thieving. We couldn't wait to see him and to see him smile. George was also a money lender and very big in numbers. He was one busy man and from four in the morning till eight he ran and banked the gambling and drinking in the whorehouse. It was the only after-hours club around here and so was very busy. George was into everything, man. His woman, Cynthia, worked the whorehouse, too, he was getting cash from every direction. Lieutenant Herlihy got some of that money for protection but George had plenty left over, you should see that cat's clothes . . . and the cars he drove and the other women he had.

There was a bouncer on the front step but he didn't stop me! The whorehouse was nothing special-looking, a regular three-story house with plenty of furniture and corny paintings and thick rugs. If you walked in the first time you'd think you was in some rich doctor's home. George took over two of the rooms downstairs for his club, the girls worked upstairs; it wasn't crowded in the livingroom but the club rooms were packed with men drinking and talking loud; in other rooms there was a heavy crap game and hookers walking around but nobody was paying them much mind.

George was wearing a pink shirt and black pants and alligator shoes. He pointed a finger that had a big ring on it at me.

"You looking for me, little man?"

"We all are."

"Who's we?"

"The Dragons."

He teased, "Oh yeah, the Dragasses, world famous."

"We were busy tonight. Manchu said you'd be very interested in what we did."

"Hey, can't it wait?"

"Manchu said you'd be very interested."

"Where is he?"

"Outside in the truck with the whiskey."

George walked very fast now, he was rubbing his hands together like he was ready for a big meal . . .

George looked in the back of the pickup truck and began shaking hands with all of us. "Hey, where's your leader . . . hey Manchu, you been so busy, huh?"

Manchu said, "We got eighty-five cases."

"You tired, you guys tired?"

"No, why?"

"I'd like you to unload it right here, put it down another basement. I can sure use every drop here at the club. You can't have too much stock. Of course I'd like to hire you to unload my delivery. Say . . ."

"Huh."

"How about thirty dollars a case, thirty bills for each case you get in downstairs before Herlihy or one of his crooked cops comes by. I'd like not to pay that man. Then it's okay, a deal?"

"It's okay."

"And you're not too tired?"

"No we're not tired one bit. Let's go, Dragons!"

We divided equally what George the fence paid. Three hundred and sixty-four dollars each—a dollar a day for a year. The most money we made so far. We were really happy and strutting around because after a couple of days the whole neighborhood knew and they were buzzing about us. Not only was it a clean job but it was pulled off some Jew who didn't live in the community, and it was always nice to see a smart white guy get the short stick. Not even a cop questioned us, although it was known the Dragons cleaned out the Jew. Maybe he wasn't paying protection because the cop on the beat couldn't have cared less, hell they didn't even go near the closed-up bar. The only guy who came round was George, who took Manchu for a sweet ride in the Caddy. When they got back, Manchu's smile was as wide as Bedford Avenue. See, George had put Manchu right in the slot, right in the action, tomorrow he was going to be the top numbers runner and pick-up man. Also Ray was picked to hustle crap games, Ray has a tremendous personality—man, he could lead a blind man to a crap game and get him interested . . . see Manchu and Ray are getting ahead . . . and Manchu said George told him there's room for all and we'll be in too and we owed it to that whiskey pick-up . . . believe me.

With the bankroll in my pocket I started dropping in the whorehouse, the whores were very nice to me, Cynthia too, but I was a little nervous of going upstairs with her so I stayed away. I thought maybe she charged more than ten and I didn't ask how much more.

All the women were busy so I went across the hall to the bar, and there was Herlihy. He was sitting at a small table with a bottle and glass, he was smoking a big fat cigar and he looked mad; funny, his face was red all over but his small ears were white as snow. He waved me over but I made believe I didn't see him, then he shouted me over.

"Big man, Tim?"

I shrugged.

"You been dipping in here every night so I hear."

I smiled, it was true and you couldn't lie to a guy who had informers everywhere.

"You fall into an inheritance?"

"My old lady hit a number," I lied.

"I didn't hear that."

"She hit it at work, she hit it there, Lieutenant."

"She's working."

"Right," I said.

"Then she's not like her son, she likes to work."

"I don't know if she likes it."

"You like working at night?"

"Not many jobs at night."

"Oh I don't know, here, have a drink, Tim." Winston Phillips, the bartender who worked for George, brought over a glass. Lieutenant Herlihy pointed to the bottle, making believe he was drunk, but he wasn't drunk. Me, I just tried not to show I was scared.

"Here, Timmy, this is called the lieutenant's bottle, see the red tape, that means it's special, not the turpentine mix that Winnie usually gives the cops. This is quality, kid, so don't insult me. Drink it up."

I did. I made a funny face.

The lieutenant laughed for a second, then got grim again.

"You don't like it?"

"I like beer better."

"No kidding this is sweet, very sweet, tastes almost like wine to me, you know what I mean?"

"No sir, tastes like whiskey to me."

"No, Tim, it's sweet like wine, in fact Jewish wine like Manischewitz, it's the Jew's stock. You know that better than me."

I made a dumb face.

"Amazing nobody knows anything—the Yid, George, Manchu, you, of course, don't know shit. I know a little but not enough. How much did you steal—twenty, thirty cases or more? I bet it was more. I'm watching your eyes kid, and I haven't hit the right number. Fifty . . . jeez, it was more than fifty."

I shrugged.

"You don't want some more whiskey?"

"I'd like a beer."

"Hey, Cynthia," he called, "bring a beer and bring your ass over."

Cynthia smiled at me and smiled at Herlihy, in this place you get a big smile for a bigger price.

"This kid is a big customer, he's throwing money around like it's going out of style."

"Not to me, Lieutenant," she made like she was insulted.

"No kidding. You don't like Cynthia? You like George, don't you, Tim, you know he only handles top merchandise. Hey you like Tim, Cynthia?"

"I dig everybody, Lieutenant."

Herlihy said, "Put my bottle back, I'm going. Keep it warm, Cynthia . . . Be seeing you, Timothy."

I was glad to see that Irish bastard leave. I went after Cynthia and asked her price and what do you know it was the same as the others so I went right upstairs with her. She said wasn't it great to see Herlihy walking around like a bull and she kept saying it makes me happy to see him so mad. I was happy just seeing him leave and have Cynthia leaning on me and taking me into a nice clean bed; there were two dressers and a big chair in there but after a few minutes I didn't care what the damn room looked like . . .

HAROLD ROBINSON

When George found me at the luncheonette, I was sipping orange soda and reading the box scores in the *Daily News*. He said, "Let's take a walk."

I kept my mouth shut. Finally he said, "You know how many blocks are important?"

"Huh?"

"I mean fuck Manhattan and Queens and the rest, this is where we live."

I nodded.

"Fifteen square blocks—that's our turf and we don't have to fight on it or for it. It's there for us to get rich on."

"Yeah."

He smiled. "I know every bar, every store. And I know people living in Bed-Stuy want action, they need some kinda action. Okay . . ."

"I was born here, man, I know that."

"Damn, that's all you ever have to know, these fifteen, sixteen blocks is it—that and the precinct house." Then he pointed to his car parked near a pump and there was no ticket. It was a pink caddy convertible. Oh man!!

"Fuck walking, let's take us a ride."

"How old are you, Harold?"

"Eighteen, I'll be nineteen in two months."

"And you're the leader, right?"

"Yeah, I run the Dragons."

"That was a sweet deal we just had, I appreciate it. The customers like the whiskey too."

"Yeah, it worked out smooth."

"I hear you shared the money."

"Right."

"You guys are really together."

"It's a small club, only seven."

"That's the best kind of club, if you're in trouble you can get the other guys to come in. Are you in trouble?"

"No."

"You was in the big rumble in the park."

"Oh yeah, that was something."

"There going to be more battles like that."

"I hope not."

"Why?"

"Too big, too crazy, didn't know who you were beating down."

"John Ellis is one of your Dragons."

"Right, why?"

"Hell, I know him since he was a little shit, his momma works for me a long time. She's a fine numbers lady."

"Right."

"How old is John now?"

"Eighteen."

"He reliable?"

"Oh, yeah."

"Hey, I may have two Ellises working for me now."

I smiled.

"But first I want you. I want you to be my top runner and pick-up man. What do you say."

"Fuck yes, when do I start?"

"You'll start tomorrow morning. I'll drive you around and show you just what you do."

"Man, thanks George."

"Don't thank me. I think only about myself. If you help me out it's even better for me."

"Sure."

"You know I'm watching you all the time, I'll let you know if I'm not happy."

We were driving past the burned-out bar, George drove past real slow.

"Boy, you really pissed on Herlihy."

"Yeah, great, wasn't it?"

"But we don't keep on pissing on that white bastard." George turned to me and added, "The fuzz are very important to our action. We don't really fuck with Lieutenant Herlihy and his crowd. Cops are important to me."

"Yeah, okay."

"See, if they don't help us out, we can't have the crap games going, the whorehouse gets axed, the girls get arrested, everything can be tight as a drum. My car needs a lot of gas, Harold, and I got me expensive tailors. So I treat the lieutenant with respect because he has power I need, we need. Without his protection, without his cops' protection, without every fucking one of them on our side taking some dough these streets become a deserted gold mine . . . nothing comes out right without handing out bribes . . . okay?"

"Okay."

"You explain this to your Dragons, I don't want anybody sassing the fuzz. They'll look away if you guys get into two-bit trouble."

"Sure, okay."

"The cops respect me too because I'm getting big, and they'd rather deal only with big operations and give the little hustler trouble."

I nodded.

"I been watching you awhile and you're going to be okay. Maybe better than okay. You're a good listener, that's important in a new scene. So you definitely want in?"

"Definitely."

"I hear rumors one of your guys is joy popping."

"Yeah, Sugar, only him."

"He's out, I don't want him near any of my business."

I shrugged. "You're right."

George asked, "Any questions?"

"You won't laugh?"

"Nah, go ahead and ask."

"Where you buy your clothes, man?"

George didn't laugh. He answered seriously, "I'll drive by the fancy stores now, I'll answer that question today, Harold man."

Every once in a while George would come by in a big car, sometimes a Caddy, sometimes a Lincoln Continental, and take me for a ride. It always meant a new deal for us to discuss. Going for a ride was not, you know, like the movies have it—rubbing you out. When I went for a ride, it was a promotion to some new gambling thing . . .

"Hey, Manchu, how come you ain't got a car yet?"

"I don't know."

"You saving your money, man?"

"I ain't burning it, what do you mean?"

"I mean the street is where you're pulling in money and the street is where you should keep it in action. You should start lending . . ."

George patted my shoulder, "Man, you're still a good listener. Deal with junkies when you shylock. You won't get burnt, make 'em put up security—they're into plenty of stealing, so make 'em put up, say, two TVs for security. You lay fifty bucks on and if they don't pay in a day or two the sixty bills they now owe you get it up to seventy and eighty and if they still don't pay just cash in those TVs, make yourself even more profit and don't lend that junkie money again. This is important, once he doesn't pay put him on the shit list but don't use any rough stuff. The security is the rough stuff."

"Sounds cool."

"It is cool. It's better than hijacking. Hijacking trucks is about as dumb as rumbles. You quit rumbles, you ought to quit opening up backs of trucks. The fuzz are watching out for that. Keep it cool, man."

"Okay, George, thanks . . ."

"Hey, you're okay, Harold man, you're really growing up . . ."

And I guess I was, I wound up making a lot of money on those few minutes of advice.

As usual I was out all night and I couldn't sleep after driving with George and then working all night. Timmy used to say I was lucky that my father was home most of the time. Didn't mean shit though if all he did was drink and sleep and be more and more quiet. I didn't mind him being quiet, I remember when he had the loudest mouth in the world . . . Anyway I didn't feel like seeing him or listening to my mother warn me I was going to be arrested, though she didn't mind now that the rent was paid on time, so I went to the luncheonette. It was closed, it was only about six in the morning, and who's sitting on the curb but my man John Ellis.

"Hey, John, what's going?"

"Man," he said, "I can't believe it."

I sat next to him. John was waving a big fat cigar.

"My mother gave me this."

"Your brother."

"My *mother*, man, she said she was proud as hell of me."

"Why?"

"George is her idol, because of him she puts bread on the table, now we got butter for the bread because of me. Well, because of you hurrying me in numbers. Boy, she ain't yelled at me in a long time and, man, now she gives me a fucking cigar!"

"I'm glad for you."

"Yeah, I can't wait for this day to start."

"Me neither."

And we sat there and I think we were both thinking about the way things were going to be. We sat there until the luncheonette opened up.

You don't need much of a reason for a rumble when you're doing nothing, just hanging around killing time. School is shit and nobody goes much any more and there's only jobs sweeping and cleaning and the bastard over you thinks he's Mr. Big Shot and dumps on you and they pay you peanuts so it doesn't take much to get mad and feel like wasting somebody. The War Dragons' first rumble came about when two Apaches fooled around with Sugar's club jacket.

That ended up in a two-minute bopping with all seven of us against six of them and they ran and limped out of our neighborhood and believe me, they didn't come back.

See, usually a rumble doesn't last long. But there's plenty of energy you use up before and after the battle. First you spend time planning about it, deciding when and where the action will be; the rumble itself is really over fast—sometimes it seems only a minute—and then afterwards is the best time when we relax—drink cheap wine, smoke a pack of cigarettes, and talk about it. So far we always win. It's like talking about what you did on vacation and had a very nice time.

We don't carry zip guns, but we always have knives, which we won't use unless the other club pulls out their blades. Mainly we use fists and garrison belts. We've had rumbles in hallways, backyards, on the roof, one right on this street in front of the candy store, and two times behind the public school playground. All told we've had eight rumbles and the Dragons have been a club for more than two years; that's about average, I bet.

Some reasons for a rumble could be name calling, you know *them* calling your club faggots or dogs; also going to a party outside your own neighborhood is asking for trouble—see, this club might throw you out of the dance and you don't fight then but plan it for the next weekend sometimes when every one is off from school and work. Or the opposite. We don't like clubs coming to our socials either so we may make the first move, sometimes just sneering. Giving a dirty look can set things off especially if everybody has been drinking a little.

Sometimes you just talk about a rumble because there isn't anything else to do. Man, it's a boring life if there's no wine, no cigarettes, no action, and a good rep is very important, so rumbles can be one way of establishing yourself.

Here's a funny thing. Sometimes we get real dressed up for a rumble. The fuzz doesn't dig us fighting because if you get hurt bad or even killed that looks like the lieutenant and his precinct ain't in control. And no fuzz bastard walking the beat or like Herlihy likes it known they ain't hot stuff. So we walk to where we're going to kick ass, dressed in our partying best, clean clothes and good shoes not sneakers or work boots. When the prowl car sees us walking neat and clean they figure we're socializing. And man are they wrong.

The night before the big rumble in Prospect Park I brought over a jug of wine and two packs of Chesterfields. All the Dragons were glad to see me.

Timmy gave the big smile. "Hey, a real party time."

"Yeah and this isn't from that bastard Herlihy either."

"I'd drink it anyway—after all, man, he was our coach."

"Well it's from George, I ran errands for him today."

Ray started tapping around doing his special dance. "If George was my coach, I'd play ball for him on any court."

"Right, right," Sugar shouted.

I added, "George had five other jugs like this one and two cartons of Chesterfields and was off to a party. Two hookers were in the Caddy."

"Damn."

"You hear more about tomorrow?"

"Not too much."

"What if it rains?"

"We get wet but we go anyway."

"All the other clubs going?"

"All of Bed-Stuy, the Apaches, the Princes, all of 'em."

"No kidding."

"Remember when we chased the Apaches to the Williamsburg Bridge?"

"What a laugh, what a bunch of faggots."

"Well, tomorrow they're with us."

"Comanches too? I thought they were on dope."

"Tomorrow we're turning it on with everybody black, the other side is white. It's very simple, Sugar."

"Anybody carrying guns?"

"I hear some are, nothing definite."

"Wow, this is it."

"What time we supposed to be there?"

"Ten in the morning."

"Should we save the wine?"

"Nah, we'll get more tomorrow."

"Tomorrow is a holiday. It's Memorial Day."

"We'll find some wine. We can always open the liquor store."

"It's really going to be big, huh?"

"The biggest yet," I said, "I'm sure of that."

"Tomorrow we duck bullets."

"They duck the bullets."

For the big rumble, for our first real war, we wore our club jackets and carried softball bats but no gloves or softball. We wanted everyone to know our names, see our names—War Dragons. Hell, we couldn't wait for the subway to get us to the Park and those fucking paddys. The train was crowded and the passengers were giving off funny looks but they had nothing to worry about, it wasn't any of them we wanted to slam.

The day was hazy and hot and the grass still wet and squishy. Nobody was saying much, we really felt like foot soldiers. An older dude called out, "Eight across marching rows." And shit everyone listened to him. I looked around there were about thirty, forty rows of marching clubs. Most guys were wearing their club jackets like us. There was real excitement in the air as we started marching across the field. The sun showed up and lit up the place and I thought here was one beautiful sight. So far I only saw Tim and Tiny in front of me. But today it didn't matter if we weren't all together today. All these fighting clubs were like *one*, like one fist. A couple of park attendants saw us coming and ran away like fat rabbits. They'll definitely call the cops. But it's too late for fuzz because here was the parade ground and over the next hill was a big sloppy circle of white bastards. Now everybody starts shouting, waving fists and sticks and throwing curses around. We can't wait to get at them. I want to smash those punks by myself. Next I hear gunfire or fire crackers. I don't know or care. I've got my eyes on one guy and I head right for him and start swinging with my bat until he goes down a bloody mess. Someone is biting me and I shove the prick away and aim for his balls while he's down. I've lost my bat but I start swinging with my fists and bloody some bastard's nose. Chains are swinging in the air making whistling noises, someone is grunting like a stuck pig and I hear somebody crying like a fucking baby. I'm looking to hit anything and I'm sweating like hell.

"Cops, cops," somebody yells. I hear some more gunshots. Cops, cops. Look at those guys come. And it's like a movie, you know, like the cavalry coming to the rescue in a cowboy movie. There are about ten cop cars heading straight for us. Behind the cars are mounted police waving billies and behind them walking very fast are hundreds of fuzz. The parade ground gets very crowded. I finally see a white guy lying on the ground. I try to knee him but clip him in the ear. He calls me a nigger, and I kick him again. A couple of cops are running over and I wave good-by. And as I run away I'm laughing and laughing like I'm on some great drunk. And still laughing I jump the turnstile and take the next subway back to Bed-Stuy.

By three o'clock the Dragons are back safe and sound finishing off the wine, smoking the last cigarettes and talking all at once—only Sugar and Ray have a few visible scratches and bruises.

"Man, that was great."

"Biggest rumble in history. Man, I want another one. More, more."

"The Dragons did okay. I was in the front row," Ray boasted.

"We all got in a few good swings. Nobody struck out," I said.

"No more wine?"

"Shit."

"Can we get more?"

"Let's try."

"Later."

"Okay."

"Who's got a butt?"

"Here."

"Maybe our picture will be in the *News* tomorrow."

"Right."

"There'll be an article about it."

"Yeah."

"It was on the radio. I heard it."

"No kidding, what'd they say?"

"Gangs battle it out; they say there were nine hundred guys there!"

"Hey," I said, "everybody scatter."

"Why?"

"Everybody scatter and come up with stuff for the party."

"What party?"

In a few hours we have a party. Everybody contributes and I don't mean girls.

This is a party for Dragons only.

"Okay," I called out, "scatter."

And we did, touching each other, smiling, looking seriously for stuff. Here was a very good day, that was going to be even better.

Five of us are still around. No, we don't call each other the War Dragons any more. Not for a long time. We haven't been a gang for twenty years. Man, we're in business pure and simple. No rumbles, not much hassling and we gave up on hijacking years ago. George was getting bigger and bigger, a real executive type, and me and Ray trailed along and right behind us—Teddy, Timmy and Tiny. And we started moving in as the Italians lost muscle here. See the whiskey got us the good rep and we were connected right away. It was right then the Dragons disappeared. We were young guys dreaming of getting ahead. The street was our only way and George called out, "Here, boys, follow me." And that was all we needed.

Teddy, Tiny and Tim are still with me every day working numbers and we are into gambling at after-hours clubs. George now banks four of these spots and Teddy among other things picks up the cash every night. Tim is in some college in Manhattan now. That's right, *college*. He got a high school diploma when he was in the can and he wants to be an accountant now. Maybe he can work for George when he finishes. Tim was always reliable and smart. No problem with him. Tiny still dresses like a scarecrow, in rags, you know, nobody can figure what he does with his money, he don't gamble or drink or even screw around. Tiny and Teddy are both reliable and not about to fuck up either.

We usually have a pizza together every day where the old luncheon-ette used to be. Now it's a pizza and custard stand—it's still a good place for meeting and joking around but what a big difference! Except for Tiny we all dress cool and flashy and there's plenty of cash in all our pockets. And the women around here are always ready. Always.

We don't talk too much about the old days—you got to think of today. And how five Dragons made it. Five out of seven is not bad odds in Bedford-Stuy. You know, when we were a fighting club with only seven guys it was like a family. We were all brothers and looked out for each other and so even today I feel lousy about Sugar and how he got heavy into drugs right about the time of our whiskey ripoff so George didn't want him around while he was on drugs, which was one hundred percent right. Sugar kept promising to stop but then he met up with another gang—the Lions, who were out of the fighting scene too, only they were strung out on drugs and so Sugar happily joined them. Instead of a jacket and emblem, he just got a dirty needle and poison and man, he was really hooked. He kept getting busted and promising to beat the habit, but after a while nobody believed him. Shit, he didn't want to change. And the fuzz nailed him on armed robbery and he got seven to ten at Attica. Tim writes and sends him money. I send cash through Tim but I don't like to think about it. The chance was there for all of us and Sugar just fumbled it away . . .

John Ellis got into a militant thing and then into a smaller, wilder, more militant group. He changed his name and started talking nothing but offing cops and we all backed off. It was like a weird religion got inside his head. His group you know became wilder and wilder and decided to rob banks to get funds. One time they fucked up and when they came out of a bank they just hit a hundred cops that were staked out there, cut them down.

You know we went to John's funeral and without talking it over before, we all showed up in our old Dragon jackets. See, we were still loyal and saying so long to an old friend.

Oh, Ray was always a slap-happy guy good for laughs—a natural comic, who ended up smart-funny. He used his comedy to be the best and most famous crap game hustler in Brooklyn. And when he rolls those dice Ray is *The Black Cat*. And like me he's into shylocking. Ray is still funny, but now he's got plenty to be happy about. Last time I saw him Ray joked, "Hey, Manchu, after all this time you'd never guess what I saw."

"What?"

"An honest cop."

"You're kidding."

"No, there was this honest cop and the cops and all of us were chasing him off the Brooklyn Bridge. What a sight, what a fucking dream."

"That's better."

"That's much better." He grinned. "Isn't that a fucking nightmare, an honest cop . . ."

Man, that would be a nightmare. You know the militants aren't wrong, but the percentage of their changing things is not good. When you've been kept down so long you're either fighting and then getting gunned down, or you're dozing on drugs because you give up or you take what's offered—use it the best you can and keep on going. Look, when I was a kid I could fight fair or with chains and blade—either way was okay with me. I was very good with my fists and some say I could've turned out to be a pro fighter, but instead of all that I went into business . . . just like other citizens . . .

I haven't been in a real fight for a very long while—been arrested twice for possession of gambling slips and once I was busted for fencing stolen merchandise and I was out of the can inside of six months. And that is my criminal record. In the twenty years since that funny old Jew's whiskey was swiped I been on the streets not leaning against some lamppost, not nodding in some hallway, but working, digging and hustling and so far I've lasted.

I don't miss the rumbles, I don't miss being hungry, I don't miss that feeling that the sun will never shine on me. I could never get out of high school, so without the good rep I could've never been free of rumbles or not got caught up in drugs but I had the rep and

I was in real business on my streets. Sure this neighborhood looks worse than ever, more buildings got burned down and not carted away, we still don't get much garbage pick-ups and you can hear fire engines and cop sirens day and night. But the sun does shine on me now and I like it. I like it a lot.

RAY BALLANTINE

Sure, I see Manchu all the time and when we see each other, man, we sure as hell smile and punch each other around. Hey, if we get arrested tomorrow me and Harold still turned out better than anybody else we grew up with . . . by far, man.

Manchu was the leader of the Dragons, not only because he was oldest and the best fighter, but, see, he listened to ideas if they were good and he wasn't quick tempered . . . you know, he didn't jump right in and that helped us because when you don't lose your cool you can pick the right place and time to kick ass. You know to this day, there's problems, I still talk it over with Manchu.

Me, yeah, I never stop talking, running off at the mouth—I could talk long enough for a world record. Old George says I'm the pied piper of street craps. Well, I do my thing, my dance, click my heels and give 'em my smile, impress 'em with my beautiful threads, and the suckers are marching from all over. See, the cops like success since they're getting bigger payoffs than usual so everyone is happy. And, of course, for a price the bars and all the stores tip off people to see me if they want action. I run the crap games at the main cathouse every night and there's plenty of action and plenty of girls so there's never any hard feelings. Also when it comes to rolling dice I am the master so I don't have to cheat. Years ago I got named the Black Cat which is still true.

Harold introduced me to the money-lending game, which is a terrific side business, since I'm always in the cathouse and always with guys losing money, it's only natural for me to know which cat is down and out and who's a good risk. If they don't pay it back quick with the right interest we don't break arms or legs, *nah*, don't have to, we just don't let 'em back into any action and then they're well known around as bad risks. Believe me I'm paid back and fast . . .

If I had three wishes it'd be going to a cathouse every night, rolling crap and making money like it was going out of style. Harold decided to hit that whiskey and my three wishes came true. Damn . . . the good old days is bullshit, for us it never was the good old days.

THE BONDS OF SOLIDARITY

This network tells the story of a gang of boys who, as they grew up, became involved in the organized crime in their own neighborhood. The gang, as a web of friendships, preceded any criminal involvement. The gang's first big criminal action—vandalizing and burglarizing the burned-out bar—was carried out strictly on a partnership basis with equal sharing of the responsibilities and of the profits. This equal sharing seems to reflect the fact that the gang was first formed on the basis of friendship. The gang, however, is more than just a social club. In effect, the gang becomes the family-surrogate for youngsters in areas like the one in which the War Dragons grew up. Their life is lived on the street and it is the street that, while it offers fear and uncertainty to them as it does to others, also offers protection. Gangs such as this one begin very early in the ghetto child's experience. The War Dragons actually began when most of its members were in elementary school, and even in that early period the main outlines of the code of behavior that gang membership would instill began to form: toughness, daring, willingness to show bravery in the face of pain and treating all that happens within the gang as privileged matters. Children are socialized to the gang's bylaws very early and those norms of behavior become implicit directives for behavior. The child-member soon learns that he must project an image through his words and his actions that convey to fellow members his acquisition of those characteristics. That image becomes the self he feels will be tolerated, welcomed, admired and valued by his gang mates and through it they will measure his worth.

What the childhood gang offers to these youths is an introduction into the street life as a member of a group so that he doesn't have to face it alone. The gang is a buffer. The street life itself is a search for trust, and many of the activities in which members engage are trust-building and sharing tests. Youthful members share forbidden activities that, as they move into adolescence, escalate into minor law breaking. The trust relationship is built not only by sharing the excitement of the activities themselves but by sharing the knowledge of the activities and learning to keep it among themselves. The members become co-conspirators with a shared code that includes silence. Loyalty to friends in the gang also becomes part of that code, and the two—silence and loyalty—join to establish the members as insiders with everyone else as outsiders. It is interesting to note that the important factor that led to the demise of the gangs was hard drugs. The addict is, as we have seen so frequently in the networks, unreliable since his dependence on drugs is more compelling than his loyalty to his fellow members. Also, drugs are extraterritorial, taking the addict out of the neighborhood in search of money and pushers. The gang is territorial in nature and roaming members are useless. Many gangs disappeared as heroin addiction increased but they are coming back again in Bedford-Stuyvesant (and elsewhere) as youthful heroin use is reduced.

While the gang produces these bonds of solidarity, it also provides an arena for status assertion—finding one's place in the hierarchy of the street society—which is much more important in areas like Bedford-Stuyvesant than it is in middle-class sections. Childhood is important in middle-class areas as well, but the greater mobility of the middle class—with its opportunities to find new statuses in the changing scene from the neighborhood, to the high school, to the college, to the job—allows the mistakes or failures of one period to be covered if not forgotten in new opportunities to prove oneself. Not so for the ghetto youngsters, whose neighborhood associates are the audience he will know throughout his life, so that his adult status comprises the memories of his childhood, not only for him but also for his neighbors. As a result, the "rep" that a youngster establishes is likely to stick with him throughout his life and will remain the measure of his worth, to himself and to his associates.

Those characteristics later to become important in adult life in the streets are the ones that are prized in childhood: toughness, loyalty and daring combined with the ability to "hustle" or make it with one's wits. The street rep develops out of a combination of these characteristics, and out of one's failings as well, which are exhibited on the street. Membership in the gang proves that one can be trusted, but even once that trust is established, it is necessary to constantly assert one's status characteristics within the group. From studying the War Dragons and data we have on Luis Santos' childhood gang (discussed in Chapter 4), we can make some assumptions about how such gangs are structured. First, they are more equalitarian than one might assume. There are leaders, but usually the leader does, in fact, lead and not rule. Second, status is determined by words as well as by actions. Much of the gang's time is spent in talk about—expectantly or in retrospect—the actions they will or have carried out, and in these sessions, verbal ability becomes important. Insults, slights and recountings of past deeds follow a very well-established pecking order and giving or receiving insults is a mark of one's position in the gang. There are also categories or classes of status within the gang. At the bottom are the "faggots"—not homosexuals but individuals who are on the fringes of the gangs. They do not possess, value or exhibit those characteristics that lead to trust. Next are the "punks," "jerks," "creeps," or "assholes"—the members who possess and exhibit the minimal qualifications for membership but who, like Tiny in the Dragons, do not possess or exhibit them with any consistency and so serve as the butt for jokes and provide a stratum for diversion by other members. The largest group are the regular guys, the members who can be relied on for all of the characteristics valued by the gang because, in street terms, "he has balls." Above the regular guys are leadership categories that mark those who fill these statuses as a step above the regular guys. First there are the "tough guys," whose physical exploits are of a higher order than most members'. They have fought more violently, against tougher or older antagonists or have greater physical strength than other members. Then there are the smart guys, those members who are more intelligent, have greater street sense or are shrewder than their fellows. Finally, there are the "crazy guys"; no risk is too great, no danger too much to face and no challenge impossible for these members. They are the ones who take the greatest chances in any activity whether it is jumping from the roof of a warehouse into the Passaic River, as Willie C. Squires did in his childhood in Paterson, or, as we shall see in a later network, exhibit the "berserk," no-holds-barred, fight-to-the-end, no-terms-except-unconditional-surrender, uncontrolled behavior of "Crazy Joe" Gallo. Each of these types has leadership potential and the leader draws something from each. The leader is usually one who is tough but also smart. If a member's chief qualification is that he is smart then, like Timothy Minton of the Dragons, he will often be an adviser to the leader who has some "smarts" but who is also tough. If he is just tough, then he becomes the gang's best fighter but usually not its leader because leadership demands shrewdness as well as strength. The "crazy guy," however, is often a leader because of the terror he can strike in his fellow members and in the gang's audience. But such leaders seem to be rare, at least in our experience.

The persistence of these childhood relationships into adulthood is a vitally important factor in the formation of organized crime networks. We found throughout our research that the links forged in childhood are very enduring and that the trust generated within them is often the only relationship of that sort the adult crime activist can remember. Also, those traits valued in the gang are also the characteristics that are important in the organized crime network: loyalty to one's fellow members, dependability in terms of silence to the police and to outsiders, and being trustworthy to the people with whom one works. As was true with the War Dragons, these characteristics are first developed and tested in the childhood gang and they keep members together into adulthood, often in the same neighborhood where the gang began.

There are other lessons to be learned from this network as well. Of particular interest is the role of Lieutenant Herlihy, the PAL coach who was an original corruptor of the boys since it was he who drafted Timothy Minton into cutting or picking up the police percentage of the payoffs from street gambling. Herlihy's role is interesting from another perspective as well; his relationship with the organized crime activities of the neighborhood, from the street gambling to the operation of the "whorehouse," shows a pattern of symbiosis in which police seem willing to allow low-level, low-risk crime to take place if they can thereby keep crime activists under surveillance and make a profit at the same time. The activities that seem to be condoned—minor theft that does not include violence, gambling, prostitution and loan sharking—are all activities that do not draw much heat; they do not have the public or official condemnation of drug pushing or armed robbery and so are "tolerable." But the complicity of the police, the failure of the school to reach these youngsters and the broken structure of most of their families underscore the most significant aspect of this network: *not a single force in the neighborhood where these boys grew up presented a vigorous deterrent—a serious threat, a danger, a fright or a compelling alternative set of values—to those of the street society, which justified most of their activities.* One can imagine that in a few cases there were lectures from family, perhaps ministers and certainly from teachers; but these would naturally count for little to boys who could weigh against them the norms they shared with their gang-peers and of the older crime activists out in the neighborhood's only place of hope and excitement, the street.

Protecting My Man's Back: The Prison Court and Recruitment in Organized Crime

As we have seen, the childhood gang can serve as an incubator in which delinquent behavior grows into criminal partnerships. But not all childhood gangs in the ghetto produce criminals, nor are all organized crime activists graduates of youth gangs. Throughout the various networks that we observed, we found that prisons and the prison experience are the most important locus for establishing the social relationships that form the basis for partnerships in organized crime, both among blacks and among Puerto Ricans. The Italians do not form their criminal partnerships in prison, both because they do not go to jail as often as blacks and Puerto Ricans do now and because they form their organized crime networks on the Mafia-oriented basis of kinship. It is, in fact, these kinship-structured groups that afford the protection that precludes arrest and conviction of Italians.

We have long known that prisons are self-perpetuating institutions because they reinforce existing criminal attitudes and because they provide many opportunities for learning new criminal techniques as well. But we have not been aware of the great extent to which criminal partnerships are formed in prison, nor have we been aware of the mechanisms that operate in prison life to promote formation of these partnerships. In our study we found that the common practice in prisons of segregating prisoners informally by race produces a number of closely knit social groups—the prison "courts"—in which organized crime partnerships are first created and which then structure similar relationships outside the prison.

In describing the prison network, we have used two different accounts of prison experience by two of the field assistants, one black and one Puerto Rican. Actually, each was in a different prison; one in Green Haven, and one in Attica. The events taking place in each prison were so similar, however, that we have included the two prisons in this narrative as one institution. The locale is upstate New York and the time is early 1972, a few months after a major rebellion in which a number of guards and inmates were killed. The characters in this network are briefly described first.

Luis Santiago, a leader among Puerto Rican prisoners, is a Puerto Rican male in his late thirties. He has spent fifteen to twenty years in New York prisons.

Angel Parilla, a follower of Santiago, is a Puerto Rican male in his twenties. He works in the prison bakery, where he can obtain yeast.

Pascual Colon is another of Santiago's followers and a friend of Parilla. He is a Puerto Rican male in his twenties.

Juan Rocque, a junkie, associates at times with Santiago and his followers. He also associates with other junkies. He is a Puerto Rican male in his twenties. He performs communication functions for Santiago.

Jesus Hernandez, a relative of Luis Santiago, is a Puerto Rican male and is in his late teens. He receives protection from, and has been adopted as *compadre* by, Santiago.

Raymond Atkins, a black male, is in his thirties. He is a "bandit," an aggressive homosexual, who attempts to assault Jesus Hernandez.

Billy Reagan, a white male in his twenties, is a pill freak. He is a friend of Juan Rocque. Because both Reagan and Rocque have been stigmatized by other prisoners as junkies, they are able to maintain their friendship despite ethnic barriers among prisoners.

Frankie Henson, a black male in his twenties, is a homosexual prostitute. He treats Raymond Atkins as his pimp.

Trenton "Mau-Mau" Williams, a black male in his thirties, is an inmate lawyer. In street life he was a successful hustler. He was a leader of the prison riot, and the prison administration and other inmates treat him as one of the most respected inmates in the prison.

Jorge Marrero, a Puerto Rican male in his thirties, formerly was one of the most respected of the Puerto Rican leaders. He is now in solitary confinement in another prison for his role as a leader during the riot.

George Watkins, a black male in his thirties, is a winemaker and an entrepreneur. Jo-Jo Smith is his friend.

Ben Hicks, a black male in his thirties, is a porter in George Watkins' gallery. Hicks takes advantage of the mobility his job permits to assist Watkins in winemaking.

Daniel McChesney, a white male in his twenties, works in the prison warehouse. He is a snitch. He supplies apples to Watkins and Hicks for winemaking.

Jo-Jo Smith is a black male in his late twenties. George Watkins is his friend. Smith plans to operate in Watkins' neighborhood when he is released on parole.

"Crazy Joe" Gallo is the well-known organized crime leader who was gunned down in Little Italy in 1972. Gallo became acquainted

with Parilla and Santiago a few years ago in another prison. Tales of Gallo's exploits have been popular in prison lore.

Wayne Newcomb, a black male in his twenties, has set up heroin deals while out on parole.

Sergeant Thomas Harrison, a white male in his late thirties, is an ambitious guard. He was recently transferred to the prison. He supplies heroin to the prisoners.

Walter Bishop, a black male in his twenties, is Wayne Newcomb's friend. He is an outside contact man for prison heroin traffic. He has also been in the prison as an inmate.

Jose Rivera, a Puerto Rican male in his late teens, is a member of the Young Lords youth gang. He has attempted to politicize Jesus Hernandez and Santiago and his followers. He was raised as a ward of the state and has served a sentence in a reformatory.

Albert Dowd, an older white male inmate, instructs other inmates in various criminal techniques and skills.

Stanley Mierkowicz, a white male in his twenties, was a leader of white prisoners during the riot.

Most of the life of a black or Hispanic professional criminal is spent in the confines of the urban ghetto. There he is shielded from the authorities by the protective coverings of an entire culture. Many of his neighbors accord him respect if he is successful, even if they are aware of the criminal activities he is engaged in. Others may fear him or disapprove of him, but no one would expose him to the police, whom they all fear. Unlike the white professional criminal, however, the black or Hispanic criminal inevitably spends one or more periods during his career away from the shelter of his urban neighborhood. New York State's maximum security correctional facilities are located from fifty to several hundred miles from New York City. Each of these institutions houses many men from urban areas and constitutes a vital training ground and organizational meeting place for the participants in urban organized crime.

The philosophy of American penology that was held in the early nineteenth century, when the first modern prisons were built, was based on the principle that a criminal must be isolated from the bad companions who led him into wrongdoing. Accordingly, silence became the first principle of prisoner conduct and physical isolation the first principle of the architecture of early American prisons. The architecture remains. A majority of New York State's maximum security institutions, which are the heart of the state penal system, were built over one hundred years ago. Physical isolation is still the major fact of the inmate's life in these institutions, as inmates spend sixteen to twenty-four hours a day alone in cells measuring about nine feet by six feet. Silence is still required at meals. Far from being isolated from other criminals, however, today's inmate lives in the ultimate criminal milieu. Not only does he in many cases live side by side with the same companions he knew on the streets, he also lives in a society where the racism and harassment by authorities he experienced growing up are reproduced in an intensified form.

Just as in the ghettos, the black or Hispanic man looks to his brothers for protection from violence, whether from the authorities or from others in his predicament. The material poverty that many knew outside is also more intense inside, and survival in a condition of severe deprivation depends on the same skills for which many have been incarcerated. Conversely, success in fully surviving the harsh conditions of prison life can be the most important training that a black or Puerto Rican can receive for later success in criminal networks outside.

In the early days of April, the weather upstate is still bitterly cold. Above the enormous wall surrounding New York's most fortresslike institution, the onlooker can hardly make out the line between the top of the wall and the slate gray of the sky. The prison yard has been virtually closed for four months, however, and today the inmates are grateful to venture outside, even inadequately protected as they are by their thin, gray, hip-length prison issue coats. The yard is broken up in several places by crude fences improvised of string and scraps of wood. These fences delimit areas the prisoners call "courts." In one of these courts, Luis Santiago, Pascual Colon and Angel Parilla are busy building a fire in a makeshift tin stove. They have brought into the yard two tin pans, a box of rice, some dried beans, a jar of coffee and a can of tomato sauce. It is late afternoon, and dinner is served in the middle of the day. Supper in the prison is both meager and not compulsory. Many inmates do not attend. They find their own fare preferable, but they are not always able to cook. Packaged food is available at the prison commissary, but cooking is forbidden in the cells. This chance to cook a meal is rare, though not so rare as the chicken served for lunch. The chicken was virtually raw and many prisoners could not eat it.

Luis Santiago lets Colon and Parilla do most of the work and sits quietly, smoking. The customs of the prison unequivocally allot this small, string-bordered square to him. Technically, four people must band together to obtain a court, but Santiago, Parilla and Colon merely paid a fourth party three packs of cigarettes to join in their request. This rectangle abutting the masonry of the cellblock that forms one wall of the yard is now the territory of these men. No one but a very inexperienced inmate would venture into the court without their invitation. This space is theirs. The dynamics of prison economy and prison life in general hinge on the extraordinary sense of value that scarcity imparts to seemingly trivial possessions. A man's cell and its contents are his own, but he cannot share them since he is alone in the cell. Thus, this small area is the entire open property of these men. For the hour or hour and a half a day that they are allowed in the yard, this is the only place where they can socialize freely and without unwanted interruption.

A tour of the various courts in the yard quickly reveals the first rule of inmate social organization, *ethnic segregation.* New York's prison population is composed of three groups—white, black and Hispanic—and the prison courts all reflect these divisions. Since the early 1960s the prison population has changed drastically from over 85 percent white to a large majority of black and Hispanic prisoners. Although the prisons farther upstate have a slightly higher percentage of whites because they receive convicts from rural areas, whites still compose less than 40 percent of the inmate population.

Less than 10 percent of the inmates are Puerto Rican. Though they

are often lumped together with blacks in the eyes of both white inmates and the white prison administration and staff, Puerto Ricans
tend to associate primarily with each other. Among Puerto Rican
prisoners, no man is more highly respected than Luis Santiago.

Only in his late thirties, Santiago is nevertheless older than most of
his fellow Puerto Ricans. He was arrested in 1959 for a daring and
skillfully planned robbery, thus entering prison with some credentials
already established. Though he has been outside a couple of times in
the intervening years, Luis Santiago has spent most of these years in
one or another of the upstate prisons. In that time, he has seen the
radical change not only in the prison population but in convict attitudes as well. His seniority as an inmate and his accumulated
experience and understanding of prison life make him respected by
other Puerto Ricans, by the general population and even by the
administration. In terms of prison life, he has prospered. At this
moment, he has taped to the inside waistband of his trousers a sum
of nearly $100. In an institutional society where no inmate is sup-
posed to have any cash at all and most men work for wages totaling
about $7.50 a month, Luis Santiago is an extraordinarily wealthy
man.

The fire lit and the coffee made, the men settle back to wait for the
food to cook. Parilla stores the unused foodstuffs in the food locker
located near the court. Pascual Colon begins to tell about how he
"burned" a guard the previous day after the showing of the movie
In the Heat of the Night.

Though Colon is a close associate of Santiago, he does not receive
the deference from the authorities that Santiago has earned by his
cool and uncompromising attitude. Colon is loud, funny and given to
boasting about his sexual and hustling prowess. He is a natural target
for harassment and maintains continuing feuds with certain guards.
He had verbally provoked one of them on the previous afternoon as
he was entering the movie. Afterward, while marching to his cell with
his "company," a housing unit of about forty inmates, he was sepa-
rated from the group and subjected to a shakedown for contraband.
Colon elatedly recounts the guards' disappointment on finding him

clean. He had anticipated their move and had ditched his "shiv," a homemade knife he had obtained from a friend in the metal shop, almost under the guards' noses. The searchers were infuriated when they found traces of the tape that had secured the knife to his side. They knew he had been holding a knife but were unable to prove it. Early this morning, the guards searched Colon's cell and they found a "dropper"—an illegal heating coil used to make coffee and heat canned food in the cells. Many inmates have droppers—indeed, much of the food sold in the prison commissary is intended to be heated. But the rule against droppers is often selectively enforced in a case like Colon's. He is now threatened with confinement to his cell, but his satisfaction with having so cleverly duped the guards the day before outweighs this threat.

When the rice and beans are cooked, the men eat avidly. Simple though the meal is, it is at least hot, fully cooked and not served on half-clean dishes. After the men have finished their supper, other inmates seem to feel that Santiago's court is now ready to receive visitors. The first to enter is Juan Rocque, a thin intense young man who is peripherally attached to the court. It was Rocque who accepted the cigarettes in return for adding his name to the request for the court. Rocque is a long-time heroin addict and, as such, can be looked down upon by men incarcerated for more imaginative and/or challenging crimes. Rocque, however, is an intelligent man and is sometimes party to the various hustles that operate out of Santiago's court. He is always looking for some kind of action in hopes of hustling a fix. Heroin is undoubtedly the scarcest and most valuable good in the prison economy. Tonight, he has no special business with Santiago or with Parilla and Colon, who often function as Santiago's agents, but he habitually includes the court in his rounds. He is relating some trivia from the grapevine when a second visitor makes a more dramatic entrance.

Jesus Hernandez, a young man of nineteen, slightly built so that he looks even younger, bursts in looking extremely agitated. The abruptness of his entrance is ignored because the men in Santiago's court know he is a relative of Luis Santiago. Hernandez had arrived at the prison a short time ago and had joined the general population after being processed only days before. His arrival had created some stir in Santiago's court for reasons other than his kinship with Luis. Hernandez had never been in prison before and probably had been sent all the way upstate because of the violent nature of his crime. He had been convicted of a youth gang slaying in the Bronx and possession of a number of guns. The combination of his youth and slightness of build, his proud bearing and his exploits in the street gave him the beginnings of quite a reputation.

When questioned as to why he is so excited, he seems extremely reluctant to speak. He is given smokes and coffee and a chance to relax while Pascual Colon holds forth again, this time with an account of a sexual exploit that the others have heard many times before. Finally, Hernandez, on Santiago's urging, begins to tell of a homosexual assault he suffered that morning on his work assignment.

After he had entered the prison, Hernandez was transferred to the general population and assigned to work in the metal shop, the prison's main industry. The metal shop is a hated job for several reasons, and the members of Santiago's court had all managed to wangle more desirable jobs during their time at the prison. Besides being full of heavy, inadequately safety-equipped machinery, the shop is hot and dirty and little or no training is provided in handling the hazardous equipment. The worst aspect of the metal shop, however, is that it has three or four times as many workers assigned as can possibly use the machines. The shop is known throughout the prison as a notorious lair for "bandits," the prisoners' term for aggressive, violent homosexuals.

On his first day in the shop, Jesus Hernandez was approached and ostensibly befriended by Raymond Atkins, a black in his thirties, with a large build and considerable strength. He offered to teach Hernandez how to use the machinery and gave him a pack of cigarettes. Since cigarettes are the standard form of currency in prison, this was a very generous gesture, but one that Hernandez accepted to his later peril. On the next day, Atkins again offered Hernandez a pack of cigarettes. Now Hernandez became suspicious, but he accepted the cigarettes anyway. Shortly after giving away the second pack, Atkins told Hernandez that he now owed him some repayment, perhaps in the form of sexual favors. When Hernandez refused, Atkins and two other men abducted him from under the eyes of the supervisory personnel, who were accustomed to disregarding such matters anyway. Atkins and his cohorts had not reckoned, however, on the fierceness of Hernandez's reaction. The chance passing of a guard and a burst for freedom saved Hernandez by the narrowest of margins from being branded a punk, possibly for the rest of his prison career.

Luis Santiago has not stirred while listening to the story. When Hernandez has finished telling it, Santiago immediately turns to Angel Parilla, requests and receives Parilla's shiv. Though there are no guards near, the transfer is made quickly and surreptitiously, the movements seeming no more than casual gestures. Santiago gives the knife to Hernandez, and the men quickly tell him how to conceal and when to carry it. Hernandez will later be delighted and fascinated with his new possession, but he seems primarily relieved for the present. To know anyone inside when entering prison makes "jailing" much easier. To find the protection of Luis Santiago is quite a piece of good fortune.

Shortly after this business has been completed, Santiago clears the court of everyone but his young cousin. They are not close relatives and had never met until a few days previously, but Santiago is acquainted with the young man's mother. Their conversation discovers other common acquaintances and family lore. Though Hernandez has never been in Puerto Rico and Santiago left the island many years ago, they trace their parents and grandparents back to the same village. Santiago ends their conversation by wryly observing that Hernandez might have just acquired a *compadre*.

In Puerto Rico, a *compadre* is an older man who serves as a child's patron or sponsor. He is usually chosen by one's mother or father for his knowledge and connections in a given field. Sometimes there is a baptism or initiation ritual involved. In an important family, the younger man may be made a godchild of the older man. Once the *compadre* is chosen, however, the younger man has only begun to be admitted to his *compadre*'s business or field of acquaintances. The apprentice must now prove himself, and, as he does so, he is gradually introduced to his *compadre*'s *compadre* and friends and is trained in some business. Outside of Puerto Rico, the system is not so formal, but Luis Santiago's and Jesus Hernandez's relationship is beginning within the vestigial framework of the customs of the old country. The progress of the relationship will depend on how quickly and perceptively Hernandez learns to jail, that is, to understand and survive in prison society. His toughness and aggressiveness, as demonstrated by the crime for which he was convicted and his resistance to the bandits, as well as the leadership ability shown in his youth gang, are an impressive beginning. If he can emulate his *compadre*'s cool manner (Luis Santiago is called "ice"), he can learn to advance himself quickly, both in prison and later outside.

In the yard next afternoon, Juan Rocque pursues his rounds with more than usual alertness in his eyes. He has heard rumors of an impending heroin transaction, but he cannot ascertain anything beyond a general report. For an opiate addict, the goals of prison survival are simple: (1) obtain heroin, (2) if heroin is not available, obtain morphine, which is easier to find, (3) in the absence of the above, obtain any of dozens of pills with an opiate base. In the prisons nearer to New York City, heroin is much more available than in the upstate prisons, but Rocque has long since run out of schemes to get himself transferred. In the upstate prisons heroin is a very scarce and valuable good, and addicted inmates must rely upon various substitutes such as pills, which can be smuggled out of the prison medical facilities. The medical care in the prison is slipshod. One way in which the doctors register their contempt for inmates is to assume that every man on sick call is merely after something to get high. Thus, tranquilizers are relatively easy to obtain. Some men receive them regularly and carry them out under their tongues to sell for cigarettes in the yard. The inmate nurses can sometimes develop a relationship with a staff nurse and pilfer a quantity of pills. Other drugs available on the prison market from time to time include marijuana, "222," a codeine-based pain pill imported from Canada, nutmeg, and cocaine. Cocaine is even more expensive than heroin. The use of cocaine is a pinnacle of conspicuous consumption in prison and raises rather than lowers one's prestige. Pascual Colon is an avid cocaine fancier and spends much of his time with Luis Santiago on the drug; yet, he is not considered a junkie as is Juan Rocque.

Though an addict's goals in prison may be simple, the means the addict uses to achieve those goals, at least in Juan Rocque's case, can be quite complex. Just as in the street, he must go to a variety of places and engage in a number of activities in order to score. Thus, Rocque has acquaintances in many sectors of the prison whom he contacts regularly. He knows many more people than Luis Santiago, especially many more non-Puerto Rican inmates. Just as on the outside, junkies in prison tend to associate because of their common needs and because they are branded with a common stigma.

Having failed to crack the mystery of the heroin rumor, Juan Rocque settles down in the company of a young white inmate and personal friend, Billy Reagan. Reagan is actually a pill freak, convicted for selling a variety of drugs, but both the prison community and the two men themselves view themselves as having a common interest. Were they not both drug oriented, even though toward different drugs, they probably would not associate and could not without being harassed by both guards and inmates. Reagan would be taunted as a "nigger lover" (white men in prison, both administration and inmates, tend to lump blacks and Puerto Ricans together), and they would be accused of having a homosexual relationship. As "dope fiends" they are able to converse outside the normally rigid barriers of ethnic segregation that are the most pervasive principle of inmate social organization.

Their stigmatization works in many cases to their advantage precisely because they are able to venture outside their own ethnic groups. Of course, Juan Rocque would never be trusted with actually transporting drugs or with any other task requiring that kind of reliability. As a conveyor of information, however, a vital interracial connection in the prison grapevine, he can be invaluable.

Besides his value in communications, Rocque is also known in

Santiago's court for a certain versatility, especially in dealing with people. He does not have the kind of versatility that Luis Santiago has—one involving a high degree of self-control and a sense of authority—but he has learned from his experience as an addict to adapt quickly to the range of situations and challenges the vicissitudes of the dope market present to any addict.

Rocque had actually met Reagan, for example, in a business transaction before either was incarcerated. During a drug shortage in New York City one summer, Rocque had become involved in a complex series of operations in order to score. He had traveled downtown to buy some pills from Reagan, which he resold for a profit in his own drug-hungry neighborhood. With the money earned in that transaction, Rocque was able to buy heroin for himself, at a high price because of the drought, in still a third neighborhood. Many ghetto residents have few dealings outside their immediate neighborhoods, but junkies are forced to learn how to enter unfamiliar and dangerous territory, especially during shortages. Thus, the peculiar mobility of the addict in prison society, based on a certain stigmatization that has its advantages, is something the addict has already learned outside. In this sense, some addicts have a relatively easy time of jailing, once they have begun to establish contacts.

Rocque's conversation with Reagan is suddenly interrupted by the sounds of the beginnings of a heated confrontation near one of the black courts. Luis Santiago, flanked by Colon, Parilla and some other Puerto Ricans, is confronting Raymond Atkins, the bandit who had attacked his young cousin. Atkins is similarly flanked by supporters, and an incident of racial violence seems perilously close. Not content with arming Jesus Hernandez against further assaults, Santiago has decided to inform Atkins personally that Hernandez is under his protection. Santiago's prestige does extend beyond the Puerto Rican courts and would be sufficient to impress many people, particularly because Santiago is a very powerfully built man. Atkins, however, is a butch kid, hot-tempered, also physically powerful, and with a decided taste for violence.

Atkins refuses to acknowledge Santiago's warning and launches into a stream of anti-Hispanic epithets. Though Santiago remains unmoved by the provocation and calmly repeats his ultimatum concerning Hernandez, the other Puerto Ricans, as well as the blacks backing Atkins, many of them also known bandits and butch kids, are all spoiling for a fight. By this time, there are encircling the principals a number of inmates not allied to either side (the bandits are hated by many prisoners) and armed guards observing the action from their posts on the walls surrounding the courtyard.

Santiago decides to try a new strategy when he sees the bystanders. Behind Raymond Atkins is a black inmate named Frankie Henson who has a known homosexual relationship with Atkins. In fact, Henson is a homosexual prostitute and addict who treats Atkins as his pimp. Henson performs sexual acts for which he is paid in cigarettes. He gives Atkins his profits in return for Atkins' protection and ability to supply him with drugs. Unlike punks, who are forced, duped, or paid to assume their roles, Henson is a natural homosexual and advertises himself as such by openly effeminate dress and mannerisms. Punks usually try to conceal their role.

Santiago tries to take advantage of Henson's presence to ridicule Atkins. His remarks succeed in provoking laughter among the non-allied onlookers, but Atkins begins to lose control. At this moment, a third party enters the center of the gathering to try to prevent an outbreak.

Trenton (Mau-Mau) Williams, a black leader and respected inmate "lawyer," is probably the best-qualified man in the entire prison to handle this situation. A few years ago, during an uprising in the prison, he emerged as one of the strongest and most competent leaders. Every man in the prison knows how Williams once spent many months in solitary for helping other inmates with their writs, an activity that was forbidden at that time but that Williams' persistence helped make acceptable. Further, he has just emerged from solitary again for his part in the recent uprising. Today's prisons are much more highly politicized than the society outside, and Williams is indeed very greatly esteemed by his fellow inmates. Even Atkins, who is capable of scorning anyone, is indebted to Williams for legal advice.

The situation is very hot, however, and before appealing to Atkins, Williams begins to berate the incensed inmates for being so foolish as to provoke the administration. He points to the guards on the walls who already have their guns trained on the belligerents. This argument is undeniably effective, for all the inmates know the potential of institutional violence. Having arrested the attention of the crowd, Williams proceeds to cool them out with a succinct political appeal for solidarity among the inmates. He tells the prisoners that racial confrontations among inmates play into the administration's hands, because the administration, in seeking to defuse inmate protests about conditions of prison life, tries to divide prisoners among themselves. Developing this argument he reiterates the oft-cited maxim of prison politicos that racism is the administration's chief tool for breaking down prisoner solidarity and thus destroying efforts for prison reform.

As Luis Santiago returns to his cell that evening, he is annoyed with himself for having managed the Atkins business so carelessly, though with a man such as Atkins there might have been no other way he could have handled himself. Because he had taken Hernandez under his protection, he had an obligation to Hernandez in the eyes of those attached to his court as well as in the eyes of the general community. The one trait absolutely essential to achieving and maintaining respect in prison is the ability and willingness to back up one's assertions physically. Difficult circumstances, such as the potentially explosive confrontation that Santiago had had with the hot-headed butch kid Atkins, are never an extenuation of this principle.

Prison life always verges on violence, and the man who is respected in prison must demonstrate his ability to deal successfully with violent situations. The respected prisoner must be able to fight when the circumstances of a conflict between inmates seem to require it, and he must be able to accept punishment from guards manfully. He may be called on to witness a fight between prisoners and then he must view this exchange of blows without flinching and must be ready to assist one of the men who is fighting if he is the man's ally. If he is able to use violence as a tool, not as a first resort but as a weapon that is always available to him to back up his words or to assert his rights as an inmate, then he can become successful in any endeavor he is engaged in in prison life. Without the ability to use violence, he cannot deal successfully in any prison activity and, at worst, will become prey to the savage homosexual bandits who attempted to assault Jesus Hernandez. Luis Santiago's own physical prowess and the position of leadership and respect he has attained are no coincidence.

Since he is skipping supper, Santiago is leaving the yard for a straight fourteen hours of confinement to his cell. That night he eschews shouting to his neighbors or playing cards with the man next door. The memory of Trenton Williams' intervention poses much thornier problems than the simple inevitability of his having had to confront Atkins. Santiago, along with the rest of the prison, inmates and administration, respects Williams as a stand-up guy. He is also grateful that Williams was able to intervene successfully. For all Atkins' bluster, Atkins was successfully put in his place, and the resolution of the particular situation is largely satisfactory to Santiago.

But Williams' intervention has threatened Santiago indirectly in a number of ways. The very fact that Williams had to impose himself in Santiago's quarrel is somewhat embarrassing, but Santiago is wise enough to disregard this aspect. Had the violence-prone parties been Puerto Rican, Santiago might have been in Williams' position.

More serious is the threat to Santiago's image that is posed by the entire evolution of Trenton Williams' prison role. Williams was himself once the central figure in an influential and wealthy court as Santiago is now. Williams' prison experience is even longer than Santiago's, and Williams was once, and to some extent still is, a successful inmate entrepreneur. In recent years, however, he has turned his energy to law and to politics within the prison. Influenced by the newly politicized young men coming from urban ghettos who made up an increasingly large percentage of the prison population during the riot-scarred decade of the 1960s, Williams became deeply involved in the inmates' political struggle against prison authorities and in inmates' battles for extended legal rights and protection. Williams' efforts brought him several dozen months in solitary confinement, along with confiscation of his mail, packages and law books. Jorge Marrero, a close friend of Santiago's and an important spokesman for the Puerto Rican segment of the prison population during the uprising a few years before, has had a similar experience. Marrero is now in solitary in another upstate maximum security institution, to which he was transferred after the uprising. The comparison between himself and these two men suggested by the day's event keeps Santiago awake into the early morning. Though he is not anxious to become a martyr, Santiago is aware that entrepreneurial successes are in some ways advantageous to the prison administration because they regulate explosive situations such as the distribution of contraband in an economy of scarcity. This latter realization troubles his hard-won sense of being his own man.

Inmate labor is used to maintain the prison, to meet the needs of its population and for industrial production, the latter chiefly in the metal shops. All the various jobs are poorly paid—from $5 to $20 a month. Some are skilled, some dirty and physically demanding, many almost completely idle. Some inmates consider jobs on work gangs and the prison farms desirable for the chance to get outdoors. The inmate from an urban area, however, is not likely to want to play farmer in the bitter upstate winters. For most inmates, the really desirable jobs are those which give them a chance to obtain some material profit in addition to their meager wages.

A few jobs are appointed by the administration. These are usually jobs in the front offices of the prison, working along with the administration and civilian employees. These jobs carry privileges and are considered highly desirable. White inmates occupy most of them. Traditionally, the ethnic segregation of the prisoners has been encouraged in every possible way by the prison administration, and the high proportion of whites in front-office jobs is one of the most striking evidences of this policy. The administration also assigns belligerent inmates to a certain few worker "companies" with largely idle responsibilities in order to keep the designated troublemakers in one place. Trenton Williams has escaped assignment to one of these companies since he was released from solitary. He works as a clerk because he is respected by the administration as an educated man for his legal prowess, the very ability for which he was first put in "the hole."

Most jobs, however, are handed down through a hierarchy based on seniority. Unless a man becomes known as a troublemaker, he can expect to obtain a better job eventually. Getting a particular job usually depends on personal contacts. A man about to be paroled may recommend a friend to take his job. The head cook has a say in who works in his kitchen, as do the head men in the bakery, the tailor shop, the commissary, and almost every other division of prison labor.

Luis Santiago benefits from his seniority and works as the head man in the laundry. The laundry can be an extremely lucrative place to work because of the contradictory rules of the prison. Inmates are required to maintain a neat appearance but provided with few means for doing so. The regular laundry service is wholly inadequate, even to maintain in properly clean condition the few shabby garments provided by the prison tailor shop. Most men must provide for themselves by buying a laundry contract for a carton of cigarettes a month. Thus, Luis Santiago's relative wealth in the prison economy begins with a sizable base income, technically contraband, of course, but unofficially sanctioned.

One of the workers in the laundry is a black man named George Watkins. Though he has laundry contracts of his own, Watkins' take is not as much as Santiago's, and he does not share the valuable head man's privilege of being able to move freely around the prison during work hours. Watkins, however, devotes much of his energy to another form of hustling that is traditional and profitable. He is a practiced bootlegger, known to inmates as manufacturer and supplier of some of the finest vintages in the institution. Prison booze is made from any obtainable fermentable produce and varies in strength from that of wine to slightly stronger. Once he has all the ingredients, Watkins can put together an excellent batch rather quickly, but the total process of manufacturing and distributing his product under prison conditions is a complex one involving several people, payoffs and maneuvering.

The first essential ingredient is yeast, and here Watkins must depend on Santiago's court. Through Luis Santiago, Watkins has a connection to Angel Parilla, who works in the prison bakery. In expectation of some of the finished product, Parilla steals a cake of yeast, which he delivers to Watkins through Santiago. It would be possible to deliver the small parcel in the yard, but the prisoners share an interest in keeping yard transactions down. Since guards and inmates are forced to spend months and years together, they inevitably become aware of one another's games. Two inmates seen talking together who are not known to be friends will draw attention, especially if they are from different ethnic groups. Thus, Santiago intervenes in the transaction even though he is not actively involved in the booze-making scheme. Parilla delivers the yeast to Santiago in the yard, and Santiago transfers it to Watkins at the laundry during work.

Watkins' next task is not so easy. The raw produce must come from the warehouse, where the contacts are not so easy to manage. Watkins himself has no access to even the general vicinity of the warehouse, which is somewhat set apart physically from the rest of the prison. The key man in this situation is Ben Hicks, the porter in Watkins' cell gallery. A porter's job is a very menial one but carries with it the great privilege of mobility. The porter's assignment is to keep his gallery clean and to move inmates in and out. Since the porter is assigned to the cellblocks during working hours and his tasks do not require all his time, he has a certain amount of freedom to spend his time as he wishes. Most importantly for the brewers' purposes, though, the porter has a wagon for carrying his maintenance supplies and for moving the inmates' personal possessions from one cell to another. This wagon is his passport throughout the prison. As long as he seems to be en route somewhere with the wagon, he will seldom be challenged by the guards.

Ben Hicks and George Watkins are acquaintances both from the street and from another prison a few years ago. Hicks agrees to collaborate with Watkins in an assault on the warehouse, but neither of them has a direct contact. The warehouse is the source of almost all contraband raw food in the prison, and it is almost entirely staffed by white inmates. Both Hicks and Watkins are black. For the next few days in the yard, Hicks and Watkins observe the warehouse staff and consult the grapevine in order to determine their most likely candidate for raw-produce supplier.

The basic problem for the men's scheme is that the administration has consciously placed in the warehouse jobs men who are widely known or suspected by the rest of the inmates as snitches and tremblers. A snitch is a man who informs on other inmates, a violation of the oldest and most unquestioned of inmate codes. A trembler is a man, often one who has committed a single crime of passion and who consequently does not really consider himself a criminal, who lives in constant fear of other prisoners. The snitch cannot be trusted because he sells out others for his own benefit. A trembler may honestly undertake a role in a contraband operation, but he cannot be trusted because he flies apart at the least sign of pressure. In the last few weeks, a trembler had botched an attempt to smuggle some grapefruit out of the warehouse and caused a number of inmates involved to be keeplocked. Awareness of that incident makes Watkins and Hicks doubly cautious in formulating their plan of attack.

Hicks and Watkins finally decide to try to establish a relationship with one of the warehouse staff, a white man named Daniel McChesney. There is no question in their minds that McChesney is a snitch, but that does not mean that they cannot do business with him if they go about it properly. McChesney is a man who keeps pretty much to himself. He is thought to have been incarcerated for a sex crime, but no one knows for sure because he never talks about his previous life. The stigma attached to being a sex offender often keeps them apart in prison society. This timidity plus his suspected ratting and the fact that he is white all make McChesney a good choice for the administration to put in a key warehouse position.

The administration has contradictory motives in regulating and not regulating the underground economy of the prison. On the one hand, the prison is simply not well enough staffed to eliminate hustling. Hustling in penitentiaries is as old as the penitentiary system itself. Unless the authorities allow a certain amount of inmate organization for the purposes of hustling, the result will be chaos and uncontrollable violence. On the other hand, the administration does not want anyone else running their institution. An inmate who runs a successful hustling operation can gain a great deal of influence in the prison and if he gains too much influence without exhibiting at the same time some form of obeisance he runs a high risk of being transferred to another institution and/or being put in solitary for a real or fabricated offense. The perfect way for the administration to satisfy its contradictory needs to allow hustling and to maintain control of the prison is to place informers in many of the jobs key to the contraband networks. The job favoritism shown whites also serves the administrations' interest in the same way. Since the majority of inmates are black and Puerto Rican, the big organizers are not likely to be white. Thus, putting white men in key jobs further fragments the hustling network.

The day after McChesney has been tentatively selected to supply the raw material for Watkins' still, Ben Hicks takes a trip to the warehouse on the pretext of restocking the cleaning supplies on his wagon. Before leaving the gallery, however, he has acquired another kind of contraband with which he hopes to attract McChesney's attention. Hand-drawn pornography, called short-heist, is a salable commodity in prison, and Hicks has traded cigarettes for some pictures produced by a skilled forger on his gallery. When he encounters McChesney in the warehouse, Hicks casually asks him if he wants to see something interesting. McChesney pretends disappointment that the pictures are only hand-drawn, but buys them anyway, for only a few packs of cigarettes. Hicks does not press him about anything else and goes on his way. Hicks' attitude throughout the brief encounter has been one of feigned indifference, but he is satisfied with the meeting because his relationship with McChesney has been established.

In the next few days, Hicks finds other excuses to run into McChesney. Each time, he speaks to him briefly or conducts a trivial transaction. Finally, the porter's wagon happens to wheel by the warehouse just after a shipment of apples has arrived. George Watkins' friend assigned to the front gate has had something to do with the coincidence. When Hicks broaches the subject of apple smuggling to McChesney, he does so just as he has done everything else, casually and indirectly. He does not ask outright to buy some apples with cigarettes. Rather, he drops a hint by admiring the apples and waits for McChesney to pick up on it. McChesney talks about something else and then mentions that there might be some apples to be found at a certain place at a certain time. The deal has been made, but nothing has been openly discussed.

After he has left the warehouse, Hicks makes his way back to his gallery. From there, he drops a scribe (note) over to Watkins at the laundry. Watkins checks the closet in the laundry where he plans to hide his brew until it is fermented. He then arranges to convert some of the cash he is holding back into cigarettes in order to pay Mc-Chesney. The latter would probably prefer to receive cash, but Watkins doesn't want it known to McChesney that he has cash.

The next morning, Hicks meets with McChesney one more time to arrange the specifics of the deal. This time, they must talk a little more openly, and a few complications develop. McChesney has con-cocted an elaborate plan to receive payment, involving several parties and steps. Hicks finds McChesney's scheme to be cloak-and-dagger nonsense that creates many more risks than it solves, but he agrees to most of it to keep the other man happy. In the yard that afternoon, the cigarettes are exchanged, and, the following morning, Hicks packs the apples from the warehouse and wheels them out in a trash barrel.

The difference in Hicks' and McChesney's attitudes on how to con-duct the cigarette transfer can be related to the change in inmate attitudes during the 1960s. Hicks is typical of the young, black in-mate from the urban ghetto whose posture toward the authorities has become offensive rather than smiling-at-the-man-while-picking-his-pocket. He operates on an awareness that, in terms of sheer presence, the black inmates are the largest and because of their numbers the most influential group in the prison. McChesney is more typical of traditional inmate attitudes of "doing your own time," which include attitudes of guilt and submissiveness toward the authorities. His cloak-and-dagger schemes are the results of his sense of isolation and his fearful outlook.

Next day, having gathered the fruits of his entrepreneurial efforts, George Watkins sets to work to apply his manufacturing skills. With the aid of a friend and co-worker in the laundry, Jo-Jo Smith, he carefully measures and combines his ingredients in a five-gallon pail, which the two men cover and hide on an unused shelf in the selected closet. There are always batches of hooch fermenting in any of dozens of hiding places throughout the prison. Watkins' brands are known as potent (though still more wine than liquor) and potable. In about four weeks, the rather sweet, raw-tasting beverage will be divided up into six or eight one-quart jars, distributed and consumed.

On the day when this vintage hits the market, Angel Parilla receives one quart as his fee for providing the yeast. Ben Hicks receives one jar plus a percentage of the profits in cigarettes for his versatile and mobile efforts. An unforeseen hassle in getting the goods out of the laundry costs another jar to an inmate on one of the internal gates. Hicks receives a work order from a guard as he is transporting the finished product and must deposit the wine with the man on the gate, for a fee of one jar. The remaining jars are sold for cigarettes, mostly to men on or near Watkins' cell gallery. The concentration of booze in one cellblock produces a rather boisterous night, including a keeplock on one partying inmate who decided to challenge a guard.

In terms of social organization, the most interesting aspect of this winemaking hustle is the complete interdependence among several parties required for the successful completion of the project. Although George Watkins' entrepreneurial and manufacturing abilities and Ben Hicks' mobility were perhaps the key elements in the hustle, other men were just as important at various stages of the operation. Angel Parilla, Daniel McChesney, Luis Santiago, Watkins' friend on the front gate and the man on the internal gate were all indispensable to the hustle. The success of the venture depended not nearly so much on any one man's skill or key job so much as on the cooperation among all of them.

This element of cooperation must illuminate the idea of leadership and position in contemporary inmate society. Although men like Luis Santiago may have comparatively great wealth, connections and influence, no one man can in any sense control the lives of a large number of his fellow inmates. The popular idea of a czar behind bars, which probably dates from James Cagney movies, just does not apply to the present situation. Though a man may become an eminently successful hustler, he can only do so if, like George Watkins, he is able to contact and cooperate with a number of others. The same relationships that can be mobilized for business also exist on a day-to-day basis as personal relationships. A man hustles with and for the benefit of his friends. In some cases, hierarchical relationships may be discernible in inmate groups. For example, Angel Parilla and Pascual Colon have come to depend on Luis Santiago both for his connections and for his experience and understanding. In other relationships, however, the relative importance of the individual depends entirely upon the situation and its demands. Further, inmates are isolated from one another by various prison policies—such as confinement to cells fourteen to sixteen hours a day, the racist allocation of jobs, solitary confinement for men who accrue too much power—so that inmate networks are prevented from becoming too extended, regular or structured. The basis of inmate social organization is rather the small, loose, personal inmate clique that may be involved in business but is founded as much on personal as on business needs.

The day after the George Watkins' inspired and supplied party is Saturday. On weekends, the inmates do not have to work and can spend a few hours in the yard. Luis Santiago, Pascual Colon, Angel Parilla and Jesus Hernandez are gathered in Santiago's court on one of the first pleasant days of the late upstate spring. Their mood is jovial as they trade stories about the events of the night before. Jesus Hernandez's presence affords the men an opportunity to relate prison lore with which they are familiar but the newcomer has never heard. By this time, Hernandez has been fully accepted into the court, and much of the conversation of the court has come to involve the instruction and initiation of Hernandez into prison life.

The stories of the drunken activities of the preceding night prompt Angel Parilla to recall some of the parties that were given by "Crazy Joe" Gallo in another New York prison. Accounts of the Italian mobster's eccentricities and exploits are known to many inmates. In fact, many more inmates than could possibly have done so often claim to have known Gallo. Parilla recounts how Gallo had given extravagant parties in prison and tried to befriend a variety of people. He had freely handed out white shirts and cigarettes to other inmates, including blacks and Puerto Ricans.

Luis Santiago, who had spent many months in the same institution with Gallo, takes up Parillia's account to describe an incident in which Joey Gallo was rebuked for approaching a respected Puerto Rican inmate too familiarly. Specifically, Gallo had taken the liberty of talking too freely about the man's activities outside, and he was roundly put off. Santiago points out to Hernandez that although one may know that someone is into something on the outside, he may not simply approach the man about it. Usually, such a man will discuss his affairs only with someone he considers an equal and an intimate friend.

Santiago next admonishes the newcomer not to believe everything he hears. Imprisoned men often fantasy, he explains, to the point where they believe their own stories. The number of men who claim to have known Joey Gallo is a clear enough demonstration of this facet of prison life. These men may have seen him and heard stories about him at one time or another, but they have inserted themselves into these stories as participants after the fact. Santiago then relates that Gallo had in fact been able to make contacts and to affiliate himself with a number of blacks while he was in prison. Some Puerto Ricans had tolerated him up to a point, but they were only interested in what they could get out of the mobster.

Gallo, on the other hand, had been more interested in recruiting an army of blacks in order to advance himself in his own organization. In return, he was ostracized by many white inmates and attacked in the yard on at least two occasions, once with a shiv and once with gasoline. Parilla interjects at this point that Gallo was a punk in the yard. He couldn't fight a lick. Yes, replies Colon, but on the outside he is a very dangerous man, because he has a lot of support and people to do his strong-arm work.

These attitudes of fascination and contempt for Gallo are common among black and Puerto Rican criminals. On the one hand, Gallo represents the higher echelons of organized crime that few blacks or Puerto Ricans have been able to penetrate. Just as in prison, whites on the outside control the sources and connections necessary for big operations. Without a white contact, the black or Puerto Rican trying to set up an operation in his neighborhood cannot obtain quantities of drugs, finance policy operations or dispose of large amounts of stolen goods. Conversely, the white organizations cannot prey upon the neighborhoods directly and must contract with someone in the neighborhood to handle the street-level operations. Similarly, in prison, even though whites have many of the key jobs for obtaining prison contraband, the main market for the contraband is black, and a white man with a supply must work through a black man who can feed it into the larger market. This fascination with the connections and organization of Joey Gallo is mixed with contempt for his failure to meet the common measure of manhood among blacks and Puerto Ricans holding their own on the level of immediate physical violence.

The stories of Joey Gallo eventually lead Luis Santiago into a description of prison life before the radical change in the prison population that occurred in the 1960s. Since Santiago is the only one present who was around in the old days and who saw the changes, the other men fall silent, except to question him at times.

At one time, the upstate prisons were largely controlled by white men of Italian and Irish descent. Their control was a lot more extensive than anything that exists today, and many of them were able to live almost luxurious lives while incarcerated. One penitentiary in particular, situated almost on the Canadian border, was known as a gangster institution. Santiago remembers that when he first went to prison there were so few Puerto Ricans that some of them used to eschew speaking Spanish and pretend that they were Italians.

One reason that inmate organization was more highly developed at that time was, of course, the lack of racist divisions among the inmates and the consequent greater freedom for hustlers to run large operations. Another reason is that men used to be sentenced to much longer terms and consequently had to adapt more completely to prison existence. With the modern plea-bargaining systems, plus the huge increase in drug-related arrests and convictions, many more men are sentenced to much shorter terms. Although these men may return again and again, their commitment to a particular prison society is much shorter.

The principal reason that the Italians and Irish were able to live as they did in prison, however, related to their connections and organization outside. Traditionally, white crime organizations protected their members from the authorities in every way possible. The white professional criminal has always been much less likely to go to jail in the first place. For the black or Puerto Rican criminal, prison is an inevitable stage of his career. If a member of a white crime network was convicted, both he and his family would be taken care of by the organization. The physical well-being of the men in prison was taken care of from the outside. Joey Gallo's extravagant parties were the result of his connections outside.

From the standpoint of organization within the prison, the whites were used to strict hierarchies and in fact were able to bring them in almost intact from the outside. Finally, it may be assumed that the prison administrations were much less afraid of the important white convicts than of black inmates and allowed them much greater leeway in organizing and controlling the inmate population. Whatever the reasons, it is certain that in the past prison populations were much more highly organized around important leaders and their courts than they are today. Although Santiago's court is recognized for a certain amount of wealth and connections, its sphere of influence is much more limited than that of the courts of the Italian and Irish leaders of the past.

Luis Santiago describes the scene in those days when a member of an Italian "family" arrived in prison. He would be met almost immediately by friends with cigarettes, shoes, pajamas, underwear. When the black or Puerto Rican convict enters prison today, he is likely to know someone in the institution from the street or from a previous jail term in a different institution, but he may not be able even to see them for days or weeks. He must depend not on a protective organization but on personal friends with careers similar to his.

The days when white men controlled the prison, however, are definitely past. Santiago remembers when it was forbidden even to set foot on a white court. The guards would immediately lock up such an offender. After the population began to be overwhelmingly black and Puerto Rican, this primacy of whites in the yard could not continue, even if their preferred job status could and did. One of the turning points in Santiago's own experience was an incident in another institution where several blacks simply began walking on a white court. The white occupants of the court were too outnumbered to react, and a tradition disappeared in a day.

The heroin deal that Juan Rocque had gotten wind of did not materialize until a few weeks later. Rocque finally is able to score from his friend Billy Reagan, who has bought the stuff from a black inmate named Wayne Newcomb. Newcomb has been around the prison for some time, but he was released a few months ago on parole. He has since returned as a parole violator. While he was on the street, he had become involved with drugs again and realized that he would probably be returned to prison when his addiction became apparent to his parole officer or when he failed to show up for his regular meeting at the parole board. Before that eventuality occurred (his needle tracks showed up on his arms), Newcomb arranged with a friend to smuggle some heroin inside.

This deal also began in another way quite independently of Newcomb with the transfer to the prison of a guard named Thomas Harrison. In New York State, corrections personnel are promoted solely on the basis of written civil service examination. After three years, a guard may take an examination for promotion to sergeant. If he passes, however, he is placed on a statewide list and is given the first available job in his new category. This system makes it likely that a promotion will entail a transfer to a new facility, and many guards have strong local ties that they do not wish to abandon. Harrison is more ambitious than family-oriented and thus has a somewhat different orientation than many guards. The average guard is drawn from the upstate, rural population. He comes from an agricultural community and often works in the prison alongside his brothers, cousins and uncles. The gap between the guards and the inmates can be seen in the forms of entertainment occasionally provided at the prison. Much of the live music brought into the prisons is country/western music played to largely black audiences.

The family ties keep many guards in the prison from engaging in heroin traffic, even though it can be profitable. When Harrison arrived at the prison, however, he had no such inhibitions, and it was he who made the initial overtures to Newcomb. After the sergeant and inmate had known each other long enough that they could work together on some viable basis of trust, Newcomb informed Harrison that he knew of a source of heroin outside and that the two of them could turn a handsome profit. Inside prison as well as outside on the streets, traffic in heroin is risky but far more lucrative than any other kind of illegal operation. The scarcity of the drug in the upstate prisons and the large numbers of incarcerated addicts make pushing a volatile activity. For this reason, Newcomb includes as few people in his planning as possible and no other junkies, until he is ready to sell.

After he has made his intentions clear to Sergeant Harrison, Newcomb writes a letter to his wife, who informs Walter Bishop, the man with whom Newcomb has made an arrangement during his time on parole. A few days later, Newcomb receives a visit from Bishop during regular visiting hours at the prison. Bishop informs Newcomb, according to an agreed-upon code (there is a guard present during the visit), of a post office box he has rented under a fictitious name.

That afternoon, Newcomb relays this information to Harrison. Shortly thereafter, Harrison receives in the mail the key to the post office box and instructions for picking up the dope at a specified place outside the small community where he lives. Harrison receives a money order for his payoff at the post office box, where he could not easily be traced. Sometimes, relationships between guards and inmates became personal and trusting to the point where the inmate's wife will send a money order directly to the guard's house, but

Harrison's and Newcomb's relationship has not advanced that far. After he has been paid, Harrison picks up a package at the chosen drop spot and delivers it next day to Newcomb. Newcomb then keeps some for his own consumption and sells out parcels to a few junkies like Billy Reagan who further distribute the scarce drug to the main population of users. Newcomb's motive for acting as a wholesaler is his fear of creating an incident in the yard if he simply began hawking his product openly in the midst of the strung-out junkie population of the prison.

Indeed, the delicacy of distributing the heroin to its eventual consumers is in many ways the most difficult stage of this hustle. Besides the very real danger of the retailer being mobbed if he is not careful, selling anything in prison is extremely difficult. The accepted maxim is that if one can hustle in prison in an atmosphere of constant surveillance by the authorities and utter skepticism from the inmates (there is no more suspicious consumer than a convict), then one can hustle anywhere.

Undoubtedly, many criminals learn their trades or hone them to professional skill in prison, both by learning from experienced practitioners and by undergoing the rigorous training of hustling within the prison. Wayne Newcomb's deal illustrates also that hustling in prison and on the streets can have very immediate connections. As a result of shorter prison terms and the tremendous amount of discretion that has accrued to the parole authorities, the modern participant in urban crime is often involved in a steady alternation back and forth between jail and the street. Also, many of his friends are involved in the same sort of career. Wayne Newcomb's relationship with Walter Bishop exists both inside and outside. Bishop was able to aid Newcomb effectively because he had been in the prison itself and knew the problems involved in the operation intimately. Newcomb himself set up the deal during what amounted to a sojourn from his prison life. For many men, prison itself is merely a microcosm in which the problems and pressures of the outside society are intensified. The course of their daily lives runs through stealing, hustling, pushing, prostitution, gambling, harassment by the authorities of a different culture and the constant possibility of violence. The only possibility of survival in this world, just as on the outside, is to form alliances and friendships for mutual protection, and in many cases these relationships span the wall between inside and outside.

Besides having gained acceptance in Santiago's court and being treated as Luis Santiago's *compadre,* Jesus Hernandez has also formed relationships with other Puerto Rican inmates. In particular, he has become friends with a young man his own age named Jose Rivera. Although the two had not known each other on the street, they are both from New York City and have much in common—street lore, music, a couple of mutual acquaintances. Hernandez had been deeply involved in his gang in the South Bronx. Jose Rivera is a member of another sort of organization, *Palante,* the Young Lords political party. From his experience in the party, Rivera has become highly interested in politics and in his Puerto Rican cultural heritage. Since he and Hernandez have become friends, Rivera has been trying to awake these same interests in Hernandez, with some degree of success. A certain tension, however, has become evident between Rivera and the members of Santiago's court. Hernandez has begun to feel certain contradictions between the jailing that he is learning from the older men and the political approach to jailing that he is hearing from Rivera. Though Rivera is the same age as he, Rivera has spent several years in a state reformatory and has already formulated his ideas and practices for surviving in prison.

One afternoon in the yard finds the two young men and a few black inmates listening to the tales of an older white man named Albert Dowd. Such interracial groupings are rare in the prison yard but they do occur in exactly this kind of situation. Dowd, a skilled safecracker and lock and burglar alarm expert, is telling his war stories, accounts of crimes he has committed and explanations of his technique. Traditionally, war stories are shared with anyone who is interested and the telling of war stories is one of the most common instances of temporary dissolution of ethnic segregation in the yard. Information on any sort of criminal skill or profession is available in any prison to anyone who wants to learn. Murderers, armed robbers, con men, junkies, safecrackers, forgers and car dealers all have a special area they can teach to those interested. This process is known as educating or giving you an inside.

Hernandez and Rivera listen closely to Dowd until he finishes and the group disperses. They discuss what they have just heard for a while, until Rivera begins to talk about other kinds of education. Although Rivera managed to finish high school while in the reformatory, he is not referring to formal education. The *Palante* is but one of numerous political organizations that exist in the prison. Black Panthers, Black Muslims, Five Per Centers, Maoists, all have a political line and many believe they have a task to enlighten the inmate population to their conception of political reality. Classes in black history, Arabic and African languages, and law are taught in the yard, even though all these activities are hated and feared by the administration and persecuted accordingly. Rivera has heard of a black history class and wishes to organize a similar one in Puerto Rican history and culture.

The rapid change in the ethnic makeup of the prison populations in New York State was occurring at the same time as the turbulent development of minority consciousness that swept the United States, particularly the cities, during the 1960s. The parallelism of these two developments was no coincidence, for both were the result of the mushrooming of the urban ghettos. The closed society of the prison is a much more charged atmosphere than the fragmented life of the ghetto, and the development and spreading of political ideas was much more extensive inside than outside. In the modern prison with a large number of inmates from urban areas, politics is one of the most pervasive topics of prison life.

Carrying on political activity in this upstate prison, however, is almost more difficult than hustling, though the two activities can overlap. With a minimum of fourteen hours a day in their cells, most prisoners read to fight boredom. Books and periodicals dealing with radical politics and black and Puerto Rican revolutionary consciousness are extraordinarily popular, but they are strictly proscribed, on the grounds that they are not rehabilitative. An inmate can obtain a copy of *The Godfather* from the prison library, but in order to read *The Autobiography of Malcolm X* he must wait his turn and then pay several packs of cigarettes for the chance to hold a battered copy for one night.

In their advanced stage, however, prison politics can and do pose a threat to hustling. One example is a man like Trenton Williams, who was once as successful a hustler as any man in the prison but who has now abandoned hustling for law. Though he still is a member of the contraband economy of the prison, as every inmate must be if he is to survive the physical privations of his existence, Williams now devotes his time to working on his and others' legal problems and to studying and teaching law. As a result of his change in activities, Williams is one of the most admired and respected inmates in the penitentiary. The fact that he had already proved his mettle as a right guy and as a successful hustler ensured that when he became interested in law and politics he would attract a large following. On the other hand, if he had continued his hustling, which inevitably includes a certain amount of exploitation of others, his credibility as a political convert would have been difficult to establish. Prisoners live too close together to be able to fool each other over a long period of time.

The comparison that was forced on Luis Santiago at the time of the near skirmish that Williams resolved, in large part on the basis of the respect he commanded among all the inmates, is very obvious to Jose Rivera. Having been partly raised and educated in a state reformatory, he has already learned to understand prison life in political terms. He joined the Young Lords while incarcerated as a youthful offender. Rivera is still respectful toward his friend Hernandez's older benefactor, but Rivera's tone becomes insistent when he talks politics in Santiago's court. The older men are sometimes a bit irritated or uncomfortable during Rivera's diatribes, but they in turn respect the younger man's integrity, and political conversations become an irregular activity in Santiago's court.

When he is not trying to make a point, Jose Rivera asks the older men questions about the history of the prison, particularly of the bloody uprising a few years before. Since most of the prison was transferred around the state after the riot, most of the older men had not participated, but they know many stories of that and other instances of organized resistance over the past fifteen years.

One of the most remarkable aspects of the uprising was the unity that emerged among all segments of the prison population. Whites, blacks, and Puerto Ricans all worked together during the few days in which they controlled the prison. Each group contributed a leader to the central committee—Trenton Williams from the black inmates, Jorge Marrero from the Puerto Ricans and Stanley Mierkowicz from the whites. The riot proved to be the greatest blow to ethnic separation and mutual distrust in the history of the prison. Even though the prison populations were scrambled after the rebellion, this consciousness of unity still survives in many individuals. Though political thoughts and feelings in the prisons started largely with men like Malcolm X who emphasized black solidarity, one of the results of that consciousness has been to break down racial and ethnic barriers. Today, even white inmates who still maintain their privileged jobs recognize a common interest with other inmates against the prison administration.

From the administration's point of view, political activities pose the greatest threat to their control that they have ever faced. Most of the guards and administrators, not to mention higher authorities, openly blame the riot on the political activities which preceded it. For these reasons, an inmate who hustles is much less likely to be put in the hole or transferred to another facility than one who engages in political activity.

In order to see in perspective the political consciousness and growing political solidarity in the prisons, however, it is necessary to look at the evolution of political actions since 1960. In that year, the inmates of another New York penitentiary staged the famous "good time" strike. Their goal was for the right to have a specified amount of time taken off their sentences for good conduct. Back in 1960, this strike was carefully planned months in advance by all groups within the prison. There were similar strikes in 1962, in 1963 and a bloody one in 1965, and, in 1967, the good time was finally granted. Literally busloads of men went home on the retroactive recognition of their good time. The lesson the inmates learned has stuck. They know now that if they stay together and persist in their struggles, they can improve their condition. Otherwise, they can only hope to prey upon each other.

George Watkins, the winemaker, and Jo-Jo Smith are close friends. Sometimes they engage in business together. Both work in the laundry and they pool their contracts with other prisoners. One week Watkins may do most of their contractees' laundry, or, if Watkins is busy hustling the ingredients for a batch of hooch, Smith will handle Watkins' contracts that week. Their mutual hustles, however, are the result rather than the foundation of their friendship. They have lived in adjoining cells for some time, and they first became friends through talking and playing cards through the bars. (It is impossible to see directly from one cell to another, but one can hold a mirror out into the gallery and look back into the next cell.)

When Jo-Jo Smith first came to the prison, he had never before served a felony sentence and had a difficult time of jailing. For the first few months, he was moody and depressed, coping, though with difficulty, with the fact of his four-year sentence. He had been involved in a number of petty criminal activities in his Brooklyn neighborhood and had served a one-year sentence on Riker's Island. The experience of being shipped upstate for several years completely disoriented him, however, and he withdrew into himself. Since Watkins was in the cell adjoining his, Smith got to know Watkins but very few others during those first months.

Watkins is a gregarious sort with many friends among the blacks in the prison. Besides the renown he accrues from his winemaking, he is an excellent athlete and plays on a number of the prison's organized teams. His athletic ability inspires respect and also affords pleasure to the other inmates. At first, Watkins was hesitant in his judgment of Smith. Since Smith was reticent and unwilling to talk about himself, Watkins was unsure whether his cell neighbor would prove good people or a punk if the test ever came. On the other hand, when Smith did emerge at times from his depression and boredom, his conversation and manner seemed sufficiently manly. Watkins remained open to the other man, and the two developed a limited relationship based mostly on passing the long hours of confinement in their cells.

As the months passed, Smith adapted somewhat to prison, but he was still subject to periods of intense depression. Eventually, he confided to Watkins that he had not been communicating with his wife. When she finally wrote to him, her letter merely informed him that she had met another man and wanted a divorce. Smith's reaction was violent. The next day he refused to leave his cell and provoked the guard who was ordering him to report to work. He was sufficiently belligerent to earn a severe beating, which he endured without relenting in his refusal to cooperate. He was confined to his cell for the next two weeks.

At the end of that time, Smith seemed to have reached the other side of his depression and disorientation. The stoic way in which he had resisted the guards had been observed and admired by the other men on his gallery. Henceforth, Jo-Jo Smith was known to the other prisoners as a stand-up guy, one who sticks to his principles, whatever they be at the time they are tested. Watkins was quick to inform his neighbor of the impression that he created, and Smith in turn began opening up to other men in the yard.

Soon after these events, Watkins was able to obtain a job for Smith in the laundry, quite a desirable change from the metal shop, where Smith had been assigned when he entered the prison. As a laundry worker, Smith was soon able to hustle a number of contracts and thus establish a place for himself in the prison economy. He also widened his circle of acquaintances greatly and began playing on the football team of which George Watkins was the captain.

In his conversations with Watkins, Smith lost his personal reticence and began to tell stories of his life outside as well as discussing his plans for after his release. Like many convicts, Smith dreamed of advancing himself in criminal activity and of seducing beautiful women. By this time, he had arranged to divorce his wife, but he was still troubled about his young son and swore to obtain custody of him on his release, despite Watkins' advice that his criminal record would make that impossible.

In his hustling activities, Smith was proving himself an able and reliable businessman. Before long, he and Watkins established their informal partnership in working their laundry contracts that freed Watkins to concentrate on his winemaking problems. Already the two men had begun to talk about working together in various schemes when they returned to the city. Watkins had been convicted for his involvement in an organized theft ring specializing in office equipment. The previous operation had depended on a fence who was connected to white organized crime. Watkins' and Smith's dream was to set up an independent operation.

The relationship between these men works to their mutual advantage in both offensive and defensive ways. From the standpoint of protection, each one knows that he is never alone. If there should occur a dangerous situation in the yard—for example, a contraband transfer in which trust among the parties involved is less than complete—then the man making the transfer knows that his friend is watching his back. It is a good thing in prison to be able to turn one's back. On the outside, also, men who have been in prison have an instinctive sense of guarding the other's blind spots. From an offensive standpoint, Smith learns from Watkins that special brand of psychological judo that is so pervasive in prison relationships. In a situation of complete powerlessness, a prisoner must always be able to defend himself physically. In order to accomplish any "constructive" enterprise (and, of an inmate's options hustling is one of the most challenging), a prisoner must resort to guile. The skill of a hustler is not to coerce cooperation but to convince others that they are being given an opportunity for their own benefit. This skill depends on being able to perceive another's personality and to manipulate it on its own terms.

In prison, where men live very close together, the refinements of

these games become incredibly intricate. On the one hand, it is difficult to completely deceive someone over an extended period of time.
Between two men such as Watkins and Smith, any sort of deception
becomes almost impossible because of their daily intimacy and the
minimum subsistence level of their living circumstances. In relationships with less intimate acquaintances, psychological judo becomes a
real test of one's personality precisely because complete deception is
an unlikely possibility. Although inmates play many games, they are
also playing for real. A man who has survived the prison experience
is likely to emerge with a very highly developed sense of social interactions.

The friendship between George Watkins and Jo-Jo Smith is an
example of the absolutely crucial role that prison plays in black
criminal relationships. The way in which prison strips a man down
materially and psychologically ensures that prison-forged relationships are very strong, often the strongest in the black criminal's life.
Puerto Ricans also form strong bonds in prison, but they also rely
heavily on kinship ties, such as those between Luis Santiago and
Jesus Hernandez.

In Jo-Jo Smith's case, however, we have seen how prison can strip
a man completely of his ties to the outside world. Smith has had a
chance at family responsibility and lost it. His family was simply
assumed by another when he was incarcerated. Many other men are
able to maintain loose family ties because of the extended family
structure that exists throughout the urban ghettos. In this situation,
when a man is forced out of his family responsibilities, as commonly
happens, whether the cause be unemployment or incarceration, his
children will be supported by a grandmother or an uncle. The street
orientation of the urban black male is the background out of which
the durability of prison-forged ties grow.

Prison is a demanding environment, and men who have seen each
other's behavior in prison know what the other is capable of. For
many months, Jo-Jo Smith was an unknown quantity to George
Watkins. When Smith began to emerge from his destructive self-
absorption, however, he gradually began to earn the respect of

Watkins and others. By proving that he was not a physical coward, he satisfied the first criterion of manhood in prison. In his subsequent activities, he established his personal integrity and his ability to act decisively in challenging situations. Finally, after some months of involvement in prison activities, he established a reputation for reliability and for openness and generosity toward his friends. On the street, one man would rarely have the opportunity to know another in such a total way. The depth of personal involvement that characterizes prison relationships makes them likely to continue beyond the prisoners' date for "maxing out."

Thus, shared prison experience provides a basis of trust for risky activities outside. The fact that the black criminal, unlike the member of white organized crime, is almost certain to spend some time in prison makes the prison experience the common denominator of organized crime among blacks. Not only do men learn to work together, they make contacts that will later afford them access to otherwise closed neighborhood networks. After many months of living beside George Watkins, Jo-Jo Smith is soon to be released on parole. Watkins must stay inside, but Smith will now be able to gain entrance into Watkins' old neighborhood and whatever activities are in progress there.

Normally, it would be very dangerous to go into a strange neighborhood and begin asking questions, but Smith now has a certain amount of credentials as "good people" on the basis that he has done time with Watkins. The mere fact that he has done time establishes that he is not a cop. If he can establish that he has known Watkins well, he may be granted access to guns, drugs, fences, whatever is going on in the neighborhood. As we have seen before, the basis of network formation among black and Puerto Rican crime activists is "being connected." The prison is where many connections are made.

The most pervasive principle of prison social life is racial segregation and ethnic succession is taking place there as well as in organized crime. The whites, blacks and Puerto Ricans each band together into their own courts, and whatever social life goes on in prison—talking, playing games and the like—goes on largely within these groups.

Prison administrators encourage the segregation of the prisoners into racial groups by giving the white prisoners all the best jobs, thereby elevating them in prestige and material advantage above the blacks and Puerto Ricans. Blacks and Puerto Ricans are perhaps less segregated from each other in prison life than they both are from the whites; but even between blacks and Puerto Ricans, segregation is the rule.

Thus, for Luis Santiago, Pascual Colon, Angel Parilla and Juan Rocque, most social interaction occurs with other Puerto Ricans. Luis Santiago provides his followers with leadership, advice and the material advantages that arise out of his many successful "hustles," and his followers in turn provide Luis Santiago with protection. Angel Parilla and Pascual Colon are friends with each other, and both of them have other friends among the prison's Puerto Ricans. It should be observed that when Angel Parilla gets out of prison, he will be able to go into Pascual Colon's neighborhood, with or without Pascual Colon, and upon establishing that he is a prison friend of Pascual Colon, he will be admitted to conversations among criminals that he would otherwise be denied access to. Thus, prison life can provide a man with street-level "credentials": testimony that he is not a cop, and perhaps that he has valuable criminal skills.

Although prison segregation is pervasive, it is not altogether total and complete. Drug addicts, for instance, are despised in all the courts. Because of the low status they all share, together with the basic needs that they shared even before coming to prison, which often enough led a Puerto Rican addict to come into a black or a white neighborhood during a drug shortage, or vice versa, they tend to mix in prison somewhat regardless of race. Thus, although Juan Rocque spends most of his time around the Puerto Rican court, it is often he who is chosen as a courier when business transactions are carried on between the Puerto Rican court and one of the other courts. Moreover, segregation also breaks down somewhat when it comes to telling "war stories" and passing on criminal skills. Thus Albert Dowd, who is white, will tell anyone who cares to listen, regardless of race, how to crack a safe. And prison uprisings can be the most devastating destroyers of segregation: during the rebellion of a few years ago, Stanley Mierkowicz, a white leader, Trenton Williams, a black leader, and Jorge Marrero, a Puerto Rican leader, all worked hand in hand, and there was a spirit of complete unity among all the prisoners in the penitentiary. It seems likely that some prison administrators believe segregation to be an effective way of keeping prisoners in line: after the rebellion, nearly the whole prison population was reassigned to other prisons; when fresh batches of prisoners were brought in, they didn't know one another and therefore fell more or less naturally into the segregated patterns that were expected of them.

The prison network, particularly the courts, which are childhood gangs grown up, is an ideal-typical model of nearly all the criminal networks that I have described outside of prison. In prison, presumably because of the close quarters and the constant presence of authority and the nature of captivity itself, the rules that govern relationships among men delve even more deeply into their personal lives. Thus, behavior, rules, values and sanctions seem more intensified. In most of the criminal networks we have described, it would be fair to say that the chief rules governing relationships are (1) don't tell the police, or anyone who likely would tell the police; and (2) don't cheat your business associate out of money. Of course it is also true that a person who fails to act firmly in any instance will probably soon be bereft of whatever criminal fortune and influence he has, but this is almost as true in the legitimate business world. The only real difference would seem to be that in the legitimate business world the means of recourse tend to be less violent than in the criminal world. By contrast, however, in prison it is an offense to be a "creep" or to "punk out" of any fight whatever.

What prison relationships—particularly the small, intimate courts —most resemble in the "outside" criminal world seem to be the relationships that we discovered in the two youth gang partnerships found in our networks—in the War Dragons, discussed above, and in Luis Santo's childhood gang, discussed in Chapter 4. In those partnerships, where business relationships among the parties are less well-defined than in situations where one man has most of the money or supplies and is the boss, it can be expected that, as in prison, reliance on personal qualities such as willingness to fight, to be generous, to be friendly, is very high. This is especially interesting since what stands out with greatest clarity in the networks we observed is the fact that the two chief proving and training grounds for organized criminal activity are the neighborhood and its gangs and the prison. Perhaps it is necessary for a would-be criminal to go through, at least once, a social situation where his personal qualities are severely tested and observed by his peers. Once having successfully gone through that testing situation, he can become party to criminal networks that can become established—sharing common values—where those personal qualities are assumed as requisites of membership. Thus, since these basic qualities have already been proven to exist in the individual, he can be accepted as a member of the network and patterns of interdependent relationships can be established. This is, of course, not restricted to networks in crime but is a common phenomenon in all networks where a code of behavior—a common set of values and mutual interdependence—are important.

One final aspect of prison relationships to be considered is the fact that many people share incarceration as a common experience to the extent that they know each other before, during, and after various jail terms. Jose Rivera, the young politico who befriended Jesus Hernandez, formed very close relationships during his reformatory term, in this case more politically than criminally oriented. Many men go through an educational system together, from one level to the next. In these cases, prison friendships can be very similar to the "old school tie" in which an Etonian prime minister picks another Etonian to serve in his government because he knows that he can rely on certain values and standards of conduct from an earlier shared experience.

PART THREE

ETHNIC SUCCESSION IN ILLICIT ENTERPRISE

4

THE CUBAN CONNECTION: ORGANIZED CRIME AND KINSHIP IN EL BARRIO

✠

MANY OF the features that characterize black organized crime networks—the importance of street society and prison experience, the role of women in crime operations, and the still-emergent and so somewhat indistinct patterns of organization—were found to exist among Puerto Ricans as well. In large measure, this basic similarity results from the fact that Puerto Ricans share the same ghetto streets and so are subject to the same social and economic forces that shape the development of blacks in organized crime. In the case of the Puerto Ricans, however, there is another aspect to their organization which they share with Cubans but not with blacks: the greater importance kinship plays in the establishment and maintenance of crime networks. Thus, we found the same criminal operations involving numbers, narcotics and the sale of stolen goods, again each with its own leader and loosely organized into a network by the presence of "my man" in each of the separate operations. What is important here, however, and what marks Hispanic networks as different from the black ones we have just seen, is that among Puerto Ricans

201

and Cubans "my man" is often a relative. In the course of our field research, we managed to identify and study one large but loosely organized Puerto Rican crime network by tracing out linkages among a group of people related by blood and marriage. It soon became apparent from this network and from others we observed that the Puerto Ricans in organized crime resemble the Italians in a number of other characteristics as well as the importance of kinship as a basis for network cohesion. While following out these relationships, we came across the extraordinary story of the "Cuban connection," the new drug importing and distribution system, which has a number of important implications not only for the pattern of ethnic succession in organized crime but for the American drug scene as well. Then, through another set of relationships within this network, we were able to look at a minority industry that is in the process of moving from an openly illegal status to a position of at least quasi-legality. The "gypsy cab" companies we observed operate in ghetto sections of New York City but both the industry and the enigma it presents are problems in every major urban center where such "cars-for-hire" operate despite the fact that they are not licensed as taxis. It is important for us to look at this industry here because it serves to illustrate the complex interplay of public demands for service, the blocking of legitimate minority demands for economic mobility, and political expediency in organized crime.

The Puerto Rican network is based in East Harlem, a section variously known as Spanish Harlem or El Barrio ("The Place"), and in the Red Hook area of Brooklyn, but it has its drug contacts in the Cuban community in the upper Broadway section of Manhattan. Both East Harlem and Red Hook were once dominated by the Italians, and the names of famous Italian-American organized crime figures—Ciro Terranova ("The Artichoke King"), Joey Gallo and Joe Profaci—are associated with them. Today the two sections are becoming increasingly Puerto Rican, and the control of organized crime there is moving to the new residents. The transition here, however, seems much more gradual than we have seen in black areas of

Harlem. The Italians are moving out or being driven out more slowly, and in some cases, particularly in the numbers, they are selling Puerto Ricans concessions, pushing back, for a time at least, the eventual takeover of control by the Puerto Ricans. In narcotics, however, the Puerto Ricans seem to be establishing new contacts with Cubans who are bringing drugs in from South America and bypassing the established Italian-controlled drug traffic from Europe.

Not only are the Spanish-speaking groups moving more slowly to displace the Italians, their organization for crime seems much more Italian in origin or at least character than the blacks'. Kinship, as we shall see, is as important an organizing factor among Puerto Ricans as it has always been among the Italians. There are even some older men who seem not unlike the *uòmini ríspettati,* the men of respect who are the "godfathers" of Italian-American organized crime. Perhaps the source of similarities is the proximity in which the Puerto Ricans have always lived with the Italians in East Harlem and in Brooklyn, or perhaps it is their common religion and the emphasis that their religion places on the family as an institution; in any case, the similarities are apparent. But if the Puerto Ricans seem to resemble the Italians in organized crime, the Cubans are almost a copy of them. In the Cuban neighborhoods in Manhattan, which stretch out along Broadway between 145th and 161st, and in the Cuban sections of Brooklyn and the Bronx many of the characteristics I found to be part of the early experience of the Lupollos in Little Italy seem to be reappearing among the Cubans. Like the Italians before them, they keep crime out of their communities even while organizing it elsewhere in the city. They do not allow drug pushing or prostitution in their neighborhoods. They are, we are told by our informants, more clannish than Puerto Ricans, less likely to flaunt their wealth than blacks and much better organized than either group. Some of our sources insist that these characteristics are the result of the fact that Cuban rebel groups organized by the CIA have transplanted this organization into crime; a more likely reason is the close working relationship Italian-American and Jewish gangsters maintained with pre-Castro Cubans in Havana. In either case, the Cubans are moving rapidly upward in organized crime and are rarely found on the street level for very long. Again like the Italians, most Cuban organized crime figures have legitimate fronts to cover and augment their crime activities.

Our information on this network originally came from Luis Santos, one of the Puerto Rican field assistants, in the form of an autobiographical account of his childhood in East Harlem describing how he became involved in organized crime. His description of these experiences shows many similarities to what we have already seen in the story of the black childhood gang the War Dragons in Bedford-Stuyvesant. In both cases the importance of street society as a locus for network formation in organized crime is apparent. But there are important differences as well, and these differences seem to be related to the more recent migration of Puerto Ricans to mainland cities and the consequently greater retention and unity of their cultural heritage and language. Through Luis Santos, we learned of Clemente Sanchez, one of Luis' childhood friends who has become a very successful drug pusher in East Harlem. Sanchez operates his narcotics activities through his brothers and sister, and by comparing the success of his operation with that of Luis, we learn a good deal about the importance of "being connected," a lesson reminiscent of the difference between Bobby Hassan and Jimmy Brown in Central Harlem. Again, however, "being connected" seems to involve kinship relationships much more frequently among Puerto Ricans than it does among blacks.

From Clemente Sanchez, we traced out the network in two directions. One was to his uncle Roberto Mateo, who operates a successful independent numbers game in the Red Hook section of Brooklyn. We were unable to find any criminal relationship between the two, however. But, when our other Puerto Rican field assistant, who lived in Brooklyn, made contact with Roberto Mateo, he discovered that Mateo has another nephew, Cesar Rosario, who sells stolen cars but also has a small drug-pushing operation. He obtains his drugs from his cousin Clemente Sanchez.

From Sanchez, we also traced the network out to Rolando Solis, a Cuban in Manhattan who wholesales drugs to Clemente. It was from Rolando Solis that we learned about the workings of the Cuban connection, the new system of drug smuggling and distribution that is challenging both the authorities and the established drug rings. Here we closed the network and set about learning as much as we could about the relationships among the individuals we knew about within the network. We did not have as much success as we would have liked to. We found it impossible, for example, to move to any other informants from Rolando Solis so that whatever we know about the Cuban connection comes from him and from Clemente Sanchez. In Red Hook, however, we did trace the links to one other action set, which I have included within this network. From Cesar Rosario we learned of another Puerto Rican in Brooklyn, Tomas Correa, who sells stolen cars and who uses the same youthful gang of car thieves who call themselves the Barracudas and the same automobile re-painter, Eduardo Paredes, as Rosario. We included Correa and the Barracudas and Paredes in the network because they are related to at least one part of it that we know of and may well be related to other operations within it as well. Thus, what I describe in this first network is a series of action sets where we are certain of some of the linkages among particular individuals, many of which are based on kinship but some of which are based on common criminal operations and a few of which are based upon both.

It was also through Tomas Correa that we learned about the gypsy cab operations because he sold a stolen car to one of the drivers in that network. I have included Correa in both networks but report them as separate ones because it was only in this one instance that we know of any contact between Correa and the gypsy cab net-work, although he undoubtedly has sold more than one car to them.

Because much of the information we have on this network is in the form of life histories obtained in interviews rather than from observed behavior, we know more about the operation of the individ-ual action sets than we do about how the total network fits together. Consequently, here I will follow a somewhat different procedure by presenting a description of each action set in the network in the words used by its leader and then, in the analytic section that follows these narratives, relate each action set to the total network to show how we feel it hangs together.

The first action set we discovered was centered about Luis Santos, our field assistant, who describes his childhood and subsequent career in organized crime. The locale is El Barrio in East Harlem and the story begins in the early 1950s. The characters in this action set are described briefly, before we hear from Santos.

Luis Santos is a Puerto Rican male, age twenty-nine. His mother came to New York from Puerto Rico in 1949 and settled in East Harlem on 109th Street between Lexington and Park Avenue. The majority of people who lived on this block came from his mother's hometown in Puerto Rico. Like the Italians before them, they brought their village with them and many of the old social patterns remain. Santos was soon enjoying what he describes as the normal growing up of a boy in Harlem: playing hooky, carrying numbers for different runners and explaining everything to his mother in terms of helping a guy at a grocery store. When his mother found out, she had him committed to Lincoln Hall for truancy. When he was freed, he was sent to a "614" or "special" school for delinquents and became in the eyes of his neighborhood friends a "big tough guy." When his mother moved to mid-Manhattan on the West Side, to a block on which only two other Puerto Rican families lived, Luis began returning daily to his childhood neighborhood in East Harlem.

He began gang fighting, "one thing led to another" and he was sent back to Lincoln Hall. In the meantime, local dope pushers began observing him and eventually he was given a job as a dope cutter, which he preferred to carrying numbers because of the greater profits involved. Upon his second discharge from Lincoln Hall, in 1958, he got together with four of his old street-fighting buddies and formed a partnership: each was to put up money so that they could buy almost $1,000 worth of marijuana. In order to meet his share of the financial burden, Santos committed a number of robberies, burglaries and muggings. The friends finally bought their marijuana, resold it all at a profit within two weeks and were ready to start again. They sold marijuana for a while and became frustrated over the fact that it seemed impossible for them to dominate the business even in their own neighborhood because the Italian from whom they purchased drugs was never willing to sell them more than a few pounds at a time and unwilling to cut off his other customers. Santos was caught and jailed for burglary for a few months, and in jail he discovered the far greater profits that could be made from dealing in heroin. When he got out, he and his friends each put up $250 and went off to four different places around New York City to buy four different "pieces" of heroin, which when put together gave them the kind of tidy stockpile that they would have been unable to obtain from any one dealer.

After this initial success, they tried to dominate the heroin trade in their neighborhood. However, obstacles kept coming up: some older women with whom they had been carrying on turned them in to the police and so they all got prison terms. Santos wound up addicted to heroin and was sent off to prison. On his release he returned to his old neighborhood, where he is now a numbers runner, the same job he started out in as a youth.

Antonio Rivera, Angel Rojas, Juan Rios, and *Rafael Quintero* are Puerto Rican males who grew up with Luis Santos and were members of his childhood gang.

Carmine "the Hook" Grazioli is an Italian who lives near 109th and Lexington Avenue in East Harlem and is the local narcotics wholesaler for an Italian organized crime family.

LUIS SANTOS:
ONE STREET, ONE VILLAGE

Most of the people on our block have come from the same town in Puerto Rico, or their parents did, and you get this warm feeling being around people just like you. So it doesn't matter that my mother hasn't lived here for more than ten years, I have always lived on 109th Street. Even when I was in Lincoln Hall for truancy and in real jails when I was old enough there I was, always daydreaming about the Barrio and my street. That street. And knowing that I would be going back there once I made out was very important to me. 109th Street is as good as having a family ready to take you in—I can live in a lotta rooms there. I am known there and always made welcome. For me 109th Street is the only place.

I was just a baby when my mother came from Puerto Rico and we started living in a railroad apartment with only two windows and a toilet in the hall on the fourth floor. Oh, sure, it was a tenement and the whole building stunk of sweat and piss and rotting fruit all the time, even in the winter. But I never stayed much in the apartment, I was always scuffling, making do in the streets.

I never knew my father, he had already deserted us in Puerto Rico. My mother had to have a women's operation when we first landed in East Harlem, and she never felt right. After that she didn't care much for men, she got very religious and became a Pentecostal so our apartment was filled with religious picture books and cards and statues, and holy pictures were tacked up everywhere. *Mamá* would rather pray to God than talk to me. She moaned a lot about sin and watched carefully to see how much I was sinning. I fooled her for a while until she found out—after that she really didn't want to have me around. I started to live like any normal Harlem boy. I played hooky, carried numbers from different runners, and my mother used to question me about where I got money. I would tell her I'd shine shoes or help the guy at the grocery. When she found out I was lying she would curse me—"¡ *Bestia, animal!*" then she would cross herself and bless me—"*Que Dios te bendiga.*"

I know my friends were always more important to me than family. And they feel the same. Most of our folks were living with the same broken furniture, living on welfare handouts; the radios were loud but all the TVs were beat up. I never saw a really clear TV picture until I went to a pusher's apartment when I was about ten or eleven. I hung around with seven, eight other guys, and we had ourselves quite a good gang. We wouldn't back away from a challenge and we looked for and started some good fights ourselves. None of the white teachers in school would speak Spanish plus they treated us like we were some kind of mean shit. So we either cut up in the school halls or cut out altogether. Which means we usually didn't bother to go at all; secretly the school was happy to see us running in the street, ripping off the fruit stores and any other stores on the block, but school being really bullshit they sent out people to check up why we weren't going to them for education.

Our education was on the street watching who made it and who didn't. Talking about education, I remember once when I was really a kid, me and Antonio Rivera stealing hubcaps and then not knowing what to do with the crap and tossing them down a sewer and running home to hide in our hallway like scared mice! Like I say, we were really small then so when I got an inch or two bigger, we really knew what to steal and never wasted our time with stuff you couldn't sell.

I've hung with the same guys since I was little, only depending who was not in the joint or at some rehab center. Some of the guys really had the bad luck. Like when Jose and his brother Juan were abandoned by their parents and they were given to the courts, I think, and they got sent upstate to an orphanage. They used to come back and visit during holidays but it was different, you know, when you don't see a guy every day you sort of can't really trust him the same. See, you don't know what he is doing all the time. I couldn't love them like brothers any more. Then one summer when we're all about seventeen, Jose and Juan came back and they were going to live with an aunt who had moved up from Florida. Nobody would run with them, the rest of us were busy running numbers; getting into dope, and we were really deep into rumbles. Juan and Jose only stayed around a week or so instead of two months and then they went back to the country. I bet they even live up there now. 109th Street was no longer their street and they were smart not to waste their time. I have no feeling for them at all now and I'm sure it's vice versa. I bet they even finished high school up there in the country.

The first time the truant officer spoke to my mother she beat hell out of me. Then she went to church, prayed for me, came home and beat hell out of me some more. The second time the truant guy showed, she sent me to Lincoln Hall for truancy. *Mamá* had found I was stealing and fighting, you know, the whole scene. I was no different than most of the other kids on 109th Street except I was a little tougher and smarter but she was a little crazy and a hermit and I think she really believed in God and sin and she thought Lincoln Hall would straighten me up. It didn't do nothing for me and when they turned me loose I couldn't go back to regular school but now I was in a 614 school for incorrigibles. By now because of the Hall and now the 614 school and the fact that my gang was the best in the area I was getting a cool reputation and getting noticed and approached. I was ready for anything. First you did stuff like get the bigger guys cigarettes and sandwiches and beer and they were letting you keep the change—then when they was sure of you, you got to be a numbers runner full time. That was me.

My mother moved then to midtown near the Hudson River. There were only Irish and Italians on the block and on all the other blocks so I never really moved with her. I stayed up on the street. Stayed for a while with Clemente Sanchez and his family. Clemente was one guy I liked a lot, he was very smart and he turned out better than me and I'm glad for him. At that time in my life he let me share his bed, but he didn't join in what we were doing. *Mamá* had about given up on me. I told her I was working in the grocery store and going to school but she didn't believe me, she only nodded, waiting for me to be arrested again. Which I was. Again I was dumped in Lincoln Hall but this time I was involved in a lot of the conversation in the place about how much money was in drugs. Just to be a part of the action meant more money spilling in than any full-time numbers running. And with my gang I thought maybe we could dominate a couple of blocks and really make us some money. But first we had to get cash. My mind was spinning when they released me and I almost ran the whole way back to 109th Street. Most of the guys I knew were around so we started planning . . . I was going to invite Clemente again but he was in jail now. But more than enough guys I trusted were around.

You see, I didn't have too much experience with dope—some old man had shown me how to cut it and I did it okay for him a couple of times but then he was picked up and I really wanted something for myself. First we had to get us a couple of pounds of pot. Nobody had the bankroll so we mugged, robbed and burgled like hell. I was doing numbers again just to keep eating but my eyes were on the pot deal . . . and gang fighting was really heavy so we were very busy, day and night. I was a little nervous about getting sent up again before we raised enough bills but the cops were also busy with other gangs —they couldn't concentrate on one place. In fact, they seemed to stay clear of 109th Street for about a month. Finally, we got up the bankroll; this was it. My friend Rafael Quintero bought two pounds of pot from a Puerto Rican distributor a few blocks away who got his stuff from the Italian who lived six, seven blocks from us. He was the *padrone* for our neighborhood. His name was Carmine Grazioli and everybody called him "Carmine the Hook" because he had a nose like an eagle. The Italians controlled our area; they doled out the stuff in small portions so you could only get so much from them and you could never take over even a block. They were very smart and they had everything going for them, since we had to depend on them. They had the cops, too.

Well, we unloaded our two pounds inside of a week and made a great profit. At that time we were selling bombers—really fat marijuana cigarettes—for up to $1.50, $5 bags were going for $7, $8, $10. We couldn't get much more pot right away so we wasted the profits going out drinking, you know, socializing. Then I had to start burgling to raise another ante and the other guys were doing the same. Only this time I got nailed and was in a real joint this time. Didn't stay too long because I played along and got parole in less than a year but while in there I decided how pot was really like numbers, small potatoes—heroin is the way to fast cars and fast women and the good, good life.

First day out I said to Rafael, "Now we try *la tecata.*"

"Sure, *amigo,* and where the fuck do we get heroin? The Hook will piss hisself laughing if we ask him."

I laughed. "We don't buy in our neighborhood, that's how we get a good stash. The Italians want us down forever. So we try every-where else."

"Everywhere?"

"Sure, even another borough maybe."

You know, Rafael was one guy I always wanted him next to me if I'm backed in an alley but Rafael didn't like to travel and another borough is like another country to him. Another village.

Once more I asked Clemente, who was out also, if he wanted in. But he had started a small drug thing with his family, his brothers and sister and an uncle was backing him with some money. And he wished me *buena suerte* and so I wished him luck, too.

A piece of stuff costs about $225–$250. We raised a grand this time. It was me, Antonio, Rafael, Angel Rojas and Juan Rios; we each put in $250 and we all got it the same way. The usual way. We spread our money around and got stuff easy. We did it like the Cubans do uptown in Manhattan—by jumping from connection to connection. Also your chances of getting caught are not as bad this way. Everything turned out like a birthday party; Rafael got a present from Columbus Avenue and 80th Street and I got another from Delancey Street, Juan scored in the Bronx and Antonio told me about a guy on the street in Harlem and that was it. We got up a grand of heroin and we did real well. And since we were kids we got careless, too. Once we sold the stuff we threw some big parties and I met Yvette. She was about ten years older than me, very beautiful, very wise in loving and drinking and snorting—everything I was interested in, so she taught me like a special one-on-one teacher. But she was also a junkie and not to be trusted. In fact of life, I was set up —I'm sure Yvette was hired by the Hook and his *paisans* in the neighborhood who saw we were getting big and wanted to cut us down fast; also we had a lot of enemies among other gangs we had dumped on and we had made a point not to buy a piece of anything from the local distributors so it could have been anybody that set us up. But for a week or two I was screwing my head off and really *embalao*—strung out—forgetting everything and beginning to get too deep into drugs personally.

Yvette had some girls friends and me and Angel and Juan, man, we all began to really swing with these *chicas*. Man, parties every night and in the daytime, too, plenty of smack, lots of wine, I was a real stud. One day we were all at Yvette's place and this guy comes in and starts raising hell saying he's Yvette's husband. I was really high and a little *loco* from drinking and snorting white stuff, so I called him a motherfucking pimp and *cabrón* and threw a whiskey bottle at him. I gotta give him credit, there he was in this place with me and all my friends there and he came right after me. Angel, me and Juan all jumped on him and beat the shit out of him, really wasted him—we punched him, kicked him and then took him downstairs and threw him out in the street and then went back upstairs, and started having a party again.

When I next woke up clear-headed I was in the arms of a cop who is charging me with rape and homicide. The second charge was true but the first was impossible with that *vieja puta*. I was sent to Riker's Island and left there and that is some terrible island. I'd rather be nodding out and dying slowly in some hallway than be alive in that hole. Rafael got seven to fifteen at Attica and Juan and Angel were in Elmira, five to seven. Don't ask me how come I was out but it didn't matter. I had no money, no guys to be with. I was in sad shape because by now I was hooked and I wasn't doing much of anything else. People who knew me since I was a kid looked away and wanted to forget me. Only Clemente was good, he'd slip me a few bucks but he couldn't offer me a job. I knew that. It was a very black, scary thing. I stayed around 109th Street and watched what was happening. There were big gang wars—the cops and papers kept saying it was for rivalry of turf but it was more than that. There was tries to take over drug operations too. Clemente stayed clear of the rumbles and he's really successful from his operation. He told me once he learned a lot from the Cubans watching how they copied the Italians operating, only he says the Cubans are nicer, more human, and they help you once they trust you. They're not prejudiced. You should talk to him. Clemente's a cool guy, he always did have a good head.

I'm back on the streets again, people can see I'm beating the drug thing so I'm running numbers again. It's like when I started out, but I know it's not the same. I look around and see all new kids. I hope to stay away from drugs for myself and I hope to stay away from jail. The drug scene is very violent but I have to confess I'm still attracted to the business side of it. This time if I do get an edge I'll probably get killed or kill someone . . . it has to happen that way. Still, I try to see if I can slip in. I try all the drinking clubs, show my face around, smile at the right people, you know, make myself known and available. I know it's still street hustling and, whatever happens, I'm still a street kid but I'm not ashamed.

I'm luckier than the kids who are dead or rotting in jail and even though she set me up, I still remember one time with Yvette, me, Rafael and Angel and two more women. We drove down to Riverside Park in a jalopy with fake license plates and we had no driver's license or car registration; we're loaded down with wine, chicken and ribs, and beer and drugs. So we barbecue on the grass and no cops bother us and we have one sweet afternoon. When it gets dark we pack up and toss all our junk in the garbage cans and drive back and double-park that car and never go near it again. Three, four days later, Yvette turns me in and kills whatever chance I had to make it better for myself. But I still got memories, I got my street where I grew up with me everyday.

I pay rent for a nice big clean room—but the color TV this family has has lousy reception, just like the black and white sets fifteen years ago—nothing really changes. The crappy smells and everything are still here. But I'm still around too—so if I have the street or the street has me, what's the real difference? Right? It's my village and I think I'm pretty damn lucky to be still living in it . . .

Luis Santos has already introduced us to Clemente Sanchez, his childhood friend who is the leader of another action set, a drug-pushing operation in the same area of El Barrio. The characters in this action set are described briefly.

Clemente Sanchez is a Puerto Rican male, age thirty-one. He was a childhood friend of Luis Santos but not a member of his gang. His uncle Roberto Mateo is a numbers operator in Red Hook, and it is this relationship that links the East Harlem and Red Hook segments of the network. Clemente educated himself in prison. He seems to be well-read in psychology, sociology and philosophy, and he understands how to make use of psychology; for example, he is likely to show off his gun collection to business guests. Sanchez sells narcotics, and he seems to go about it in a manner reminiscent of the Italian-American families: he employs other members of his family because they are safer and more reliable than most people and because, being family, they have less trouble "keeping the thing to themselves." He also retains a Jewish lawyer, which makes his pushers feel more secure than they would with other dealers.

Hector Sanchez is seventeen or eighteen years old, the younger brother of Clemente. He works for Clemente in the narcotics operation.

Jorge Sanchez is also Clemente's brother and he is twenty-four years old. At the time of this episode he worked for Clemente in the drug operation but since that time he has been arrested and he is now in prison.

Francisca Lopez is Clemente's half-sister, age twenty-two. She is a Lesbian and has been addicted on and off over the last ten years. She occasionally works for Clemente in his drug "factory."

CLEMENTE SANCHEZ: A FAMILY AFFAIR

Life is like the wind, in that it blows you around a lot but if you can grab some wisdom you learn how to prepare for different days, different weather. I feel bad when I see Luis walking around his own neighborhood lost and looking lousy and out of step. He's still strung out on drugs and just beginning to understand that gangs were never the way. And that's all he ever had going for him. I always understood that gangs were bad news: they bring attention to yourself when you win and mean curtains when you lose. You can't really win and there are too many other guys involved, too many other considerations. I know people thought I was acting funny years ago but I never joined a gang, even for a day.

But don't get me wrong, I was in plenty of trouble in those days. Whatever I did that was illegal I got caught and sent to some institution; other guys were nailed doing stuff on a bigger scale and getting released, but I was always being incarcerated. And I was fortunate in one respect because with time on my hands I really began to read. I got myself an education in philosophy, psychology and sociology, and I have used those books in practical ways that some of the authors and doctors would be impressed about. If not exactly pleased.

I read books that kept after you to really know yourself: see how you could be self-destructive and cancel that out—learning how to impress people with your strengths begins to give you inner strength.

Also, books do give pleasure, after a while it's like someone is talking only to you and I dug that. I still do. Most guys picked up even worse habits in joints but I learned about libraries and how you have to really shut up and read in them. I began noticing my own ideas and how life was changing, and crazy, I was getting respect for myself and others were handing out respect too. I once read a book about a terrific school where you really learn and the teachers don't only write out detention and suspension slips and don't look at you with hate and fear. When I am really high on wine and grass and I feel most happy and secure I dream of walking along this road full of trees and flowers and walking into a college and sitting down at the first empty chair and some man starts talking, lecturing, and I'm writing it all down and listening. And I have this smile, this great smile that I never had before . . .

I haven't been arrested or in jail for more than seven years and during that busy period I have set myself up in one sweet operation. About the time I was getting ready to do my thing the Cubans were beginning all their enterprises in upper Broadway. Watching how they operate is like reading one or two of the best books on how not to fuck up. First you deal only with your family, your true family if possible, so there's even less chance of bad inner trouble. You have to learn to be selective and able to adapt something big to your own small ideas. For instance, the Cubans think big in terms of big money so they can jump around, start a legit business while doing drugs too. One thing I was determined was not to be greedy or too big for my britches. I don't want anybody to get nervous or jealous of me. I only need so much to live good and that's all I was after and all I'm still after. I liked the way the Cuban big shots never draw attention to themselves; they drive around in old cars, even Volks', no flashy Caddies or Lincolns, you know, like the blacks do. They don't have to build up their image, see, they got inner conceit you know, they know how good they are and their community knows it. Why keep blowing your own horn? You know it is a traffic violation if you blow a horn for no reason.

Right. The Cubans are like the Italians, they don't let dope into their neighborhoods and they would kill you if you tried to use one of their women. I can sense it and feel it; they are very secretive people. They probably learned all this stuff from the Italians who used to run Cuban crime for Battista before Castro, but there's something not as uptight about the Cubans like Italians. Don't get me wrong, Cubans are not as open and very friendly as your average Puerto Rican—for example, you come on this street with money, wave it around, sure enough in an hour or two you'll get what drug you came for—not too many questions asked when most people around here see money. A Cuban wouldn't deal with you for days, if at all, he's naturally suspicious and cool to all strangers. But once he trusts you you're really in.

I've got a Cuban contact and we have a nice relationship. Like most very successful Cubans he's into another operation half-legit— he's partner in a jewelry store. The Cubans are the best in receiving and turning over stolen jewelry and watches. My man's store sells this stuff at reasonable prices since most of the stuff and the gold, etc., is stolen. I once got a beautiful watch for $40 from him. Like I say, they're human people; if it was an Italian he would have charged me full price for the watch.

I got two brothers and a sister and so I don't usually need anybody else for what I deal in. We got our own small factory where we cut and bag the stuff; we store it in my basement. There's a steel door and I got the only key. My brothers are younger than me, still wild, still liable to get into trouble, but they listen to me and they can see how good we got it and they try real hard not to screw up. That's all you can ask and like I said before, in a family the brothers and sisters try harder if they really are together in the idea. Whenever I do need others for some running or other things, I only choose from my neighborhood—we all are from the same town in old Puerto Rico, so people here can be trusted the same way again. Luis understands that. It's one law of all the streets.

Psychology is very important to me and I try to use it wisely. Let me give you an example. One of my brothers used to be a gun freak; he never used one but he had a collection of about twenty guns. I dismantled them so they don't work, but I put them in a velvet case in our house. Once we had a guy, a fellow Puerto Rican, who was very slow paying full price for what we sold him. I invited him over one night for a drink, we never talked about this debt, he mentioned it once but I brought up a different subject. Then just before he left and he was full of good cheer and wine I showed him my case and named every gun. I also told him about all kinds of bullets that are sanded down to make wounds even more painful. Like I said, none of the guns work but this guy is suddenly nervous and shaking. I pushed him out the door saying goodnight *Mr. so and so* instead of just using his first name. Next morning before breakfast he was back at my house with the cash.

You know, that's a true story and it's a story that can be told a couple of more times. But after the first year or so we had no more trouble with anybody about money and we never had to rough anybody up. *The threat of violence is far worse than actual pain,* a lot of books will tell you this. And that is the truth.

You know how politicians always seem to know the answers and are always acting so sure of themselves. That's called projecting a good image. Right? Right. Well, in any line of business you must have the good reputation of delivering the stuff at a fair price plus a good image is important. You got to project confidence. Even if it's only small-time business. In that way a small business is no different excepting size to a big corporation. And you know how corporations faint if their image gets lousy from some reason. They spend millions for public relations and advertising. I only spend a little. I got a lawyer, a Jewish lawyer, whose office is on the Grand Concourse. I can call him anytime. I pay him a retainer. And all the people who I deal with know I got a full-time lawyer. So even if I never call him except to say "Happy Jewish Holiday" it pays. People think we got a solid thing going—which we do. But the lawyer helps our image and since it's true he can also help us when we do get into trouble.

I enjoy going to the Cuban restaurants in the 150s for a couple of reasons. You can always meet some new connections; sometimes plain people coming back from Latin America bring a little stuff they want to unload privately.

The Cubans get stuff from practically every part of South America but they are very good with cocaine. And now cocaine is going to become very big—the blacks all use it and I understand that even the college students are moving to it from grass and hash. Imagine, if the blacks give up heroin for cocaine and the whites start to use it instead of pot—imagine how those Cubans will score. That Cuban connection has got to be the biggest thing going in the next couple years.

I got to know some bartenders and waiters up there. It's amazing how much of all drug trade is now from Latin America. My friend Rolando says the Cubans were organized by the CIA to attack Castro and then moved to drugs. It could be, you know. The Cubans are very original also. They discovered synthetic heroins like angel dust or gold finger some time ago, which was a very successful idea—even junkies liked it. I think now Cubans start with synthetic heroin to get a nest egg and then deal with real stuff. When they first brought angel dust out it was like dynamite, all the guys on the street started buying it up and it looked for a while like the Cubans were going to take it all. But after a while it died out like a fad. Now they use the synthetic only for beginners.

I also like Cuban food and enjoy the relaxed atmosphere. All Cubans make a habit of visiting a lot of restaurants—Spanish, Puerto Rican, Cuban, Chinese-Cuban—to find out who is traveling to South America and especially who has come back. Some restaurant owners have made themselves by selling interests in their restaurants to guys who are these pushers. I would never move from where I live but I do admire the way the Cubans live, their neighborhoods are not beat up like ours. They do business with a large Puerto Rican clientele but they do not in any way encourage socializing with them. The reason is that there are lots of Puerto Rican detectives and cops. They have lots of stores, all busy making profits. The people seem much happier. There's little or no drug taking in the Cuban area, everybody has a business sense. I really like to be around them. Like new ideas. Sometimes I hear something I can use. Outside of the few revolutionary goofheads who are still around, they are mainly exiles who don't want to go back until Castro goes. They sit in the restaurants and talk about returning to Cuba and fund raising and dances to raise money. They all are interested in how to get weapons. They prefer army-type weapons, machine guns, even bazookas. But they got it so good here they won't ever go back.

Okay, the world is complicated and scary but you should never jump at the first choice offered, you have to lie back and wait. You must always play it cool, be *cara palo*. Patience is not a sin. If I ever have kids I'd like them to have a real education. Reading and understanding subjects can make you much more clear-headed. I was lucky that I had the right temperament for reading. And being locked up I had no choice and then when I got into it you couldn't lug me away. I know there'll be more problems with spies and narks, there always are, but I've got a good chance to survive. So far I've stayed away from using hard drugs for myself because I am really content to be busy with a small operation and I hope my family can straighten out even more, so our business can be even more successful. By now I have sixth sense about who and what to stay away from and so I must be doing all right and I hope it continues this way . . .

Through Clemente Sanchez we met Rolando Solis and in interviews with him found out something about how the Cuban connection operates. Thus, while we feel certain that he is part of a larger network of Cubans in organized crime, all that we know about that network is what Rolando told us and the only other Cubans we could identify were those he mentioned. We did, however, apply our usual methods of checking on reliability and validity to that information so that we are confident that it is accurate.

Rolando Solis is a Cuban male, age twenty-seven, who has been in the United States since his family left Cuba in 1959. Solis is now an established narcotics dealer working as a waiter in a Cuban restaurant. He is also part owner of a jewelry store that sells jewelry that has been remanufactured from stolen gold. He began his career in the lowest level of organized crime among Cubans, selling stolen goods from door to door, running errands and just waiting for an opening. Then, when he was noticed by El Hombre ("The Man"), an established leader in Cuban crime circles, he moved to the second level. He became a waiter in a Cuban restaurant where South Americans often meet to deal narcotics as part of the new Cuban connection through Miami, which is now bypassing the established, Italian-controlled European connection. Some day he hopes to rise to the top level like "El Hombre" and he describes his dreams here. Solis is Clemente Sanchez's contact in the Cuban drug connection.

ROLANDO SOLIS AND "EL HOMBRE": THE CUBAN CONNECTION

I have two goals and I consider them both possibilities within my reach. I am confident because here on 155th Street and Broadway I am among my fellow Cubans and they are a race who truly take care of one another. Because many are successful here they can help others get ahead. We are a proud people and can enjoy a countryman's success.

In the beginning I was watched and talked to by a man I revere. This man is the most successful businessman in our neighborhood.

He said to me, "Rolando, you look like you are ready for anything, to do anything. Don't be so intense, it's crazy to be in a terrible hurry to go nowhere. Slow down your mind and your dreams."

I wasn't being fresh, believe me, but I answered quickly, "I am in a hurry, I have nothing, and so many around me have plenty."

He was not given to anger and he replied softly, "When one is calm and intelligent, matters always go better and on a more straight line."

"I don't know if I am that way. I don't know if I can act that way. What do you think?"

He touched my shoulder. "I'll tell you the truth, we are watching you, I am watching you myself. After all, we are all Cubans. You'll start by doing small jobs for me; do them well and stay calm and you will not be on the streets long."

"I will try, I will really try."

I was slap happy that someone grand like him was talking to me like a *padrino*. I couldn't believe it. But I did believe he noticed that I was ready for trouble just itching to do any dumb thing that excited me. The Man could sense that restlessness and his people don't want me for a street kid in their business. In truth they don't like Cuban boys to act in these crazy ways. In some ways this is snobbery on their part but also good sense since I'd rather not be just an errand boy either. So I try to be patient and not do anything foolish.

Then one day I'm approached to go around door to door and start selling cloth and knickknacks. I remember to smile a lot at the ladies and be polite to their husbands. In a day or two I'm a serious peddler and I sell terrific and don't steal one cent. Everyone starts calling my name out in the street and nodding to me.

One day the Man strikes up a conversation with me again and this time he wants to know how come I don't go out more with Cuban girls. How do you like that? They know everything about me but I don't get mad. I say something funny and he laughs and tells me to stay in the neighborhood more often at night. "Plenty here for young men," he cautions. And frankly I listen to him much more carefully than I would to my own father. My mother is dead in Cuba; my father works hard in a dress factory six days a week. He's just happy to be alive so it's no use talking to him or learning from him. I don't have any trouble with my father, we get along okay, but I can't admire that kind of man.

Next I was handed a job as assistant manager of a laundromat. A very busy laundromat. It was sweaty, hard and long hours of work. I felt like I was suddenly copying my father, knocking myself out at some dirty factory. But since I was acting nice to everybody it got real easy to be nice and I stopped bitching even to myself. I got to like the owner and the customers a lot, there was a lot of joking around.

One night after work El Hombre stops me in the street and invites me to his casino, you know, his little social drinking club. I think he's a silent partner of this place but of course I don't ask. It becomes a night I'll never forget. When we get there it's already crowded with plenty of other rich businessmen but it's not a noisy place at all. Many of these men, and some will call them gangsters, give large amounts of money to the exile causes. I saw one numbers guy give $5,000 cash to the cause and he got a standing ovation. Everyone is quietly drinking, mostly beer, and there is some laughing but it's not loud, you know, it's a high-class casino. When we first arrive El Hombre stops at a table to talk with another old man about some guns—carbines and machine guns they will ship to Florida and then to Central America. I am proud that he trusts me to talk in front of me, but I am not into this revolution thing. I think we Cubans must make our life here, in America.

"Okay," he says to me at the table, "from now on you're a waiter up the street. It's a very important place for connections. Others will begin talking and teaching you . . . Rolando, what is the business you really want? Numbers?"

"Numbers is okay," I say carefully, "I know there's real money in it but drugs is my dream. Even synthetic drugs if they're still around, to begin with. That's what I really want."

He nods. "When you come into the business it won't be on the street level. Everyone agrees you're a good risk—my lieutenants, other scouts, and me, we all agree. You understand. First you work the restaurant and what you hear and see and are told will be a college education for drugs. When you see all the connections then we help you set up. Now, my friend, will you be patient enough now?"

I grin. "I want to be like you."

He laughs. "In what way?"

"I want to drive an old car and have cash in my pocket for any car in the world."

He laughs again.

"And I want to be smart enough not to be hit by the police."

"Good."

I look around the room, hardly anybody is left, it's getting late; the bartender is yawning. I say, "One thing more."

"Oh, what else?"

"I want to help another dumb kid like me one day."

"You had the hungry look but you were not dumb, Rolando. You got the patience and control now. One day we'll start you off with enough capital and you won't have to begin paying back until you're doing okay."

So my two goals are these—to be well fixed in the drug connection with Latin America and to be part owner of a restaurant. I really love being a waiter. I love the feeling of a good restaurant; it has the air of a festival, people are happy and the smell of food and the noise is all of one cloth. I know now I really like people, it's not an act any more. I even like serving them our good food. It's not greedy to have two goals because it's not good to have time on your hands. My customers are beginning to trust me and they've begun to ask do I know where they can unload a small portion of cocaine. It is how the Cuban connection works. People fly here from South America, they bring small amounts of cocaine or sometimes heroin. They come to the restaurant and I direct them to where they can sell it. No big shipments, no chance for a big raid, just small operations. But ten people can carry more than two and if two get caught there are still eight left. I know one Ecuadorian diplomat who is now a millionaire on what he makes bringing in small amounts of cocaine—even his children do! They will bring it back to this country—fourteen, fifteen ounces each—and cocaine is selling for $70 to $100 a spoon—they can pick up $30,000 or $40,000 each person who comes in. So now this man has gone to deal dope and he gets all of his friends to bring back some. Meantime, the Cubans go around from restaurant to restaurant picking up from these travelers. Latin Americans have always smuggled, it's like in their blood. I found the Ecuadorian when he came into a jewelry shop that I have a piece of. He wanted to buy a gold cross for his mother. When he spoke with me I felt he was a man one could talk with. I gave him a good price on the cross and we began to talk. I told El Hombre about it and he smiled and asked me to make the connection with the Ecuadorian. That was a proud moment in my life when I handled the transaction without a slip. I feel I'm on my way. Soon I'll have my own apartment. And one day I will help another wild Cuban kid. That was not an idle promise. How can I ever forget that man's kindness to me . . .

From our initial contacts in East Harlem, we traced this network into the Red Hook section of Brooklyn. Here, in an area where the Puerto Ricans are now rapidly replacing the Italian population, we located and observed the other segment of the total network. This part of the network, which is entirely Puerto Rican, links with the East Harlem segment through Clemente Sanchez's uncle Robert Mateo, who is a leading numbers operator and well-respected resident in Red Hook. It was in this area that we had to stop field work for a period of time in 1971 when Joseph Colombo, Sr., was shot at an Italian civil rights rally and the police announced that the Gallo faction of the former Profaci family in Brooklyn was responsible. The shooting was done by a black who seemed to have connections with the Italian syndicate. For a period of time the entire Red Hook section of Brooklyn was tense as everyone waited for the certain retribution that would come. Police surveillance in Red Hook was so intense it was impossible for our field assistants to operate for a while. Eventually things returned to normal but on April 7, 1972, Joey Gallo was killed in a clam bar in the Little Italy section of lower Manhattan.

We found a number of action sets here, each with its own leader.

The first action set is the numbers operation of Roberto Mateo, a Puerto Rican male in his late forties. He runs his own "book," an independent *bolita* game. His territory is near what was Joey Gallo's neighborhood, but he tells how the Italians used to sell franchises to Puerto Ricans and how he has managed to remain independent. Heavy police surveillance of the Gallos in Mateo's neighborhood led Mateo to adopt some rather technologically advanced ways of operating his business: numbers runners record the bets of their players on cassette tape recorders, then play their tapes over the telephone onto another tape recorder located at Mateo's headquarters. Pressure due to police surveillance of the Gallos also has led Mateo to encourage weekly players rather than daily players. His customers are mostly factory workers from his immediate neighborhood along with local restaurant employees, cab drivers and gas station attendants. He also hires housewives at $50–75 a week to handle the telephone calls as they come in from his runners. Mateo wants to continue to operate independently and he is prepared to use violence to free himself from the Italians or from blacks if need be. He is frequently approached by people who live in his neighborhood, who seem to hope or expect that he will be able to help them out in one way or another, lend them money, get their children or husbands out of jail, and he operates very much like the local Mafia "man of respect" used to in dispensing such favors. He is the uncle of both Cesar Rosario and Clemente Sanchez.

ROBERTO MATEO:
A BROOKLYN ELDER

Let me give you some examples of how I am considered in my neighborhood. Perhaps while you are here you will even see others coming for advice. I cannot always do anything but still they come every day and many times through the years I have been of service. This morning I was able to aid a mother whose only son was arrested for armed robbery. I was able to help raise the bail and sometime today I will arrange for a good, cheap lawyer. Occasionally I can get those in trouble out without bail, but not her son for he has a record of too many previous arrests. And yesterday a man comes to see me and tells very bad stories about his landlord—it is not the first time I have heard stories about this landlord. I will soon have a discussion with him about new water pipes and a new boiler. I think he will listen carefully to me. Other landlords do.

Yes, this has always been an unusual book. Unusual in the sense that I have been in the *bolita* for many years and not one day have I ever paid protection except, of course, to the police. And every year of my operation I have been an independent. I have owed no one anything and never had or required a partner. That I do exist is a small miracle in this day and age—it is similar to a small store doing wonderful business though the rest of the street is loaded down with big-time supermarkets.

This neighborhood is located in the total area of the Brooklyn Mafia. Joey Gallo lives not far from here. Before him the Colombos used to sell concessions to Puerto Ricans to run the numbers for them. The Italians provided the money and took care of the police and the Puerto Ricans ran the operation. Then they split the profits. Now some of these Puerto Ricans have become independent because the Italians do not control the police as they once did. Me, I never paid off the Italians. I still hear many things about Gallo, that he tried to kill Colombo, that he has many *Negros* who work for him, but we have never crossed each other's path. We never had trouble once. But I have always had to be cautious because the police are always in this area. They constantly watch the Italians especially now that the Gallos and Colombos are in a vendetta. They move about in prowl cars and unmarked cars, in uniforms and dressed like sanitation men, utility company workers and, you know, telephone linemen. One has to smile for they are so easy to spot after all these years. Still they are always around and you have to move carefully.

Sometimes I think the police don't care to catch you, just to harass you with their presence. And it's true, very true, they and the times have forced us to make changes. To use tape recorders. To have our runners read off the slips onto casettes into telephones manned by our operators who also tape-record the numbers; then all the paper work is destroyed, a very efficient and practical operation is now operating.

This is a poor community, a close-knit community, working hard to make a living and now I hire many housewives to be my telephone operators for the numbers call-ins. Depending on their hours they are paid between $60 and $75. There are more applications for such jobs than I can handle but one day they will all have jobs with me. I will see to that. It shames me to see our young women whoring for the black men.

This is not good, this is a bad thing. The Italians who used to live in the Barrio, and who live around us now, they did not let their women to become *putas*. Not the Cubans either, their women do not whore and even their men who sell drugs on the street are despised by them and are thought to be small and mean people. *Nunca,* where did my people learn to so despise their women to let them sell their bodies like meat in the *Marketa?* From the American Negroes, and now we are *Negros* too, even if we are white, because we live like them. That is what America has done for my people, now we are colored and we have lost our pride.

I have made other changes. We encourage weekly numbers playing so that all my runners have to be in the telephone booths far less often and so risks are greatly lowered. The deadline for numbers in Brooklyn is one o'clock, the winning numbers are the last three digits on the mutuel handle from Belmont or Aqueduct, whichever is running, of course. Also, *Nucara,* where you bet one number only, is very big. Yes, from such simple facts I have made a splendid business and an equally fine reputation.

One reason I never had trouble with the Italians was I stayed in my area and they had nothing to fear from me. Everybody here plays numbers—the regular people who live here, factory workers, the gas attendants, restaurant workers and cab drivers, even the police. I had no reason to go elsewhere with my runners. You can see what happens even to such powerful well-run organizations like the Italians have, they overextend themselves and are brought down to earth and under the ground. Let me be clear. I am a man of peace, I want only what is mine and nothing that is the property of others. I am no thief nor am I greedy. But I will fight for what is mine. The Italians and *los Negros Americanos,* they think that we Puertoriqueños are *pendejos,* cowardly people. You should know that in Puerto Rico when someone tries to humble someone else by not paying a bet or going to the police, he may be thrown into the bay and *los bocas,* the sharks, teach him the way a gentleman should live and die: with honor.

Yes, I have a fine family; both my married daughters are school teachers with wonderful children. My wife and I are proud of their success too. When it's my birthday I receive hundreds of cards and almost as many presents; I think I receive such honors because I never left my neighborhood when I became very successful and I am interested in what happens to my fellow neighbors. And I have always tried to help those in trouble.

Of course, you must change with the times, but you must keep old things too. It would be hard for me not to wear a suit and tie and hat in every season, of course, the material is different for the weather, but the idea of a suit and tie is still important to me. I cannot put it fully into words. Except that I think it is expected of me.

Some months ago a man I had known for many years died of cancer. The chapel was very crowded and I was a few minutes late, I *thought.* But they had delayed the service until I arrived and the widow, holding back her tears, had me sit in the front row with the family. I was very honored and touched by the gesture.

Come walk with me now. I take my walk this time of day every day regardless of the weather. I think that too is expected of me. Now you will see how many true friends I have, you will see the smiles and hear the talk. It's very important for me to feel this love;

each day I bathe in the warmth of good feeling and trust of my community . . .

Through Roberto Mateo we identified another action set, the stolen car and small drug operations of his nephew, *Cesar Rosario,* a Puerto Rican male, twenty-one or twenty-two years old, who is in the automotive business. He left high school in his senior year, but he has become a specialist. He repairs hot rod engines and he also employs thieves to steal cars for their competitive equipment, such as four-speed transmissions and high-performance engines. The thieves are usually Puerto Ricans between the ages of seventeen and twenty-one. Rosario relies on two or three of them particularly; only one of his thieves is black. In most cases the thieves are saving up to buy their own high-performance cars.

Rosario also sells phony auto insurance cards to young hot-rodders and others for whom the cost of real insurance would be intolerably high. He also employs two or three young women (themselves in a methadone program) to push pills and dope for him. The girls are instructed to stay away from Rosario's garage at all times. Rosario buys his drugs from his cousin Clemente Sanchez.

CESAR ROSARIO: HOT RODS AND HOT CARS

I have always been independent, always worked for myself ever since I left high school. My uncle wanted me to go into business with him, to work in the numbers but to do that you have to want to work with people and I want to work with my hands. Ever since I can remember I have loved fast cars and any kind of machinery. Once I worked as a mechanic in a very good shop in Bay Ridge which handles only foreign cars—Jaguars, Triumphs, even Ferrari and Maseratis once in a while—but when I learned my trade I went to my uncle and asked him to lend me money to start my own shop. He was unhappy because he wanted me to work with my head. Now I have paid him back and he is happier with me. People in this neighborhood know me and every kid wants to buy one of my high-performance cars.

I also have spare hot rod parts and that interests a lot of kids, some of whom are the same guys who steal cars for me. That way I got them coming and going and I can supply them with four-speed transmissions and high-performance engines, stuff like that. You should hear them drag racing late at night; sounds like Indianapolis, only it's still Brooklyn. And since these cars get wrecked up, these kids couldn't ever get cheap insurance cards. You know you can't get plates unless you have insurance. For $10 I can get you an FS-1 that says you have insurance even if you don't. The fake FS-1 cards is very solid business and I have built up good will in this neighborhood. These kids would do anything for me. And they can keep their mouths shut.

And just for kicks I do some legitimate garage business like tune-ups, brake overhauls and wheel alignments. I got some regular customers just for that!

Mostly, though, I deal high-performance cars, I rebuild them and soup them up and I can take a stock car and overnight turn it into a quarter of a mile hot rod. Look over in the back of the shop and you will see many high-performance engines and parts—a 426 Chrysler Hemi, 426 cubic inches and 425 horsepower or a 396 Chevelle with 375 horsepower. And I know how to do the work, tearing down the whole engine, dropping in cams, boring up the motor, putting in pistons, everything can be done right here. And when the engine is finished I can sell it or I can pop it into a car and sell the entire machine to a kid who wants to drive fast.

My uncle is still not really happy with my business. He is always worrying that I will get caught, that somebody will recognize his car or that one of the kids I have out shopping cars for me will get arrested and then I will be caught, too. But it is a safe business, it really is. When I get a car and break it down into parts there is no way to identify the parts. The kids I sell to don't ask me where I get my carburetors and I don't ask them where they get their money. If I get a good high-performance car then I have to work fast and hard to convert it so that it can't be recognized. The cops around here are pretty fucking sharp at recognizing a stolen car. They don't tell by the car, they tell by the kid who is driving it. For a Puerto Rican kid to be driving a hot car is like he threw the finger at the cops. They stop him every time and that's where my good work comes in. I have a guy who paints the car with a gray primer and that way it looks like the kid bought an old wreck and is rebuilding it. Then he has the insurance card and the plates and there is nothing the cops can do. I even change all of the locks on the car — door, ignition, trunk, everything. Then if some guy comes with the police and says it's his car you just ask him to start it or open the door, and he gets really pissed when his spare set of keys won't open anything. He *knows* it's his car but what can he do?

So I'm not crazy or stupid. I don't take drugs myself but it would be silly not to see what's going on in the projects and not begin to slip into that. My cousin Clemente [Sanchez] gets the drugs for me. I got three girls working for me that sell half-loads, that is $3 bags for me. They earn 50¢ per bag and can make some loose change for clothes and stuff. They never come within ten blocks of my garage. I meet them in one of the little parks across from the projects and supply them with the bags. It's only a beginning like I say, and I keep both businesses very separate.

You know it's true I never really finished fourth grade. I'm nearly twenty-four, some guys older than me work for me, I got sometimes fifteen employees and I pay on the spot. This phone never stops ringing. The money never stops pouring in. I make 75 percent profit on my operations and I'm in demand. There's absolutely no damn reason things won't be even better for me.

The streets here are always gray and it's an unfriendly, mean-looking place. But that's okay—who wants crowds? Even the sun doesn't make things look better. But if I want a tan I'll drive to Coney Island or Rockaway. And if I want to make a pile I'll stay here because as long as there are kids wanting cars I'll always have a good business. The drugs is something else. My uncle doesn't know about it so that as long as I stay small I'm okay but if I get too successful he will know about it and that old Puerto Rican temper will come out and he will say, simple like, *Nunca mas,* no more and then I got to decide do I want to strike out big or do I want to listen to him.

From Cesar Rosario we traced the network to another stolen car dealer, Tomas Correa, and then to Eduardo Paredes, a garage owner in the Bay Ridge section who will promptly repaint a stolen car. Paredes, it turned out, also paints stolen cars with red or gray prime for Cesar Rosario.

Tomas Correa is a Puerto Rican male, thirty-three or thirty-four years old. He can't read or write. Behind a "collision shop" front, he obtains stolen cars and sells them for parts. He has an established reputation with hundreds of collision shops throughout New York City and its suburbs, and when they need parts for a damaged car they call him, knowing that he can supply them at low prices. When he gets an order for parts, Tomas instructs a group of young thieves to steal the kind of car that will fill the order. He pays them in cash. They steal the car, strip it, obtain the parts that are wanted, and leave the hulk on a street somewhere. Sometimes Correa is able to supply the thieves with master keys. Sometimes he stocks certain parts, without a firm order, in the expectation of a later sale.

TOMAS CORREA:
BROOKLYN IS THE PLACE FOR ME

Sure, this is a quiet neighborhood. Quieter than East New York where I grew up and screwed off. Then I moved here, moved in here. Even the cops don't often go down these streets. Doesn't look like a "hot" area, you know. A lot of the buildings have been half-torn down and some factories have been closed, and the kids have broken all the windows, you know. Mostly there are collision shops and garages and some junkyards further down there. It stinks from gas and fumes. A guy I know said it looks like a war was started here and then everyone got tired and left. It's not a happy-looking place. That's for sure. But I like it here and I'm up to my ears in orders, because I provide services people need and can't get from others.

Yeah, I'm doing more than all right. I don't read or write too good and I don't even like movies or TV but my shop is busy as anything, see, the phones never stop ringing and things are always happening. I'd rather be mixing in, you know, busy myself, than watching others get busy like in sports or them movies. I'm really only interested in me and my work.

The first time I got busted was by a young cop in East New York, and he warned me nicely if I keep drag-racing stolen cars I'd be in big trouble. He was trying to be friendly; he didn't consider me a dangerous criminal, just a dumb kid. And the same time a young social worker, he spoke to me in the courthouse and said he could get me a job in some Jew sweatshop and wouldn't I be happier and safer.

But I was always interested in cars and taking them apart and selling equipment and it seemed to me this was a safe and happy job. And you know there are plenty of other collision shops like mine all over the city but I got one of the busiest. I'm way up there in reputation. Hell, you're here aren't you?

One way I did listen to that cop. I never stole cars no more, myself. Now I arrange for them to be ripped off. You'd faint how fast I can get any car delivered here within an hour, by four, five reliable guys who know I pay on the spot for what I want. I even got master keys for some makes.

By far my favorite car maker is Ford. They are very careless in their factory and it's easy to work over their models—they only have door tag identification which is a cinch to remove with a five-sixteenths-inch wrench and they don't stamp their engine block or water pump either. So here's a fast rundown, I look out in junkyards for old-make Fords, even Chevys, but mostly Fords, about '65—or the junkyard dealers call me.

Now we bought this car from the junkyard only because we want the door tag so we get rid of the old hulk right away, just push it out on the highway somewhere. Then I got a guy who gets a registration for this old junk and I got a registered car but there ain't no car—at least not yet.

When I get the car I remove the door tag, then I make a call for a stolen car brought up front; and we weld #6 screws on the tag and then screw the junkyard car's tag into this door from the side and put everything together again. We used to put the tag on with liquid lead, you know, just take off the old one and put the new one on right over the same spot. But the cops got wise to this and they used to stop cars and pick at the door tag with a nail and sure as shit, it would come off.

Next I call a garage in Brooklyn where my man Eduardo will paint a car for me (whatever color is in the registration) for $20; sometimes he will do the inside too. He's fantastic, cheap, fast and a beautiful painter. It usually takes only forty-five minutes to get it painted and then you can't tell the difference unless you look at the inside or you remember the inside. Sometimes I have Eduardo change the inside too. I know other guys like me use Eduardo too but he always says "yes" to me and I have never had to wait on him.

Now if some guy spots the car and says it's his or if the cops pick it up, they check the registration, right? Well, they see that this car was registered two, three months ago and how the hell could you register a car three months before you steal it? Man, I love those Fords and they are good to me. And the Puerto Ricans here, regular people, are often looking for a car, one of my cars, see, they have an accident with their auto and rates go sky high. You know insurance companies—so my cars are in demand.

Often my guys steal cars, strip them and leave the rest of the heap on streets half a mile away—you see those cars around everywhere . . . I'm on call from at least fifty legit collision shops who know I can supply them with parts for their repair jobs; they never ask no questions, they just want the parts supplied. And I am one great supplier. Sometimes I'll strip cars just to have some extra parts on hand but not too much of that. You see it's so easy to get a car to strip, why not wait for the phone orders?

Shit, you can't blame the guys who run those collision shops. You know how the insurance companies screw them. And those adjusters who work for the insurance company are all crooks too. They get their cut on every job. You know, you wreck your car, you take it to a garage and leave it there and nine times out of ten the insurance adjuster goes there and he tells you to leave it in that collision shop. You know why? Because he has a deal with the shop owner. He gets a piece. What can the shop owner do? He can call me and say, "I need a front end for a Cutlass or I need some glass for a Mustang." I tell him I have some used but good parts that he needs and he don't ask me where I got them. If he goes to one of the distributors it's 100, maybe 200 bucks for a part I can supply him for $50. When he puts it on your car you don't know the difference and you're happy. The shop owner is happy, the adjuster is happy counting his cut and most of all, man, I am happy. And I'll stay happy here and answer the phone and keep calling others . . . no doubt . . . Brooklyn is the place for me!

Finally, from Tomas Correa we learned of the *Barracudas,* a gang of young Puerto Ricans who steal cars for Correa. While this is a fairly common type of crime among juveniles, it is a highly organized and widespread operation in this network. Here cars are stolen on order meeting requests for particular makes, models and even colors. We learned from the Barracudas that they also steal cars for Cesar Rosario, thus making this part of the network, at least, fairly well linked.

THE BARRACUDAS

We're no gang exactly but we are together and we work slick together. We call each other the Barracudas. Sure, we're like some basketball team—you know—we practice all the time, we got regular plays and we score . . . so far we never lose, which means so far we ain't been caught.

See, we know Tomas or Cesar is going to call so we get ready for them. We would never hit a car in our own neighborhood—that's stupid and just carries attention to yourself. Okay.

See, we're always cruising around late at night, usually between midnight and five in the morning. We get on the highways and drive all over, but hardly ever into midtown or Manhattan itself. They keep the good cars in garages there and besides, the streets are loaded with cops looking for muggers. But we'll drive as far as Staten Island, usually we stay in Queens. I especially love the Brooklyn-Queens Expressway and the Grand Central so we usually get off one of them exits and real fast find us a nice, quiet residential neighborhood—a car farm that's only five or six blocks from an entrance to the highway. Then we could get a car or see what's available so that we can wait and pick it when we need it. See, cops aren't around too much on the dog hours—midnight to five . . .

And then we begin to stake out a place and start to plan heating up a special car. We know the kind of cars Cesar and Tomas order so when we find one we go back to the same farm two, three nights in a row. We watch the car and we get to know what time all the neighbors shut down and go to bed. We know this farm pretty damn good in three nights, believe me. Pretty soon we've got a few cars staked out and sure enough, there's Cesar calling for a car.

There are five of us in two cars. The lead car parks up the block, the back-up car waits at the far end of the street. Then me and my friend walk over to the car we're going to hit. My buddy fakes lighting a cigarette or taking a piss while I push out the little window on the driver's side, from there I pull down the big window and crawl in —this way the door is never opened and no fucking alarm is going to buzz off—next my buddy goes in the window on the passenger's side. I have brought my own special package, a complete ignition switch with a key so now I pull away this car's ignition wires—connect them to my ignition, switch my key in my ignition box and we are ready.

I don't switch on any lights as we take off very slowly and I'm watching to see the lead car's brake lights flashing three times. So now the coast is clear and my car lights snap on. The lead car is always on the left, the back-up car follows, keeping maybe a block and a half away to make sure nobody follows or to jam somebody who is following. Very soon, man, we are on a pretty empty highway heading back to Brooklyn.

But sometimes funny things happen. Once we were just leaving a place in Kew Gardens with a car, a good one—it was a Cadillac or a Continental—and just as we flash on the lights, a Volkswagen comes around the corner, stops and makes a U-turn and starts coming after us like hell. It must be the owner of the car or somebody on the block who knows the car and he is mad, man, and he is going to get us. We start really moving then but these are small streets and he keeps up with us. Then the back-up car begins to earn his money and he starts chasing the Volks. About two blocks away he rams into the side of the Volks and pushes the motherfucker right up on the curb and into the front door of a fancy apartment building. What a crash! Lights go on all over the block and we get out of there as fast as we can. We take the car to a garage Cesar rents for this purpose. And it is there we strip the car. You know them jungle movies where they got hundreds of tiny fish that can eat a person to the bones in two minutes? That's the way the parts on this car disappear. I know that kind of fish ain't a barracuda but for me it's close enough. See, we got plenty, plenty of tools to do all the stripping . . . poff goes the front hood and with hydraulic jacks you got the car lifted and two horses shoved under it holding the machine while its guts pour out— here comes the transmission and engine at the same time—the differential and everything else Cesar uses. Of course, we take the stereo if there is one, and the same with any bucket seats and the tires. We throw in some old seats and put on old tires, usually, and with a tow truck or any other kind of truck, we shove the heap outta this neighborhood. Before we leave the car we break the windows and kick in anything that hasn't been kicked in, and now it's somebody else's garbage.

Then we usually go back to the garage and shoot the shit until Cesar calls, about seven, and takes over. We get $125. Then we go out for breakfast and that night the Barracudas are out shopping more cars, finding the new farm and checking out . . . and very soon Cesar or maybe Tomas will be calling again . . .

Analysis of the Network

This network describes some linkages we have seen earlier in black networks and some new and interesting ones we have not encountered so far. Luis Santos has a number of significant links with people he grew up with in his East Harlem neighborhood. Throughout his childhood he ran with a gang made up of other Puerto Rican boys. The first time he was released from Lincoln Hall he was looked up to by his peers as a "big tough guy." This was the beginning of his credentialing and the first step in bulding a "rep." Later, he was observed by older criminals in the neighborhood who hired him to do odd jobs such as picking up policy slips or cutting dope. Eventually, he went into partnership with four of his childhood friends. Here two patterns of relationship that we have seen and will see often are found. The first of these is the *childhood gang,* which is a crucible in which strong and enduring friendships are forged. These friendships persist and form an important basis for the later association of crime partners. The second is the recruitment of youngsters into organized crime by experienced, established older criminals. The first step in the recruitment process seems to come when the youngster comes to the attention of older criminals as the result of his behavior on the street. The entry-level jobs are fairly menial— picking up numbers slips, fetching sandwiches and coffee. This apprenticeship system, in which the youngster is given some minimal responsibility and observed, allows him to gain both competence in crime and, just as important, a chance to develop a reputation that can lead to advancement. A third type of relationship is suggested but we do not have enough information yet to analyze it with ease. When Luis was in Lincoln Hall he learned, among other things, that there was big money in heroin, a lesson he took with him when he was released. The importance of reform schools and prisons as both recruitment and schooling centers for organized crime is suggested here but not as fully as in some of the other networks we observed.

The story of Luis Santos is also revealing as to the difficulties of "unconnected" young blacks or Puerto Ricans seeking to establish control over crime activities in even one block of their neighborhood. Carmine the Hook controlled the local drug supplies and refused either to sell a large stash to any one group of Puerto Ricans or to decline to sell to other groups. In this way the Italian mob kept control. In order to break the stranglehold, the youthful partners had to go to all parts of the city, picking up small amounts here and there in order to get enough heroin to deal on even a moderately large scale.

This episode in the life of Luis and his friends is filled with violence, duplicity, informing to the police and conspiracy. It shows how and why men who attempt to enter the drug trade seem willing to engage in more blatantly antisocial behavior than men who confine themselves to the numbers or to dealing in stolen goods; the money is better. Luis Santos robbed, mugged and burgled in order to put together his share of the initial partnership bankroll. There is more money to be made faster, but the risks are also greater.

An interesting comparison is drawn between the narcotics efforts of Luis Santos and his childhood friends, operating in partnership and presumably on the old ganglike ties of friendship and camaraderie, and the far more successful narcotics efforts of Santos' friend Clemente Sanchez. It seems somehow not unexpected that the downfall of the old gang of childhood friends should have come at the hands of a group of older women they fell in with. Carelessness and foolishness, along with daring, seem appropriate to such a gang; they are loosely organized and largely leaderless. By comparison, Clemente Sanchez is cool, clever and deliberate, an able psychologist who more often gently threatens violence than resorts to it. His narcotics operation, far from being a loose and informal partnership, is run very much like the Cuban and Italian syndicates he respects and emulates. He employs relatives to the extent he can, because they are safer and more reliable and because, being family, they can thereby "keep the thing to themselves." Like any good small businessman, he retains a lawyer to make sure that things keep running smoothly. Of particular interest is the fact that again like the Italian crime families the parents of many of the childhood friends who make up this network came from the same town in Puerto Rico. And kinship, of course, is quite obviously more important as a basis for organization here than we found among blacks.

These two operations within the network—Luis Santos' early and unsuccessful attempt to corner the drug market in his neighborhood and Clemente Sanchez's successful, kinship-based organization in the same area—are highly instructive as to the importance of "being connected" in organized crime. Clemente not only has set his brothers and sister up in his business, he has links based on kinship with his uncle Roberto Mateo in Red Hook and through Rolando Solis with the Cuban drug connection. In both cases, Clemente has a personal relationship with one man in the other segments of the network, and it is this relationship, one frequently described as having "my man" in some other set of operations in organized crime, that seems to tie various operatives together.

Roberto Mateo is an interesting crime operative for a number of reasons. He is, first of all, an employer and sees himself as such. He employs a number of neighborhood women to handle the telephones in his numbers game and he describes this role as one in which he is helping his countrymen to find work and avoid less acceptable occupations as prostitutes. He is also apparently the occasional benefactor of his neighbors who get into some kind of trouble—for example, a family that needs money to get a son out of jail. He is, in many ways, similar to the older Italian-American organized crime figures who were and to some extent still are viewed as patrons by their less affluent and powerful co-ethnics. He also appears to be an innovator, trying new devices such as the use of tape recorders and weekly rather than daily betting as a means of improving and protecting his business. Of particular interest is the fact that he has managed, or at least seems to have managed, to avoid domination of his enterprise by the Italian-American crime syndicate that controls the area in which he operates.

Tomas Correa and Cesar Rosario are both small entrepreneurs with successful stolen car and car parts businesses in the same section of Brooklyn. Their businesses are, at first glance, independent of each other but a more careful examination reveals some interesting linkages. Both Correa and Rosario use the Barracudas, a gang of youthful car thieves, to steal cars for them. And both use the car painter Eduardo Paredes for fast, efficient and inexpensive repainting of the stolen cars they sell. Paredes represents a phenomenon in organized crime that we have met elsewhere in our networks, notably in the locksmith Richard Williams, who works in Thomas Irwin's boosting and fencing operation in Central Harlem: the small craftsman who sells his skills on a regular basis to people he knows to be criminals. Such craftsmen, who are hired as independent contractors, just as anyone might hire a locksmith or a painter to do a job, provide expertise without which many crime activists would find it difficult to operate effectively. These craftsmen seem ordinarily to have only one link to each criminal network, namely, the one man who knows them and hires them. It is at least possible that within crime networks it is a source of power to possess the right contact with such a craftsman and, as in the case of purchasing guns, to be able to act as "Mr. Middle." Thus, a car thief might well feel dependent on the person in his ring who knows where to get a stolen car painted quickly with no questions asked.

Both Correa and Rosario feel that they provide a valuable and otherwise unavailable service to their community. In both cases they cite the inequity of insurance rates and practices, the high cost of cars and automotive parts and the poverty of their neighbors as justification enough for their illegal businesses. They do not steal cars in their own community because they feel a part of it but also, of course, because it would be far more dangerous. Rosario is also a small dealer in drugs, which he obtains from Clemente Sanchez. Here the kinship linkage within this network becomes apparent, for Rosario and Sanchez are cousins, both are nephews of Roberto Mateo.

One of the most interesting sets of relationships in this network is the growing power of Cubans in organized crime. Both Clemente Sanchez and Rolando Solis describe a tightly knit, efficient organization of Cubans who seem well on the way to controlling the drug traffic even on an international basis. The Cubans seem to have learned from the Italians or at least from the same cultural and religious sources as the Italians the importance of kinship and community in successful organization of crime. We were able to pick up enough information on the Cuban organization in this network and in some of the others to draw some preliminary generalizations about Cuban involvement in organized crime. First, the Cubans appear to be much better organized than either blacks or Puerto Ricans in organized crime. There are a number of indications of this in this network. Cubans are rarely found at the street level—pushing dope, whoring or boosting—except during their initial entry into organized crime. Seemingly, these early experiences are an apprenticeship in much the same way that an executive trainee in legitimate business firms may spend a period of time "in the plant" to gain first-hand experience. Most of the actual street operatives for the Cubans tend to be Puerto Ricans and, to a lesser extent, blacks. Cubans also seem to be closely tied to each other by a sense of ethnic-national identity. This comes out in a number of comments by our field assistants in various reports: "Cubans are friendly and do not compete with one another," "They help each other out," "Cubans are more clannish than Puerto Ricans," and "The Cubans have a family thing going just like the Italians." We might speculate on the reasons for this cohesiveness.

The recency of their migration from Cuba and the conditions under which it occurred do seem to suggest that there might be a greater affinity among Cuban exiles than among Puerto Rican migrants and certainly than among blacks, whose migration history is lost to most individual blacks. The Cuban exiles do tend to represent a group whose common political and economic interests could hold them together more closely than other groups. Also, the Cuban migrants tend to be lower-middle and middle class in origin, and so many business and professional workers came to this country. This might explain both the better organization and the often observed fact by our field assistants that "Cubans are much better businessmen than Puerto Ricans." Finally, the historical record does indicate that Italian-American and Jewish gangsters were active in pre-Castro Cuba, so that the experience of Cubans with American organized crime literally began before their emigration and may have provided a model that they seem to be following. It is interesting to note that some of the features of the Cuban involvement in organized crime in this country—their unwillingness to let crime, drugs and prostitution penetrate their own communities, the rejection of conspicuous consumption and the flaunting of wealth, and the lack of involvement of females in crime activities—are a pattern that existed among Italian-Americans a generation ago. The "Mustache Petes," the old men of Italian-American organized crime, behaved in precisely this manner and it is they, rather than the modern generation of Italian-Americans, who would have had contacts in pre-Castro Havana. There is no way to assess the assertion of some of our informants that the disciplined organizational development of Cubans in crime results directly from their CIA training for the Bay of Pigs invasion and similar military and paramilitary ventures. It is obvious, however, from a number of the field reports we gathered, that some of the same people are involved in gun running and dope running and that both activities seem peculiarly oriented toward restaurants as meeting and dealing centers.

The experiences of Rolando Solis with "The Man" also illustrate another principle of Cuban organization: there seems to be a much more structured hierarchy of authority in Cuban crime groups than we have found among blacks or Puerto Ricans. The lowest level comprises the recent exiles or youngsters just coming of age. They are the street workers I have already described. The second level seems to be recruited from among these apprentices and they are the dealers who combine legitimate or semilegitimate business roles with crime activities. They are the waiters who negotiate drug sales, the small business operatives who arrange the sale of stolen goods and so on. The highest or leadership level is suggested by the presence of "The Man," his mention of "lieutenants" and the aspirations of Rolando Solis to reach that level. Once again this set of hierarchical statuses is very similar to those found within Italian-American crime syndicates.

Finally, there is the Cuban connection itself. If our information is accurate, and I am confident that it is, this new route for drugs from South America should have some important effects on the drug scene in the United States. The most important effect will be the continued displacement of Italian-American syndicates from the international drug traffic as this new connection replaces the older one that came through Europe. The "street" implications of this are enormous. It not only means that new patterns of wholesaling will be established, changing the ethnic balance of power in organized crime, but also means that cocaine may very well displace heroin as *the* street drug. There are other implications as well, but more evidence from some of the networks presented later is necessary before they can be adequately developed.

Viewed as a total network, these two sets of criminal relationships seem little more than a loosely structured net of separate criminal enterprises—drug traffic, numbers and auto theft rings—held together by kinship and mutual gain. Actually, it is out of just such a mixture— particularly when, as in this case, a number of the links are strengthened by kinship bonds—that a cohesive crime organization can grow.

5

THE GYPSY CABS: ORGANIZED CRIME OR MINORITY BUSINESS ENTERPRISE?

✠

DURING THE course of field work in Brooklyn, we learned from Tomas Correa that he had sold a stolen car to Frank White, an owner/driver in the Superfast Cab Company in Manhattan. Through this initial contact, one of our field assistants traced out and observed a complex web of relationships in a burgeoning new venture into minority entrepreneurship that has been developing in a number of American cities over the past decade. Usually called "gypsy cabs," it involves the use of automobiles for hire as taxis despite the fact that they do not meet the legal standards and conditions for taxicabs. Through the use of a variety of semi- and openly illegal practices, the "gypsies" operate in ghetto areas where legally licensed taxis seldom venture. Despite the patent illegality of the gypsy system, many cities have now tacitly accepted the practice while admitting to its illegality and publicly calling for regulation of the new industry. The history of how gypsy cabs came into existence, how and why they continue to operate, their role in ghetto life and their relationship to organized crime activities illustrate the mixture of legal, semilegal and illegal activities that make up that segment of the American economy we call organized crime. The story of gypsy cabs is also an object lesson in the social chaos and conflict that can result when the legitimate aspirations of minority groups are blocked and they resort to illicit and illegal means to escape poverty.

Since 1937, there have been a set, limited number of taxicabs legally eligible to cruise the streets of New York City looking for passengers. In that year the Haas Act was passed, limiting the number of outstanding taxicab licenses or "medallions" to 13,566, which were then purchasable for $100 apiece. Since then a number of medallions have been retired, leaving the actual total at large in 1973 at about 11,700.

The rationale for limiting the number of cruising taxis was presumably (1) to ensure a healthy, stable, prosperous cab industry, unthreatened by a glut of cabs surviving marginally as business enterprises and by the cutthroat competition that would probably result; and (2) to ensure that although the public might never be the beneficiaries of too many cabs vying for their business, they might at least not be the victims of drastic shortages.

Over the years this system made rich men out of many medallion holders: the value of a single medallion went from $100 in 1937 to highs ranging between $25,000 and $30,000 in recent years and some fleet owners dominated the industry, holding hundreds of medallions. For twenty years or so the system seemed to work reasonably well to keep cabs on New York City's streets, or at least on those streets of highest public visibility, in the midtown, downtown, and white residential sections of Manhattan.

However, New York is a big city. It encompasses far more than East Side, West Side, Broadway and Wall Street. And as the years passed, into the late 1950s and early 1960s, the failures of the medallioned taxi industry—which has come to be known as the "yellow" cab industry, after the color that all its cabs are now required to be painted—became more pronounced. As crime, and more importantly the fear of crime, increased, more and more taxi drivers steered clear of New York's black and Puerto Rican areas. It was a plain fact that during these years attacks on cab drivers began to increase markedly, especially in black and Puerto Rican areas and especially after dark, and so finding a yellow cab in Harlem at night became increasingly difficult. But at the same time the same fear of crime, along with other factors such as marginal increases in employment and prosperity, served to enlarge the demand for taxi service in black and Puerto Rican areas. As the early 1960s became the late 1960s, that demand, along with so many other long-stifled aspirations, began emerging out of the ghettos with fresh articulation, and with a persistence backed by emerging political power.

Medallioned taxis have never been the only way one could get a car legally to take you someplace in New York City. Rather, they have been the only cars legally entitled to pick you up off the street when you flag them down and to measure the amount you will be charged on a meter. It has, however, always been possible to look in the classified pages of the phone book, find a "car service," a "public livery" service or a "radio car" service, call them, and arrange for one of their cars to pick you up. Charges for the service are computed at either a flat rate or at a rate determined by some kind of "zone" system (for example, if you go from 23rd Street to 28th Street, that's one zone, but if you go from 23rd Street to 146th Street then that is about five zones and will cost you five times as much). It has also always been possible for an entrepreneur to go into this kind of "public livery" business easily. He has not had to purchase an expensive medallion; rather, all he has had to do is (1) obtain an "O" (taxi) or a "Z" (special omnibus) registration and license plates from the State Department of Motor Vehicles, which will issue them automatically on proper proofs of ownership and insurance; and (2) purchase the appropriate equipment such as a two-way radio for his business. From the late 1950s onward "car services" based on two-way radios and telephone orders began to proliferate, not only in ghetto areas but also in quiet white residential neighborhoods of the outlying boroughs, where yellow cabs seldom cruised and where old people especially were in need of door-to-door transportation. These car services were perfectly legal operations so long as they did not pick up passengers off the street or carry taxi meters, practices limited to bona fide medallioned cabs, and many services abided by these rules and continue to abide by them today.

However, it is easy to see how such car services might not fully satisfy the needs of many citizens for quick, convenient, personalized transportation, especially in ghetto areas. For they require both a phone call and a wait, and for a man on a Harlem street late at night or for an old woman trying to get home from a clinic or from shopping, neither of these are very satisfactory preconditions. Moreover, zone systems are more cumbersome and more difficult to understand than simple meters. While it's true that in some cities all taxis operate on zone systems and that in many other cities cabs are available only on a telephone basis, nevertheless, it's easy to understand how in a city where metered cabs cruise in profusion "downtown," ghetto residents would demand similar service for their own heavily populated, intensely urban areas.

It is equally easy to understand how it might have come about that "car services," unmedallioned public livery vehicles, began picking up fares off the ghetto streets. It is so easy to do. There's the man or woman out there on the street corner, flagging you down. You look in your rearview mirror and there are no cops anywhere in sight, or if they are, they're not paying attention. Moreover, there certainly aren't any yellow cabs around to complain. It only takes a few seconds for you to stop, for the guy to jump in, and then you're off. You've done the passenger a favor, and since for the moment you've had no radio business you're also improving your income a touch. Undoubtedly this is how the gypsy cab was born. And, considering the demand, it's easy to see how such street pickups could have become standard practice for many "car service" drivers, or even how many men could have taken to driving or buying public livery cars on the assumption that a good portion of their income would derive from hails off the street.

What might be somewhat more difficult to explain, and where current gypsy operations are most obviously in open violation of the law, is how taxi meters finally found their way onto the dashboards of so many "car service" vehicles and how these same cars can blatantly post their meter rates on their doors, just as yellow cabs do. To really understand this requires considering the social climate of the 1960s and the relationship between political power and law enforcement. For an unmedallioned vehicle to have a meter and to post its rates on the door were and continue to be illegal acts. Neither is it the type of marginal or covert illegality that is difficult to uncover and even more difficult to prove. The meters and posted rates are there for anyone to see. But it was and continues to be true that black and Puerto Rican neighborhoods needed the gypsies, because yellow cabs were also violating the law by *not* picking up passengers in ghetto areas. In fact, it was, and is, commonly charged by blacks that they even had trouble being picked up *downtown* by yellow cab drivers fearful of being asked to drive to Harlem. The police were not pressured by City Hall to make arrests of gypsies since the political consequences of pressing the issue were not acceptable to politicians. Remember also that this was the period of widespread unrest and even rioting in the ghettos and neither the politicians nor the police were anxious to provoke confrontations with ghetto dwellers. And so, once again, the characteristically American accommodation with crime in the ghetto—which holds that so long as ghetto residents keep it among themselves and it doesn't spill outside, it is not a major problem—prevailed. The two voices that most men will heed are the voice of their own conscience and that of police, and in the 1960s neither of these was telling "car service" drivers in the ghetto that they mustn't pick up their brothers and sisters.

And so out of "public livery" status, out of radio-dispatched, unmetered "car services" grew the gypsy cab industry. Today it is flourishing, one of the few minority-group enterprises that emerged out of the 1960s "push" to do so—and, needless to say, without any poverty program help at all. Go to any of the black or Puerto Rican parts of Manhattan, to Harlem or El Barrio or Broadway on the Upper West Side, or up into the South Bronx or the Grand Concourse, or over to Brooklyn, in Bedford-Stuyvesant, or even in downtown Brooklyn, and you will see them. Indeed, in these neighborhoods they will seem to be everywhere. No uniform shiny yellow on the cabs here. Rather, every other color that to an owner's eye looks handsome—fire engine red or metallic blue, a fair number of purples, and lots of two-tone jobs: They are big old cars, with their rear ends hanging down, or their front ends, always bad suspension somewhere, and dents—and always with the rates posted on the side, just like the yellows except slightly cheaper: 45¢ the first fifth-mile, 10¢ for every fifth thereafter, and decals all over saying "car service," and even a couple of little lights on the roof, "proof" that this is a real live taxicab. And inside you will see, attached to the dash where it is supposed to be, the meter, and behind the wheel a black or Puerto Rican face.

To give some idea of the numbers and value of this industry: the yellow, medallioned cabs of New York numbered, in 1973, about 11,700, and these 11,700 carry approximately 700,000 passengers daily, or 250 million passengers a year, for gross revenues in excess of $400 million. By comparison, there are approximately 15,000 "public livery" vehicles operating in the city, of which at least 6,000 are full-time gypsies, with thousands more operating as gypsies on a part-time basis. As a group, public livery vehicles are estimated to carry 400,000 passengers per day, with annual revenues in the neighborhood of $300 million. Since perhaps 70 percent of public livery business derives from street hails—that is, gypsy operations—it can be estimated that gypsy business amounts to a conservative minimum of $200 million annually. Thus, in the course of a few short years the gypsies have grown to a size where they might be thought of as formidable competitors to New York's yellow cabs.

This is not how most gypsies think of themselves, however. Rather, because they serve neighborhoods where yellow service has been poor or nonexistent, they feel that they operate essentially side-by-side with the yellows, as a complementary transportation system. But it can hardly be doubted that the gypsies have hurt the yellow industry. The yellows have lost "fringe" income and large numbers of drivers to the gypsies. And amid these losses and the uncertainty generated by the unresolved status of the gypsies, the price of yellow medallions has plummeted, from highs over $30,000, to $16,000, $14,000 and now perhaps a great deal less. During 1972 more than 300 medallions were simply turned in to the New York City Commission, without any compensation to their owners at all. There are many reasons for the sorry state of New York's yellow cab industry today, not the least of which may well be its own short-sightedness in failing for so long to service all parts of the city, but the gypsies have undoubtedly taken their toll.

The yellow cab industry has not taken the gypsy threat lying down. Its spokesmen and leaders have demanded, stridently and repeatedly, that the laws protecting them be enforced. As a result, the police have in the last few years been issuing summonses to gypsies at a rate in excess of 10,000 annually. But the arrests reveal a striking pattern; nearly all are made in the midtown and downtown Manhattan sections of New York and at the airports—which are traditional yellow "territory." Remarkably few summonses have been issued to gypsies operating in black and Puerto Rican neighborhoods. Police put the matter bluntly: when there aren't any other cabs around, why stir up street trouble needlessly? Thus, an interesting situation has developed. While gypsy operations, insofar as they involve meters and cruising for street pickups, are patently illegal, they have received a certain degree of de facto acceptance by the city's law enforcement system. Just as the police use their powers—the limits of which no one understands better than they themselves—not so much to arrest all narcotics addicts, prostitutes or derelicts as to "shove" them into areas of town where their presence might seem less obstreperous than in others, so too do they use their summons power to keep gypsy drivers in Harlem, Bed-Stuy, et cetera, and not allow them to spill outside. And other government agencies have likewise dealt with the gypsies with a light hand. New York City's Department of Consumer Affairs makes little if any attempt to calibrate gypsy meters, the New York State Department of Motor Vehicles continues its policy of issuing "O" and "Z" plates on demand (and proof of insurance) and the State Department of Insurance does nothing to prevent insurance agents and brokers from encouraging gypsy businesses. The fines assessed by courts for gypsy offenses have been characteristically light: $10–$25. There exists neither de jure or de facto parity between the yellow industry and the gypsies: nothing prevents yellows from cruising Harlem or anywhere else in New York, for that matter, whereas the gypsies are rather closely confined to given territories. But within their own neighborhoods, the gypsies represent an important and accepted—if illegal—part of the city's established transportation network.

The potentially most volatile threat to the gypsy industry comes from New York's Taxi and Limousine Commission. Until 1971, New York's yellow cabs were under the jurisdiction of the so-called "Hack Bureau" of the Police Department. But Local Law 12 of that year created the new commission to regulate the taxicab industry, and the fact that this commission is a fresh, young agency—the limits of its authority not yet firmly drawn and its ambition not yet qualified—makes it the natural enemy of the confused, laissez-faire, clouded situation through which the gypsies have come to prosper. There is probably nothing the Taxi Commission would like better than to bring order out of the chaos that now exists, to bring the gypsies under its close regulation.

Toward this end the commission has made various proposals and offers, among them one whereby if gypsies would only revert to legal public livery operations, the city would make special efforts to encourage the public to use their radio-dispatch services. So far, none of these offers and proposals has done much to alter the status quo, but they have earned for the Taxi Commission the ire of both the yellow industry and the gypsies—which might lead one to the conclusion that the commission was following some kind of "middle path." This may indeed be the case, and the commission has consistently pointed to the need not only for adherence to law but also for the provision of cab service to ghetto areas. But the commission has not yet approached the point of approving (or even compromising on) metered cruising by gypsies, and until it does so it is hard to see how it is making any substantial concession to the gypsies at all, since the law already freely permits public livery car services to handle radio-dispatched calls with meters.

There has been an inconsistency in its approach that the commission itself recognizes. The commission's most effective argument in its two-year struggle to gain regulatory authority over the gypsies has been that such authority is necessary in order to protect the gypsies' riding public. The commission has gathered and cited statistics suggesting that upward of 50 percent of all gypsy vehicles are in unsatisfactory condition, that more than 50 percent are either inadequately or improperly insured, or are uninsured altogether, and that many gypsy cars carry "fast" meters, meters that overcharge. Moreover, there can be little doubt that although perhaps as few as 6 percent of gypsy drivers have ever been convicted of a felony, the gypsy cab business, operating outside the letter of the law as an illicit enterprise, is, as we shall shortly see, something of a magnet for ancillary illegal activity. Yet the inconsistency appears in this: by the commission's own admission, the public that uses gypsy cabs is quite well satisfied with them the way they are and in all events prefers them to the yellow cabs who for so many years snubbed and ignored them. Thus, so long as the Taxi Commission's schemes for regulation would deprive gypsies of their freedom to cruise with meters in ghetto areas, thereby returning this richest aspect of the ghetto trade to the indifferent and frightened yellows, the commission will stand in flat opposition to the will of the people it is claiming to protect. The one thing that both the majority of gypsies and their riding public would probably welcome is full legal recognition of their de facto function, and with such recognition they would then no doubt be prepared to accept the appropriate regulation.

The gypsy cabs of New York's black and Puerto Rican neighborhoods make up a truly "home-grown" industry of which the residents of these neighborhoods are justifiably proud. As the Taxi Commission has been quick to point out, "this activity represents a major ghetto enterprise, providing much-needed employment opportunities for some of the most discriminated-against members of our society."

Moreover, the gypsy driver "is in the finest tradition of upward mobility among the disadvantaged in our city." [1] Consider the typical gypsy driver in a black or Puerto Rican neighborhood. It is almost certain that he himself will be black or Puerto Rican. The chances are very good that he cruises chiefly right in his own neighborhood. He is in most cases a family man who has entered the business to improve himself economically. He is likely to be between thirty and fifty years old, and nine times out of ten he will be self-employed, either as the owner or the shift-by-shift lessee of the vehicle he drives. Before becoming a driver, he most likely held either menial or semi-skilled employment, although in perhaps one case out of five he drove a yellow cab. If he owns his cab, his average weekly income is $150–175, and if he rents on a full-time basis, $125–150—although these figures may be low, insofar as cabbies of all stripes have an understandable passion for underestimating their earnings, except to close friends.

The reasons why a fair number of yellow cab drivers have switched to the gypsies light up the very heart of the gypsy phenomenon and the threat it poses to the yellow cab industry of New York. In the first place there is the pleasure and convenience of working in one's own neighborhood and, moreover, of working in a car whose colors are respected there rather than resented. In the second place, the lack of regulation in the gypsy industry permits many drivers to evade payment of either part or all of their federal, state and city income taxes. And in the third place, the gypsy field offers the relatively poor man a chance to own his own cab, with the added respect and income that such ownership means. Few blacks and Puerto Ricans could possibly afford the $15,000 "nut," mortgages or no, that it takes to break into the yellow cab business.

This last reason, the evasion of the "nut," is what is perhaps most hurtful and offensive to the yellow industry. Not only does it mean that "those other guys" are getting away with something that they,

---

[1] Michael J. Lazar, Project Director, *The Non-Medallion Industry: A Transportation Phenomenon* (Taxi and Limousine Commission of New York City, 1971), pp. 28, 31.

the yellow owners, were not able to get away with, but it also means that their medallions, their chief capital assets, are threatened with devaluation. Who will want to buy a medallion if in large and profitable sections of the city you can own a cab without one?

This all makes very good sense; the justice in it seems strong, until one reflects on the fact that one of the major reasons medallions became so valuable is that political pressure from the established owners kept the number of medallions fixed, even while vast areas of New York City were allowed to go unserviced by taxicabs. In other words, the limits placed on medallion issuance implied a public trust that the holders of medallions long and consistently violated; so, say our informants, it hardly seems fair for them now to complain that their "rights" are being violated. It has always been the city's right to issue more medallions or otherwise to undercut their value.

What has happened very simply is that the political pressure long applied by the yellow cab industry to preserve its capital investments has now been challenged by a fresh and growing political force that is coalescing around the yellow industry's abridgment of its public trust. When, as must happen a hundred times every day, a policeman on 125th Street declines to issue a summons to a gypsy who picks up a fare along the avenue there, because he, the policeman, does not want needlessly to cause a scene, he is implicitly recognizing the street power, which is surely a political power, that has gathered around the idea that gypsy cabs in Harlem are legitimate and proper. Likewise, there was political power exercised in the gypsies' favor when Assemblyman Samuel D. Wright, a Democrat from Brooklyn who is chairman of the New York State Legislature's Black and Puerto Rican Caucus, called a news conference to announce that his group "cannot allow the non-medallion cab industry to be destroyed or curtailed in any matter." Moreover, he said, "The boot-strap operation not only supports thousands of families, but also furnishes much-needed transportation for ghetto residents. Our investigation found virtually no taxi service in the ghettos of New York, other than that offered by the non-medallion vehicles." [2]

[2] *New York Daily Challenge,* November 30, 1972, p. 4.

Elsewhere in this study we have seen how organized criminal activity and the aggrandizement of local political power can go hand in hand to lift a group of individuals, or even a whole stratum of an ethnic group, out of proletarian poverty into one form or another of middle-class prosperity. Perhaps no better example of this exists, among New York's blacks and Puerto Ricans, than the gypsy cab business. For here, even more so than in the numbers, we have men who are truly striving after little more than middle-class respectability. And here, more so than in other areas, we have an activity around which political power can easily coalesce: Which black or Puerto Rican does not feel entitled to the same quick, convenient, personalized transportation in his neighborhood that other parts of the city enjoy, and how many of these same blacks and Puerto Ricans have not at one time or another been bypassed by a yellow cab? The gypsy cab business is a natural if presently illicit enterprise for an aspiring black or Puerto Rican entrepreneur, and the gypsy cab issue is a natural for an aspiring black or Puerto Rican politician. The vulnerability of the yellow industry, whose monopoly exists only by virtue of a previous generation's political machinations, makes the gypsy industry all the more attractive.

Yet as we shall see, like all illegal activities the gypsy cab industry attracts ancillary illegalities to itself. This may be an inevitable corrollary of the rule that if you call a man a criminal, he tends to become one; at a minimum it highlights their cutoff from ordinary legitimacy. A portion of gypsy drivers and owners participate in illegal schemes that would perhaps scarcely occur to them were their basic operations deemed "legal." This is not to say that these men do not hope eventually to "go completely straight." But the road to middle-class respectability can be a long and trying one, and if some of the laws that bar that road appear trivial and silly and prejudicial, then maybe to the aspirant many other laws will look the same way. In the following pages we shall see how a number of gypsy drivers and owners are advancing themselves. Legality and illegality mix freely. But one mustn't forget perhaps the most basic fact of all about the gypsy industry: its customers are being served.

We came upon a number of gypsy cab networks that had dealings with the various black and Puerto Rican crime groups we observed, and three of these networks are described here. These are not proposed as "typical" of the range of gypsy operations, criminal or otherwise, nor do they in any way represent a statistical average of what gypsy cab networks are all about. Rather, the attempt here is simply to portray what appear to be three identifiable levels of illegality in the gypsy industry. The fact that many gypsy drivers starting out do not indulge in the illegalities ascribed to members of the Superfast Cab Company and the fact that many of the insurance brokers who deal with gypsies are more honest than Theodore Huntington are important facts to keep in mind as you read through these pages, but they do not invalidate the portraits here, which are meant specifically to illustrate criminal aspects and which in any case are based on reliable data, from our field assistants and other informants.

The Superfast Cab Company

In the spring of 1970, James Taylor, Frank White and Edward Wilson, all black males residing on the Upper West Side of Manhattain, in the neighborhood of 103rd–106th Streets between Broadway and Amsterdam Avenue, came together to form what they called the Superfast Cab Company. They did not incorporate or take any other action that required a lawyer, but they did agree that each of them would obtain an appropriate car, a taxi meter, and Superfast Cab Company insignia and would begin to cruise the streets of the West Side looking for fares. They further agreed that they would try to expand their business as quickly as possible so as to be able to afford two-way radios and a dispatching system, and for that purpose each contributed a portion of his initial weekly earnings to a kitty. James Taylor already owned a '66 Chevy, which he turned into a Superfast cab by having Superfast decals made up and purchasing certain other decals and two small yellow lights for his hood from a store specializing in such accessories and a taxi meter from Roberto Quevedo, further uptown, whose large garage was then—and is now—supplied with large amounts of stolen automotive merchandise by Rafael Pagan and other junkie/thieves. The meter purchased by Taylor, along with the meters similarly purchased by Edward Wilson and Frank White, were stolen by Pagan from other New York City cabs—two from yellows, one from a gypsy (to Pagan it has never mattered which).

Neither Edward Wilson nor Frank White owned cars at the time the partnership was formed, and so for them buying a car was the first big step. Wilson, who had previously driven a yellow cab in Manhattan and was looking for a way to set out on his own, to "have something" for himself and his large family, was in the strongest cash position of the three initial partners, and he purchased a '68 Ford from a legitimate used-car dealer. White, who was rather strapped for funds, bought a stolen car from Tomas Correa in Brooklyn, a '67 Ford at a fraction of the price that Wilson paid for his '68. This is how the purchase worked: Frank first went to Correa, to whom he had been introduced by a mutual friend, and then to an automotive junkyard, where for very little money he purchased a wrecked '67 Ford four-door sedan. He took the registration papers and right on the premises removed from the car its doortag and other official identifications. Then he went back to Correa, whose thieves in three days' time stole an all-but-matching '67 four-door sedan. He took the car to a legitimate auto painter where, for $39.95, he had it painted maroon and then switched the door tags. Thus Frank White, for all appearances and at a total investment of about $400, came to own a "properly" registered full-sized late model car, completely appropriate for use as a taxicab.

One thing that should be noted about this initial partnership, and that puts the Superfast company in a slightly different category than many other nascent gypsy operations, is that all three of its personnel had prison records. Indeed, although they came eventually to live in the same neighborhood, all three served time together when they were quite a lot younger, and prison undoubtedly did much to cement their friendship. Prison, it should also be noted, provided them with the range of acquaintances that led them to the stolen parts supplier Roberto Quevedo and through him to the stolen car supplier Tomas Correa—although even without ex-con friends they probably would have been able to find similar suppliers eventually.

The three friends worked hard, cruising chiefly in their own immediate neighborhood, and within a year they had prospered sufficiently so that White shed his stolen car and bought a legitimate one, which was cause for a great celebration at a local club one night. The truth is that White had been rather embarrassed by his stolen car from the first; he was not admired at all for his "shrewdness" in paying much less for a car than Wilson, but rather had been looked slightly down upon for the lack of substance that his illegitimate vehicle suggested. Prosperity also brought into the Superfast company two new owner/drivers: William Prentice, an old prison buddy who lived in Central Harlem, and Ramon Suarez, an ex-yellow driver who lived in the 103rd–106th neighborhood. Shortly thereafter the five men further expanded their venture by working a deal with one Leroy Atkins, whose affiliation with a now-defunct gypsy outfit had left him with some two-way radio equipment. The five drivers purchased three radios from Leroy (and two from Roberto Quevedo) and in addition each agreed to pay him $25 per week, in exchange for which he and his wife, Marion, would operate a radio-dispatch business for them fifty-five hours per week. Superfast began advertising, posting its new number by the phone in local groceries and bars, sending circulars around; and of course the owners told all their relatives and friends. Their prosperity increased, but Leroy and Marion grew dissatisfied with their end of the bargain, whereupon Superfast took on two more new drivers, Jose Rodrigues and Kenny Rivers, each of whom enlarged Atkins' income by $25 weekly. In exchange for the additional money, Leroy and Marion agreed to operate the dispatcher's office several more hours per week. Superfast's drivers had already discovered the importance of being available whenever their clients called.

The business continues to do well. The seven owners keep their cars almost constantly on the streets by renting them out for twelve-

or twenty-four-hour shifts whenever they themselves choose not to drive. Each owner has three or four drivers who rent from him, usually on established schedules and at set rates of $15 for twelve hours and $20 for twenty-four. This is known in the cab business as the "horse-hire" method of rental. The driver pays his flat fee and is then permitted to keep all the money he takes in during the twelve- or twenty-four-hour period, exclusive of his gas and incidental expenses. James Taylor, who drives perhaps sixty hours a week himself and rents his cab out for another forty-eight, can clear $225 in a good week. Superfast has, however, been plagued by some problems. For one, there has been the problem of keeping the radio manned. Gradually, the number of hours worked by the Atkins family has grown, and they now have a ten-hour-per-week employee; but whenever a customer calls Superfast and no one answers the phone, there is still created a dissatisfied customer. Superfast is still not really big enough to maintain a credible, wholly reliable radio business, although the radios do bring in substantial income and do provide a cover for the drivers' gypsy cruising. Another problem has been the police. The drivers have long since discovered the patrolmen they must make monthly small "contributions" to, but the patrolmen still come around with their periodic summonses, claiming that "the sergeant's putting the heat on," or whatever. Nobody at Superfast has yet made contact with a sergeant. And then there are the supra-precinct police, the Tactical Patrol Force and the Highway Patrol and so forth, who, whenever they're in the neighborhood and in the mood, cause the gypsies trouble. There's no way for a small outfit like Superfast to bribe these roving cops. Insurance has been another problem because of the large cash outlays that many insurers require and because of difficulties in getting certain ones to pay off. But Superfast has been fortunate recently in latching on to an agent who obtains low rates for their cars by having them registered in Mount Vernon and who nevertheless has found insurance companies that seem to pay off regularly and promptly. Last but not least is the problem of crime—that is to say, of crimes committed against the drivers themselves. Cab drivers have long been choice targets for muggers in New York, and gypsies, who work the black and Puerto Rican neighborhoods where many of the muggings take place, have not been exempted simply by the fact that they share skin color or ethnicity with the attackers. Five of the seven Superfast owners have been mugged at one time or another while driving, and at least four of their "horse-hire" drivers have too. But Superfast is now fighting back. All the owner/drivers now carry guns while they drive, concealed against the possibility of police inspection but nevertheless readily at hand, under the seat or dash somewhere. Most of the guns are .25 caliber. And, more importantly, they have worked out systems for helping one another out. A buddy system that is perhaps in many ways a vestige of prison life ensures that other cabs will be quick to help in case of emergency. In this regard, the two-way radios are obviously a deterrent to crime. Many muggers know that it's easy for a driver to phone in his location and situation if it appears at all threatening or after the fact of an attack. Superfast drivers have a code: if a guy gets in who appears a likely mugger, the driver will call in, "Cab 6, calling a signal 1 from Broadway and 88th, heading north on Broadway, to 104th and Manhattan Avenue." Or if the guy becomes more threatening, pulls something from his pocket or seems about to, "Cab 6, calling a signal 3 from Broadway and 101st." Or in case ultimately of attack, "Cab 6, calling a signal 5 from Manhattan Avenue and 102d." Leroy or Marion Atkins will always quickly relay this information on to the other cabs, and in the relatively small neighborhood where Superfast ordinarily operates, help is seldom far off.

It is worth noting the various criminal activities that Superfast and its drivers get involved in, ancillary to the fundamental illegality of gypsy cruising. Herminia Rivers, a prostitute, often uses Superfast cabs to get from one assignation to another, because she lives in the Superfast neighborhood and because she considers the Superfast people, in contradistinction to yellow cab drivers, "one of us." More seriously, Robert Murphy is a heroin addict and small-time pusher who occasionally horse-hires the cab of Frank White in order to peddle drugs out of it. White is aware that Murphy pushes but does not know the use to which he puts the cab. On the other hand, he should be able to guess. Heroin addicts will pay a premium to be able to purchase their drugs in the safety of a cab parked in a quiet parking lot or simply driving around somewhere, as opposed to having to purchase on the street.

Another criminal activity is the bribing of police officers, already mentioned. Still another is the evasion of income taxes. During the first year none of the drivers paid any taxes at all. Then they heard about two or three gypsy firms whose drivers had all been stuck with big bills for back taxes, and on the advice of a Broadway accountant, all except William Prentice have, during the past two years, been reporting at least a portion of their earnings to the IRS. Of the total tax due from seven owners, the various income tax bureaus now receive perhaps 35 percent. All the other drivers tell Prentice that he should report at least *something,* for their sake and the sake of the company if not for his, but they have thus far not insisted on it. The last major criminal area in which Superfast is still involved is thievery, or at least the receipt of stolen goods. Jose Rodrigues and Kenny Rivers are still driving stolen cars, obtained through Tomas Correa. In fact, Kenny has two of them: he drives one for three months, then garages it for three months, shifting his meter and radio back and forth between them, to save wear and tear on both. And all the drivers still purchase the largest portion of their automotive accessories—tires, batteries, radios especially—at vastly discounted prices from Roberto Quevedo. It happened once recently that a spare tire purchased by William Prentice turned out to have been stolen by one of Quevedo's boys from James Taylor's cab. Taylor made a positive identification of it, then all of Superfast confronted Quevedo with the evidence. He gave them a free tire, pleaded for their continued business and promised to inform Rafael Pagan and the others to steer clear of Superfast transportation. It was a rare coincidence, of course, in a city or even a neighborhood full of automobiles, and so Superfast will continue dealing with Quevedo; but it's doubtful that Quevedo could actually prevent his junkies from doing the same thing again, since there is small chance that they would even listen, and if they listened, how would they ever remember the name, and if they remembered the name, still, would they forbear if they needed the money and had the chance?

But despite the various criminal activities in which Superfast and its drivers have become at least tangentially involved and despite the illegal nature of their business itself, it is important to see that these men—all of them, to a man—are simply using the opportunities presented to them by illicit business to gain for themselves and their families the security and prestige of respectable middle-class society. They are striving for legitimacy, and it's tough to be "legitimate" in America if you're poor. The gypsy cab business, with or without its ancillary criminal activity, is the best if not the only way open to these men for "making it." They are mature individuals. James Taylor is forty-eight and all except Kenny Rivers are over thirty. Every one of them is married with children, ranging up to five children in the case of Edward Wilson. And they are running their business along lines that can only be called a model of middle-class commercial acuity: they are building up a clientele, trying to be friendly, trying to provide good service, gaining a good reputation. And, in the best tradition of American business, they are, with reference to the law, getting away with whatever they can get away with, cutting whatever corners they can.

The Black Diamond Special Omnibus Insurance Company

New York's compulsory insurance law requires that every registered passenger car, private or public, be insured minimally with "10/20/5" coverage. This means that every vehicle must be covered by insurance sufficient to pay at least $10,000 for each individual personal injury claim arising out of an accident; at least $20,000 for all personal injury claims arising out of an accident; and at least $5,000 in property damage. In the case of New York City taxicabs, which on a statistical basis have far more traffic accidents per year than the average private car, this minimum statutory coverage results in very high insurance rates, perhaps as high as $1,500 annually for a "public livery" vehicle operating today. Thus, a severe problem is presented the would-be gypsy owner, even before he gets his license plates.

Fortunately for him—although, as we shall see, not so fortunately for the riding public—the gypsy industry has developed certain evasive tactics for reducing this heavy burden.

For one thing, gypsy owners have discovered that it is possible to register their cabs out in the suburbs somewhere, where insurance rates are lower, and thereby to cut their premiums in half. For another, they have seen how it is possible to register as "school buses," rather than "public livery" vehicles, and thereby to cut premiums by two-thirds again. A school bus registered in Westchester may have to pay only $200 in minimum statutory insurance premiums annually, as opposed to the approximately $1,500 for public livery vehicles in New York City. Needless to say, both these registration practices are patently fraudulent and may result in the insurance policy being declared void when someone makes a claim against it. But prior inspection of registration claims by either the State Department of Insurance or the State Department of Motor Vehicles or the insurance company is perfunctory. And by now whole companies of agents have sprung up to serve the gypsy need and desire for low-cost, "bargain" insurance. Many drivers who insure through such agents are not even aware that they are participating in a fraud against both the insurer and the public; or, if they are aware of that much, they perhaps don't often imagine that it is a serious crime. Of course, many drivers probably simply don't want to know such things. They undoubtedly prefer to trust the claims of the agents who sell them the insurance. But the net result is that perhaps half or more of all of New York City's gypsy cabs are improperly or inadequately insured or are not insured at all.

The Black Diamond Special Omnibus Insurance Company is perhaps not untypical of the kind of company that procures for gypsies their "bargain" insurance coverage. The company is in reality just one man—Theodore Huntington, a black man, thirty-six years old, a life-long resident of Harlem—plus two employees and an occasional ac-countant. The company maintains a small office on Lenox Avenue in Harlem and another in Mount Vernon, New York, several miles north of Harlem, just beyond the city limits. Black Diamond adver-tises in the classifieds of various black papers and by Harlem word-of-mouth that for "specially qualified vehicles" it can obtain "the lowest taxi or special omnibus insurance rates anywhere."

When a driver/owner applies to Black Diamond for coverage, he is offered a package deal: both insurance and a two-way radio busi-ness for $800 per year, payable in monthly installments, with an additional $100 per annum if Black Diamond supplies the driver's radio. This is indeed quite a bargain, if one considers that Superfast drivers are paying upward of $1,000 apiece per year simply to main-tain their radio service. However, the fact is that Black Diamond's "two-way radio" business is basically nonexistent, a "throwaway" to add legitimacy to the company's operations but productive of very little income for its drivers. One employee dispatches calls thirty-five hours per week, hardly enough to maintain a service, especially over the broad geographical area across which Black Diamond's drivers are spread. Moreover, drivers are not even asked to maintain Black Diamond colors or insignia. They can bear whatever names they want. Black Diamond's main attraction is insurance.

This is how Black Diamond does it. It requires that on a year-to-year basis applicants turn over formal title of their car to one of Black Diamond's subsidiary corporations. For every two cars in the fold, Black Diamond forms a new subsidiary, so as to limit its liability in case an insurer fails to pay off an accident. Black Diamond then applies for insurance for the cab through New York's "assigned-risk" pool. Theodore Huntington states on the application that the vehicle is based in Mount Vernon (where, after all, Black Diamond does maintain a one-room office) and that it is a school bus. New York's assigned-risk pool works to ensure that at one rate or another all vehicles in the state will get the minimum compulsory insurance coverage if proper application is made. In effect, the state assigns cars that can get no coverage elsewhere to one of the various auto insurance companies operating in the state. Unless it can show cause why not, the insurance company must accept the risk. Since very little investigation of registration applications is done either by the State Department of Insurance or by most of the various individual companies to which the risks are assigned, this system virtually ensures that Black Diamond's cabs will receive low-cost insurance policies and the needed "Z" (special omnibus) license plates.

All this would be a very nice system—everybody happy, tacit understandings everywhere—if it were not for the fact that gypsy cabs have accidents. Indeed, they get into a surprisingly large number of accidents. Yellow cabs are bad enough in terms of safety, but gypsies are something else again. The poor condition of so many of the industry's vehicles combined with an unusual number of apparently incautious drivers, especially among the part-timers, result in an average of between one-and-a-half and two accidents per vehicle per year. And when a passenger in a gypsy accident files a claim, whereupon the insurer discovers that the gypsy obviously does not fit the application descriptions on the basis of which the vehicle was insured, then we see where all these neat arrangements break down — indeed, where they sometimes cause great hardship.

Louise Franklin, Etta Brown and her son Marvin, and James Strickland were all involved during the past twenty-four months in traffic accidents where a cab insured through Black Diamond was apparently at fault. All parties filed claims against the respective insurers of the three cabs involved. The dispositions of their claims are illustrative of what can happen to you if you are a passenger when a gypsy cab cracks up.

The cab in which Louise Franklin was riding went out of control and plowed into a series of cars parked along Riverside Drive near 148th Street, Manhattan. She was thrown forward, struck the glass partition and suffered a severe concussion and head lacerations. Her medical bills amounted to $1,100 and she lost time from work.

The cab in which Etta Brown and her son Marvin were riding overturned and slid into a tree on Park Drive North in Manhattan when the cab's brakes failed rounding a sharp curve. Etta Brown suffered numerous cuts, broken bones and severe internal injuries requiring extensive surgery. Her medical bills amounted to $9,000, she will be scarred for life, and she was out of work so long she lost her job. Her son Marvin was killed.

The cab in which James Strickland was riding ran a light at Lenox Avenue and 117th Street in Harlem, Manhattan, and was struck by a car emerging from the side street. He suffered facial cuts and a broken arm. His total expenses as a result of the accident amounted to $650.

In the first case, that of Louise Franklin, the insurer was the Albany General. Mrs. Franklin filed a claim for $2,500, including her pain and suffering, and they willingly paid off $1,800, despite the fact that on accepting the policy from Black Diamond they had sent Black Diamond a form letter (which never reached the cab's real owner) disclaiming responsibility in case the insured vehicle was to be used for purposes other than those claimed for it.

In the second case, that of Etta Brown and her deceased son Marvin, the insurer was the Firemen and Farmers Mutual. Mrs. Brown, through a Neighborhood Legal Services lawyer, claimed $25,000 for herself and $25,000 for her son's wrongful death. At first the Firemen and Farmers seemed adamant about not paying off a penny, since the cab, it turned out, was not a Mount Vernon school bus. But when Mrs. Brown's lawyer threatened to make a great fuss on her behalf, writing assemblymen, contacting reporters, "blowing the whistle" on the whole gypsy cab insurance racket and alleging the Firemen and Farmers' complicity in it, the company decided to settle at the policy limit, $20,000.

In the third case, that of James Strickland, the insurer was the Fundamental Assurance Society of Rhode Island. The Fundamental denied its liability categorically. Strickland thought of getting a lawyer, but the only lawyer he knew would not take the unpromising case on a contingency basis. Thus, suing the Fundamental seemed like an expensive proposition, against the limited payoff that could in any case be forthcoming. His lawyer/acquaintance suggested to

Strickland that perhaps he could sue the Black Diamond subsidiary that held formal title to the cab in which he'd been injured, but within a week of the accident Theodore Huntington had managed to transfer all of the assets of this subsidiary, "The 119th and Eighth Avenue Corporation," to another subsidiary, "The 120th and Eighth Avenue Corporation." James Strickland got no compensation for his accident, nor did he have Blue Cross or Medicaid. He barely had $650 in the bank to cover his bills. Black Diamond has given some thought to offering $300 to Strickland, simply to save face, but has not yet decided to do so and obviously may never get around to it.

In all three cases the insurance company subsequently canceled its policy with the Black Diamond subsidiary. But in all three cases, when the drivers got back on their feet again, Theodore Huntington formed new subsidiaries for their cabs and placed them through the assigned-risk plan with new insurance companies. The Fundamental Assurance Society of Rhode Island still insures cabs of one of Black Diamond's subsidiaries. All three companies continue to issue policies to falsely registered gypsies of other than Black Diamond registry. It should be noted that not only the riding public loses from such conniving but also the owners of school buses, funeral cars, and so forth, in Mount Vernon and elsewhere, who must pay for their counterfeit colleagues with soaring rates. Perhaps when the rates for school buses are driven sufficiently high in Mount Vernon, Black Diamond will move farther upstate, into fresher, safer territory.

Probably the most interesting aspect of this Black Diamond network for our purposes is that here we can see the gypsy cab industry already entering areas that might be dubbed "white-collar crime." The laws involved are more complicated, the frauds somewhat more subtle. Many middle-class people, unless they happened to be the victims of one of these arrangements, might think they were less serious offenses than, say, driving a stolen car. Whether they are or not is beside the point, however. The point is that here we see how even in the gypsies' criminal activity, the nature of their industry— providing an essential public service, requiring willynilly interaction with many of the established regulatory bodies of the government—leads them inevitably toward at least the lower strata of the middle class.

What is lacking in these frauds is refinement. It seems as though it would not be too difficult for an interested government agency to crack down on an outfit like Black Diamond. The most rudimentary investigation would turn up considerable fraud. And indeed early in 1973 an equally blatant operation based on Staten Island was broken up when it was discovered that many of the cabs involved had no insurance coverage at all—and that their real owners were ignorant of the fact and had moreover lost permanent title to their cabs in the bargain. Insurance procurers such as Black Diamond would seem to be the gypsy industry's most vulnerable spot at present. Many gypsy drivers simply can't afford to pay legitimate New York City public livery insurance rates, especially considering the frequency with which New York's admitted public livery vehicles continue to have accidents. On the other hand, if Black Diamond's fraud is rather rough and blatant, one must also observe that it is rather young and fresh. Theodore Huntington has only been in business for five years. With maturity is it not reasonable to expect that refinement will gradually come?

Victor Hidalgo and the Look Smart Livery

Victor Hidalgo was born in Puerto Rico but came to New York when he was seven, just after the end of World War II. His father was a hard worker and his mother was unusually clever, and the two of them parlayed the little money they managed to save into a successful *bodega* on Lexington Avenue in New York's East Harlem section. Victor was smart in school, occasionally brilliant, but according to the pattern of his neighborhood he finished only tenth grade. He managed to get to be sixteen without any trouble from the law, but that didn't mean he never did anything illegal. By the time he was seventeen, in 1955, he was was already running numbers for his older brother, Jorge, who was at that time a collector. He did a year of that, two years in the Army (which he liked and which taught him more about how the country beyond El Barrio worked than he'd ever learned in school), and then a year as a *bolita* collector, following his brother's advancement.

He had money in his pocket at age twenty-one, but he was not satisfied. His brother was twenty-nine, and had just gotten beyond the collector level. It seemed like a long haul upcoming in the numbers before Victor could hope to advance again. And how would he ever get out of his brother's shadow?

Victor was shrewd. He looked around to see where the best possibilities lay. It was 1960, and in East Harlem small fleets of gypsies were already getting together. They were popular. People seemed to want more of them, and the police weren't running them out. And Victor remembered all the infuriating late nights of his own life when he hadn't been able to get a yellow cab north of 96th Street. It seemed like these new, special cabs might have a real future. Already he knew he would never be satisfied with the ownership of merely one cab, like all those other slobs around, eking out food for five kids, but rather a whole little fleet, all paying money into him. It would be claiming too much for him to say that in 1960 he already could foretell the full size of his 1973 fleet, but this much at least is true: he knew from the beginning that he would be bigger than most.

He combined his own savings with a loan from his brother to buy a car and radio, and he hooked up with a neighborhood fleet. Then he simply started driving. All the time he was observing, figuring things out. And saving money. Victor Hidalgo has always been a vigorous saver of money. By the end of a year's time he knew pretty much what he had to do. He bought some stolen two-way radio equipment and with offers of lower rates lured six drivers away from the fleet with which he'd been associated. Within a year and a half he'd earned enough profits from his radio business to purchase eight late-model stolen cars, and soon he had all of these on the street with horse-hire drivers.

And so it went.

He was ruthless, shrewd and hard-working. He held his drivers to the highest standards of personal honesty in their dealings with him. He provided good service and kept his cabs in shape. And he plowed every penny he could back into the business. His pitch to prospective drivers was simply this: make as much money as with the yellows, in your neighborhood, and yet without the travails of personal ownership. His pitch to customers in the neighborhood was: no other outfit will provide such consistent service in such clean, safe cabs. Gradually he built up a large phone clientele and high street recognition for his blue-and-white striped cabs. And gradually he persuaded drivers —who often came to him owning their own vehicles and simply wanting to be associated with what he had already named the Look Smart Livery—that they would be better off simply working for him. Indeed, he arranged his fees and pay scales so that that would almost surely be the case.

By 1965 he owned eighteen cabs; by 1969, thirty-one cabs; and today he owns sixty-three. Another twenty-three owner/drivers are affiliated with him. Of the cabs he owns, nearly all are driven by men who work on 50 percent of the meter plus tips, although he permits a few stubborn drivers to horse-hire, usually to their own loss. He is quick to fire anyone who appears to be cheating on him, and his accountant thinks he runs a ship-shape business. His personal income is substantial—in the neighborhood of $60,000 per year—but much of that money goes to his mother and brother, and if he wanted it that way, his salary could be much greater than it is. Company profits were in excess of $120,000 last year, nearly all of which went for expansion of capital facilities. Thus Look Smart Livery is still growing fast.

Whatever criminal activities Victor Hidalgo formerly engaged in, he feels himself too big for them now. Too big and too important. Dealing with fences and so forth is unbecoming. Hidalgo pays his taxes, holds valid insurance policies, avoids hiring crooks. He is trying for a "high-class operation." His fleet is loaded with late-model cars and holds a license for a private radio channel. Of course Hidalgo still pays off certain policemen—but so do untold numbers of otherwise perfectly legitimate businesses. The only other illegitimate thing about the Look Smart Livery is its fundamental business activity: metered gypsy cruising. There is perhaps a certain irony in this.

Victor Hidalgo is plainly an ambitious man. He is thirty-five, single, attractive, sought-after in the upper echelons of New York's Puerto Rican community. But at the same time he is rather indifferent and even scornful toward anything but his business—or, more generally, his own advancement. He is singleminded. He has rivals but he is intent on being a leader of his industry—at the very least, of the Puerto Rican faction of it. He makes statements to the Spanish papers, addresses meetings, picks up the tab for untold numbers of "business lunches." And he is clearly interested in politics. He has contributed cash to several campaigns, made friends, offered suggestions. On Election Day his cabs have helped deliver voters to the polls for a whole slate of local, state and even federal candidates—and nearly all the men he's supported have managed to win. Part of this political involvement has undoubtedly been for the purpose of advancing his business affairs. All his chosen candidates have at one time or another expressed support for the gypsy industry. But Hidalgo has never tried to extract promises. All he has hoped for is friendship. And it seems entirely possible that he is more interested at this point in using his business to further his political ambitions than in using his politics to advance his business. But the two are intertwined. In all of this one can surely detect a striving for respectability, for escape from the stigmas of an under class; but perhaps there is more to it than that. Perhaps there is also the sheer love of power, classical and unadorned. Hidalgo already frequents his local political "clubhouse." Running for office is the obvious next step.

At this point it is unclear whether Victor Hidalgo's next ambition will be realized. There is a lot of talk in the clubhouse over whether they really want to back a man whose business still leaves him wide open to scandal and prosecution. These have been times of high visibility for politicians who've had scrapes with the law.

Yet it is precisely the illegality of his business venture that Victor

Hidalgo would like to erase by his entry into politics. He would love to be the man who got the gypsy cabs legalized. And the vicious circle in which he fears he may get caught turns him stony with anger. Victor Hidalgo has an immense temper, which he is nearly always able to control. When he is angry he stands tall and rigid, his eyes fire up and his teeth get set—in sum, he is like a gun about to go off. And when he looks that way it is difficult to imagine that somehow, someday, he won't find a way around his obstacles.

Many other shrewd, powerful men before him have mounted the same path that leads from illicit business into politics and thence into the center of the nation's life, and have faced the same obstacles or worse, and have overcome. In his heart, Victor Hidalgo knows this.

Indeed what is most striking about Victor Hidalgo's success story is how closely it follows the old American scenario—from Yankee trader to robber baron, to whiz-kid tycoon—and how much Hidalgo resembles the basic type of the American who "made it." He is the fierce individualist, the pragmatist. He is restless. And yet he is also the man who would be respectable—or at least who now thinks that he would like to be respectable—as soon as he can afford to be.

The gypsies of New York—all of them, James Taylor and his partners at Superfast, Theodore Huntington with his Black Diamond group, even Victor Hidalgo and the Look Smart Livery—face considerable perils in the years ahead. It is uncertain how much power the Taxi Commission will eventually have and what it will do with that power. And if the health of the yellow industry continues to decline—as well it might, as a result of antipollution measures, continued increases in crime, or the inroads of the gypsies themselves—the yellows will probably grow more strident for action against the gypsies. Then they will be able to present a very compelling picture both to their supporters in politics and to the middle-class public as well. The loss of the yellows would be as great a catastrophe to the city generally as the loss of the gypsies to the city's black and Puerto Rican neighborhoods. It may be that eventually some compromise will be worked out in which only the "biggies" of the gypsy world—Victor Hidalgo and others like him—will be permitted to survive. In all events one can look forward to increased regulation of the gypsies, which for better or worse will add to the expense of doing business as a gypsy and therefore drive many of the financially marginal owners out.

Nevertheless, the future of the gypsy cab industry seems, to an outside observer, rather bright. The gypsies are fulfilling a genuine need, providing an essential public service in the black and Puerto Rican neighborhoods of New York. And despite the illegalities involved—and despite the undoubted presence in the unregulated industry of some unsavory men and some unworthy practices—the instincts of the bulk of the men are honest and true. They simply want to "make it," to "have a little something" for themselves and their families and to achieve these goals without harming their neighbors. Indeed, their neighbors recognize as much. Political power is growing in their favor. A challenge is at last being mounted to the political forces that for so long preserved a yellow monopoly that failed to be accountable to so many New Yorkers. In the years to come this industry will in all probability be institutionalized as part of the "legal" strength for the black and Puerto Rican middle classes of New York. Today, however, they are an interesting case of an activity in transition from illegality to at least quasi-legal status. Present in the gypsy cab industry are all of the ingredients that make up the sociological puzzle we call organized crime in the United States: public support or even demand for services that the externally administered law defines as illegal, an avenue to social and economic mobility where more legitimate routes are blocked or nonexistent, official and political indifference or complicity and an organized network of associates in the illegal activity.

PART FOUR

SOCIAL BANDITRY AND A BLACK MAFIA

6

ANALYSES AND
CONCLUSIONS

♯

We began this study of ethnic succession and network formation among black and Puerto Rican organized crime groups with four basic questions in mind: How are black and Hispanic crime networks organized? What are the codes of rules that control behavior in these networks? What is the organizing principle in the establishment and maintenance of such groups? Finally, what is the relationship between such networks and the ethnic communities in which they operate and with American society?

By now the reader has had many opportunities to assess the cogency of the arguments I have presented and the power and pertinence of the data offered to support them. Nevertheless, in these last pages, I want to review analytically the major propositions I have put forth and then answer these questions in terms of what can be learned from the networks we observed. Having answered the questions, I would then like to suggest some possible implications of the research for social policy toward organized crime. First, however, a quick recapitulation of the major themes of the book.

In this book I have been primarily concerned with two matters.

279

First, as part of a long-range research program, I have tried to describe the complex of relationships that exist among ethnicity, politics and organized crime as an American way of life. More specifically, however, in the research upon which this book is based, I wanted to examine the proposition that over the next decade, we will see the presently scattered and loosely organized pattern of emerging black control in organized crime develop into a black Mafia. Both of these propositions are based upon the assumption that organized crime is more than just a criminal way of life; it is a viable and persistent institution within American society with its own symbols, its own beliefs, its own logic and its own means of transmitting these systematically from one generation to the next. Viewed in this way, organized crime is a functional part of the American social system, and while successive waves of immigrants and migrants have found it an available means of economic and social mobility, it persists and transcends the involvement of any particular group and even changing definitions of legality and illegality in social behavior. Organized crime (though illegal) is nonetheless a function of social and economic life in the United States, and it can also be viewed as falling on a continuum that has the legitimate business world at the other end.

I have argued that understanding how crime is organized and how it relates to American society requires studying it in operation in the community and in society. Thus, I have tried to show black and Hispanic involvement as part of the process of ethnic succession, trying to demonstrate what was common and what different in the experience of these groups in comparison to the Italians who preceded them and then to define what distinctive patterns will characterize the period of their control over organized crime. In presenting the various networks we observed, I have tried to describe them in such a way as to demonstrate what these new groups in organized crime look like, how they operate and how they are related to the social world around them and then to make some predictions about their probable future.

As in all field work, we recorded a vast amount of information, and determining what was important and what trivial, what was characteristic of and generic to all networks or idiosyncratic to one or some, and how all this related to the questions we were asking was no easy task. From the outset we began comparing the information we were getting on each of the networks so that, as the research progressed, we became increasingly aware of what we knew and what we still needed to find out in order to provide valid and reliable data with which to answer the questions. We also continuously developed and refined tentative answers and tested these with each other in our group meetings. Toward the end of the field research, I also tested our answers on a number of crime activists, community residents, law enforcement personnel and a few scholars and students of organized crime. Since our answers were drawn entirely from the field data, this raises the important question of how representative the episodes I have chosen to present here are. Each episode concerns real people in real situations and I have tried to select a sample of the network descriptions that cover the range of activities and situations we observed. The stories I have presented are factual accounts of life in these networks, and from this body of fact anyone can draw his own conclusions. The answers I present here are the conclusions I have drawn, and they are meant to stimulate thought and even elicit some disagreement or controversy; the network descriptions are the food for that thought and it is to them that we should look to evaluate our answers.

The first step in determining the pattern or patterns of organization in the networks we observed was to ask, "What brings and holds people together in these networks?" In our analyses we were looking for types of interaction that bring individuals to the point of entering into some form of criminal partnership, then lead to the formation of organized criminal networks and keep them in continuous interaction. It is these interactions that forge networks and establish relationships of mutual dependence and responsibilities among organized crime activists. From our analyses of the networks, we found two distinct types of linkages. One set we called *bonding relationships* because they serve to introduce individuals to each other and into joint criminal ventures and so bring people together in networks. The second type of linkage is what we came to call *criminal relationships,* links based upon a common core of activity in crime that keep people working together once they have joined in a network.

Bonding Links in Black and Puerto Rican Crime Networks

We identified six sets of bonding relationships in our networks. The first of these is *childhood friendship*. This relationship is quite common throughout the networks but particularly prominent in the story of the War Dragons and in Luis Santos' childhood gang of drug pushers. Although childhood gangs are an obvious place to look for such friendships, the childhood friendship does not require a gang to establish a potentially criminal relationship. Remember that after Reggie Martin and Jimmy Brown were grown and successful in their individual criminal ventures, they joined together to "launder" some of their illicit profits through a joint enterprise in a boutique. Also, Luis Santos was a friend of Clemente Sanchez, who refused to join Luis' gang but later helped him after the downfall of that gang. Although the long-term relationship that grows out of childhood friendship is not restricted to crime circles and is found in legitimate social relationships, it seems particularly potent in organized crime networks. In every case of childhood friendship that grew into an adult criminal partnership, the individuals involved were of the same ethnic or racial group and usually were approximately the same age. It seems almost unnecessary to point out that this is not the result of any innate criminality in any of the ethnic groups but rather results from the fact that street society, where youngsters meet, is based on residential patterns, which tend to follow racial and ethnic lines as well as socioeconomic ones. Reggie Martin and Jimmy Brown could just as easily have been meeting in the Grill Room of the Yale Club and discussing the formation of a joint stock venture if their childhood circumstances had been different. But youngsters growing up in the ghetto have a different set of experiences, a different set of role models and so a different pattern of life chances. One of our interviews in Central Harlem makes just this point:

Again I stress the point of making the right kind of friends, from the time you're a little kid, then building up the right kind of respect among your associates, and carrying yourself so that those people who have always known you can continue to depend on you, to think that you are okay. For every friend you have you have that much more chance to get in on deals, to make it in crime. You are able to be in touch; people will give you their address, their telephone number. Otherwise you are outside looking in—you are nobody. It's a thing in New York that people just don't take you in unless you know somebody. It's a city thing, a poverty thing. No trust. The guys who are into organized things in crime let you in only when they feel you are "cool." You got to prove yourself or have somebody vouch for you . . . Growing up in New York is important. You get to know the people involved. You make friends and you make connections. The kid in Harlem has plenty of opportunities to be turned on to crime. [Central Harlem] [1]

A second type of linkage develops when *an experienced criminal in the neighborhood sees that a young boy (or gang of young boys) possesses talent and recruits him into organized criminal ventures.* This is the most common method of recruitment into organized crime and represents the first step in criminal apprenticeship. Again, as was the case in childhood friendship, there are numerous examples throughout the networks, but the best-documented cases are in the recruitment of the War Dragons by George Gordon following their successful whiskey theft and Luis Santos' recruitment, promotion, demotion and re-recruitment following his prison terms. It was also the means by which Rolando Solis was brought into the lower echelons of the Cuban connection and from which he later moved up the ladder of criminal success. Contrasting these cases, it appears that recruitment through this relationship may be individual, as in the

---

[1] Throughout this chapter I shall include a number of unedited extracts from our field notes to illustrate points I make or positions I take. In the brackets at the end of each such extract, I have identified the network from which the extract was drawn.

cases of both Luis and Rolando, or group, as in the case of the War Dragons. Like all social relationships, however, this bonding link between and among younger and older crime activists is two-sided; not only does the older criminal seek out the younger, but the youngsters also seek to be recruited and to emulate their elders in crime. It is this role modeling that gives generational continuity to organized crime and accounts, in part, for its persistence in society.

Numerous examples throughout the observations and interviews document this apprenticeship system. In Paterson among blacks, for example:

You can know who is connected and who is involved but you can't go to them and say, "Hey, man, I want to be one of you!" You can know for certain that Joe Blow is the biggest man in Paterson. He knows me and I know him but I can't approach that man about it. If I ask him something about that directly he might cuss me out. This is the way it happens. If he has been watching me and he likes what he sees and he wants to give me a little play, he might tell me one day to go see Joe. He won't ever turn around and commit himself to me the first time. You just take this for granted that you don't approach these guys at that level . . . Well, how can you? On what grounds? What do you know about him to say something that's kind of personal, you might say? You can't just walk up to one of these guys and ask about something that doesn't concern you. [Paterson.]

This concern for being noticed and waiting to be tapped by the big men seems to operate in the same way in Brooklyn among Puerto Ricans.

I find that in order for people to put the right kind of opportunities in your path on the streets there has to be respect given to the people in positions in crime. They, in turn, must respect your ability as a person, as a hustler or whatever, in this way—through mutual respect—there is a chance that you will be given the opportunity for profit making in crime and that means you have to be connected. [Brooklyn.]

Finally, there is the simple, but telling observation by one of our black field assistants about the lack of positive influences and legitimate role models for ghetto youngsters:

The ones you see are the ones that interest you. If it had been doctors and lawyers who drove up and parked in front of the bars in their catylacks, I'd be a doctor today. But it wasn't; it was the men who were into things, the pimps, the hustlers and the numbers guys. [Central Harlem]

The third bonding type of linkage is *prison acquaintanceship*. It can provide very strong and durable links among men who have already been involved in crime and who in the prison atmosphere come to feel themselves segregated from society and find natural linkages among themselves. Once such links are developed in prison the chances of their leading to later joint criminal activity and forming the basis for organized crime networks seems to be quite high. Moreover, a multiplier effect is at work here since sometimes being a friend of a friend is enough to establish a link among former convicts. The role of prison experience in bringing blacks and Puerto Ricans together in crime networks is also an important difference between these groups and the Italians who preceded them. Prison experience, often beginning early in the crime activist's life, is found very commonly among the blacks and Puerto Ricans in the networks we have described but seems to have been absent to any sizable degree among Italian-Americans. The strength of kinship and family that binds Italian syndicates together is not found among blacks and is less pronounced among Puerto Ricans than it is among Italians. Thus, the linkages among Italian-Americans are formed early enough to provide a protective network so that apprehension and consequent incarceration seem to be less common among Italians than among blacks and Puerto Ricans.

Throughout the networks we found numerous examples of the importance of prison experience in bringing crime activists into contact with each other. Seemingly, the experience can begin quite early:

The kid who grows up in Harlem, goes to school there, and quite likely goes to a special boys' school for delinquents or whatever—he is a kid likely to be in contact with crime operatives in those places. These special schools are the places where ties are established, where a kid learns the ropes, gets to know people, etc. [Brooklyn]

Not only are these contacts active in the prison itself, they form an important basis for later contacts. Former association on the inside is a frequently cited introduction to new activities on the outside:

When if I do need him outside [prison], I go to his neighborhood. Everybody is leery of telling me where I can find him or even telling me they know him. But the minute I mention that I did time with him and where, then immediately they come around. They get less scared I may be a cop. When I get to my friend he can take me around so all the people know I'm okay because we did time together. I soon get to fit in.

. . . We have a street-level way of communicating with some guy who you knew or worked with before. This reaches all the way back to reform school and I still know some of the guys I did time with in Utah. If I want to find one of the past acquaintances I knew in prison I go to his neighborhood and approach some junkie on the corner and the following conversation transpires between myself and the junkie:

"Hey, man, is 'X' around anywhere?"

"He might be, and he might not be."

"When he is around I want to talk to him."

"He comes around now and then."

"Do you think that you can ring him up for me or tell me where he lives at? I just got out of Green Haven and we did a bit of time together and he told me to look him up as soon as I get home. Just tell him Charlie F. is out here and I would like to get in touch with him."

"Yeah, man, he just came home a few months ago from there. I'll see what I can do."

The fact that you do time clears a communications resistance to the junkie even admitting he knows "X." Second, it is looked upon as a tough life and the junkie is trying to make out in order to gain favoritism with "X" and even with you. This is also a form of name dropping in the communication system you employ. This particular individual "X" is known to me for perhaps eighteen, twenty years during one incarceration or another. This is my security clearance from being denied access to conversations about anything that is going on in the neighborhood. I can then ask "X" after I find him, "What's going on here," "Who's doing what, you think this, you think that?" "Who's dealing in guns, I know so and so who has a gun and he knows somebody who can get it from him, or a car or dope or even a job if he's connected right." [East Harlem]

Next, there is the very strong link that develops in prison between an inmate and his close associates in the prison courts I described earlier. This relationship between a man and "the man who watches my back" is one of the strongest links we have found in black and Puerto Rican crime networks and rivals childhood friendship as a bond:

And being with your own people in a 'court' is what makes it easy to do time together, your friends, your crimies, rap partners, homies, you watch out for each other like brothers. He's the kind of guy you won't hesitate to come to on the outside when there is some money to be made or at times like he says to go uptown and find out how come the money is not being made. If I get hung up and the cops are looking for me as a result of doing this he is not going to change his address and move to Sweden and all that stuff. He'll look into it, send a lawyer, see to it that everything is all right. That's the real thing about doing time together. There are ties created because you were sort of like stripped down. When there is trouble under any given moment, under any given circumstances, I will not hesitate. I will turn around instinctively and search for him. It sounds strange, but you make your best friends in prison. I could remember a time when something would go down like a strike or something like that. The guards are shooting at you, and some faggot you turned down is waiting to put a shiv in your ribs. It is like going to a shooting gallery. But you got friends. The guy in front of me, I'd watch his back; the guy in the back of me watches mine and down the line. And it was like a group of people. I can remember coming into the mess hall when the strike was going on. I had stood all day on the soap box and said what we was going to do and all that and we decided to be silent. As I walked into the mess hall, there's a friend of mine sitting over there with his brother, his real brother, and I looked at him and he was mad because he thought we should burn the place down. But he was the type of guy who said, "Well, I'm not going against his word." I said, "Keep it cool, baby," and he understood. But his brother thought I was downing him. He got out of his seat in the mess hall. I turned around to say something to him and everybody there kept saying, "Man, this guy is crazy, turning his back like that." And his brother was right there where Fritz [the author] is sitting when I looked around, angry as he can be. And the guy behind me has his hands across his chest. I looked down and said, "Let him go. Come here. I don't know you and you never walk up behind me no more." So he sat down and when I see him again he said, "I'm sorry man, I didn't know." I said, "Everything's cool on you man. You never would have gotten to me." He never got to me. I wouldn't have been worried about that. It is a good thing in prison to be able to turn your back. And that is the one thing, when you see a guy watch your back inside, I would try anything with him as my crime partner outside. [Prison]

Another type of bonding linkage is the infrequent but potent relationship that seems to exist between individuals in black and, to a lesser extent, Puerto Rican organized crime networks and *their wives or lovers*. Black and Puerto Rican members of organized crime networks involve women, particularly their lovers, in whatever criminal activity they themselves are involved in—thus, Elizabeth Dukes, one of Thomas Irwin's thieves, and the neighborhood women Roberto Mateo uses in his numbers operation. Sometimes, as in the case of Elsie Payne, Joseph Hajar's lover and associate, or Madame Stephanie St. Clair, they reach fairly high positions. Here, there is a distinctive difference between the emerging black and Puerto Rican organized crime networks and those found traditionally among Italian-Americans. Once again it may represent the strength of family and kinship among Italian-Americans but it may also be a result of the less highly organized and consequently less professionalized criminal relationships among blacks and Puerto Ricans. It is interesting to note that in our field experience we have found that Cubans, who are much more highly organized than either Puerto Ricans or blacks, do *not* use women in their crime groups. The usual reason given for this by the informants was that the Cubans are "more like the Italians."

Among the blacks there have always been women involved in numbers and dope. You find the same thing in the Puerto Rican race sometimes where they are runners in the numbers; they don't actually "run" numbers from place to place but they do have people come to their house and you leave your number and your money there. Sometimes Puerto Rican women whore too but not usually for Puerto Rican pimps. Most pimps I know are black even if their women are white or Spanish. Where you don't find any women is with the Cubans. If a Cuban woman gets into drugs or into hustling her ass, she is dead in the Cuban sections and she better get out as fast as she can. [East Harlem]

Although it happens not nearly so often as we found among the Italian-Americans, nevertheless, *kinship ties* will sometimes foster a criminal linkage among blacks and Puerto Ricans. Our experience indicates that there is much greater reliance upon kinship among Puerto Ricans than among blacks and that, once again, the Cubans seem more like the Italians in that kinship is an important element. One interesting point that did emerge in this research is that all the kinship ties in our networks which we knew to be criminal relationships were between brothers, as in the case of the Squires and Jenkins brothers in Paterson or Clemente Sanchez and his brothers in East Harlem; none was between a father and son. This could be a function of the limited size of our sample but it could also be a function of the relatively short period of time in which organized crime networks such as those we have described have been in existence in black and Puerto Rican societies. The importance of kinship ties, even among blacks, was commented on by a number of informants:

There is a great deal to the observation that trust is given more easily to a boy if he has a relative—a father, uncle, brother, an aunt—involved in crime. Many times, people want to know who a guy is, that is they want to know his pedigree. A guy is accepted more easily if he has a "crime heritage." [Central Harlem]

Family ties help preserve confidences which builds trust. Guys use their relatives in crime for two reasons: one, they are blood; two, they can keep this to themselves and coordinate among themselves. [East Harlem]

The sixth and most common bonding type of linkage in our networks is the meeting of two men, either through intermediaries or casually, who happen to be in complementary business positions such as Reggie Martin and James Mitchell or Cesar Rosario and the car painter Eduardo Paredes, and consequently form a linkage for common profit. These kinds of relationships, *premised on business,* can lead to a great deal of criminal activity. Characteristically, some of the activities are legitimate and some are illegal. But as can be seen in most of the networks we have described, gradually the activity tends to move from one form of organized crime operation to another. In some cases the linkages are ad hoc arrangements, as when a particularly good opportunity arises and two or more individuals along with their associates join together briefly for a common venture. In other cases the relationship grows over a period of time as expertise and special skills are required for the continuation of certain types of activities. In either case, what is important is that individuals involved in organized crime activities do seem to have a common set of relationships that allows them to come into contact with one another. And in these relationships, the rules of good business practice are as true as in the world of legitimate business:

Any jerk with a trigger finger can put a gun in somebody's face and get a few bucks. When someone is looking down the barrel of my gun with me asking for money, they don't request any references. But if you really want to make it you have to have a business head, to let people you work for know that you are interested and alert and that you are accepted in the neighborhood or on the streets. You have to know your business. Drug addicts, for instance, are never really successful because they are not respected—they are hooked on dope and cannot be trusted. [Central Harlem]

Criminal Links in Black and Puerto Rican Crime Networks

In addition to these bonding types of linkages in the networks, we also isolated a number of substantive *criminal relationships,* links that develop out of joint criminal operations within a network. The most common by far, just as it is in the legitimate business world, is the *employer-employee relationship*. The employer hires the employee at wages or a salary to do certain things that the employer requires of him. In nearly every one of our networks we find many such relationships: Thomas Irwin and his thieves, Joe "the Turk" Hajar and his black employees, George "the Fence" Gordon and his employees in the whorehouse, Roberto Mateo and the neighborhood women who work for him, and Jimmy Mitchell and his pushers.

A second type of criminal relationship is provided in the *partnership and joint-venture type of linkage* in criminal networks. The partners or associates share equally in the risks, responsibilities and profits. This relationship differs from the employer-employee relationship in that the two individuals involved are in association without a dominant-submissive relationship; there are no fixed leaders or followers. In some cases, however, one partner does seem to have greater authority and perhaps more influence than the others. The childhood gang often operates in this fashion and it appears that older groups such as the Barracudas do also.

A third type of relationship is that which occurs between the *buyer and seller of goods*. This type of relationship is very important in the narcotics, boosting and stolen car trades. However, we have found in most of our networks that this type of relationship exists in a number of the activities of networks. In some cases, as with Thomas Irwin's thieves, it is a well-established pattern where illegally acquired goods such as guns or cars are sold either through a middle man or directly as part of the network. In others it tends to be episodic, when an individual or group learns that someone has some "hot" goods to sell, as in the case of the War Dragons' whiskey theft.

Related to the buyer and seller of goods relationship is the *buyer and seller of services* relationship. In all networks this involves chiefly a specialized criminal skill, such as locksmithing. Other skills such as prostitution or numbers running are less specialized but still important in the networks that include these activities. We distinguish between the buyer and seller of goods relationship and the buyer and seller of services relationship because the relationships are quite different. In the case of the buyer and seller of goods, the relationship very often is the result of the availability of certain goods and a need on the part of the purchaser. In the case of the buyer and seller of services relationship, however, there is usually an established pattern so that the same locksmith or car painter, for example, is used repeatedly.

There is also a complex linkage that exists between *a leader of an informal gang and his followers.* The one significant example of this in our networks is in prison life although it does appear in other networks in some form. This relationship seems to be too informal to maintain a stable operation except in prisons, where incarceration keeps inmates in close, continuous association. Here our data are too thin on hierarchical placement, dominance, submission and other organizational features to allow us to do more than speculate that these informal relationships represent first stages in the formalization of leadership in organized crime networks.

Another type of linkage is that which exists *among and between fellow employees or among and between followers in a gang.* Although this type of relationship seldom brings a criminal venture into existence, it is often on this type of relationship that the success of a venture rests. Poor coordination of effort and a lack of cohesion in the group seem to have doomed some of the efforts described in our networks—Luis Santos' gang, for example. In a traditional legitimate business relationship this would be described as morale, or *esprit de corps,* within the company.

There are also a few relationships that are somewhat less common than the foregoing but that do emerge with some frequency in our networks and seem important to a number of the criminal operations described. The first obtains *between a granter and a grantee of a privilege,* as when, in the Paterson network, Bro Squires inherited his brother's business and his connections and followers as well. In effect this relationship defines property and territorial rights in much the same way that it seems to exist in Italian-American organized crime circles. Another type of relationship that seems to be present in our networks is that between *the giver and the recipient of a bribe or favor*. Here the basis of the relationship is the exchange of goods and services based upon mutual needs and the assumption that the exchange is in some fashion mutually beneficial. Here again this is not an uncommon activity even outside of organized crime but the relationship is an important one for keeping the networks in operation and protected:

Even to survive with the law you have to be connected. The cops will not take money from just anyone. They are in the business of being a cop to make money and they are interested in pulling in bribes, but they want it in a safe way. The safety comes in knowing the guy from who they take money. The cop takes the money from a successful man and grants him his protection so that the man can carry out his numbers or dope thing which allows the money to keep flowing to the cop. A little man is not interested in so much protection and he might turn in the cop if he got pissed or if the heat was on because he doesn't have that much to lose. If a small-time cop on the beat tries to fuck with one of the big men, though, it could mean a lot of money and he will be interfering with the sergeant or the lieutenant's take and so when the sergeant gets wind of it, probably from the operator himself who will call and ask what the hell is going on here, the sergeant must get the cop out of the way, transfer him or talk to him. Nobody likes an honest cop. [Central Harlem]

Finally, there is a criminal relationship that we did not find very frequently in our networks but did occur in some cases. This is *the relationship engendered by a simple, direct assault,* as between the policeman Reggie Martin describes in Central Harlem and the addicts he shakes down to obtain narcotics for resale on the street. We do not have a great deal of data on the use of violence and assault as techniques for compelling behavior in organized crime. In fact, our informants reported repeatedly that violence does occur but is not an important factor since it is the certainty of relationships and the mutual profit among members of the network that keeps it in operation. It is important, however, to remember that criminal business is not always tidy and consequently violence certainly does occur. There are numerous examples of violence against outsiders throughout the networks I have described, but we don't know how important violence is within networks as a means of keeping members in line.

Forms of Behavioral Organization

Once we had identified the bonding links leading to the formation of networks and the criminal relationships sustaining them, we looked at the networks again to see if we might classify them on some functional basis that might help explain how they are organized. We found that basically there are two forms of behavioral organization into which all of our networks could be divided. One type of behavioral organization characterizes what we termed *associational networks*. These are networks held together by close personal relationships among its members. It is the intensely personal network that places strong emphasis on mutual trust and is held together primarily by the force of the bonding links described earlier. We found two forms of associational networks in our field experience.

The first of these is the *childhood gang* as a beginning criminal partnership. In these associational networks, black or Puerto Rican youngsters growing up in the same neighborhood were involved in criminal activities and then through the process of recruitment became involved in organized crime as a group. The friendships and ties among these youngsters were such that they continued into adulthood. It is important to point out, however, that such youthful gangs should not be included under organized crime networks initially because although they might occasionally participate in organized criminal activities, they are not organized entirely for participation in such activities. Rather, their importance is as a beginning step and as a source of recruits into organized crime.

The partnership of old neighborhood friends is most characterized by the sharing of risks and profits, by unclear lines of authority, by expressed concern over many aspects of the personalities of the members and by the youthfulness of the partnership's members. The partnerships we saw in various networks are illustrative of each of these points. It is interesting, however, that these tend to be youthful partnerships and few probably last beyond the mid-twenties of the participants' lives. For one thing, the men involved—no doubt like men everywhere—grow apart from one another as they grow older and so begin to feel uncomfortable in the intimate confines of the partnership. For another, this kind of partnership has its perils—the youthful enthusiasm that led to its formation and created many of its norms can result in costly mistakes, errors in judgment and significant problems such as those which befall the gang of Luis Santos. But in some cases, as with the War Dragons, some members do remain as crime partners in adulthood.

The importance of these childhood relationships in building a "rep" and in forming crime networks is obvious in this interview:

You gotta have eyes to move up. In other words this has to be your goal and you have to make it known that you intend to make something of yourself and get other people to accept it. First of all you've got to have a knowledge of what you're gonna do and what you're able to do. You have to go and enlist the aid of somebody who's known to other people who help him in a way that gives him some power or show that they are interested in him or look the other way, such as the police authorities. He has to grease them or have a contact who is able to grease them or he's got no chance. You've got to be flexible in all things except in your main concern and that's got to be making money, more money, and getting more power. The power is going to come in several ways. One power is protection. You've got to have the power to pay off the police or you're dead. Another thing is somebody will sooner or later challenge your authority. First of all you have to have a reputation dating to the first time you ever entered into whatever you are doing. You probably got into it in a number of ways. You might have just been a kid and you might have just been lucky and have been noticed by the other bigger guys in the neighborhood. This is not always going to work though because you've got to do some things yourself. Somebody will come along sooner or later and will challenge that authority and unless you're strong enough or connected well enough you won't be able to maintain your position, even through force. You've got to be forceful and be willing to do things like putting your life out on the line because somebody just took $10,000 from you. You also have to always be thinking about your business and what you're going to do with it. What happens to it depends on who comes along. Everything works on the basis that you are liked, either because you have qualities that are likable or because you have qualities that are recognized, such as being a nice guy but still being a regular guy, somebody that is good to be with or a bright kid. These things lead to your being discovered. These are the things that old-timers look for. It is a tradition. We don't want nobody who is on drugs half the time taking on our business when we decide to retire and go to Florida. We don't want somebody who will let somebody from another territory come in and take over. What we want is somebody we know and like but somebody we can talk to and can get you to do what I want to so that you are learning the business at the same time. If you are not a doer, whatever you are that is what you are going to be. Once they learn that you can do something then they are willing to experiment on other things, bigger and better things because you have proved yourself. But if all you do is bring in $100 a day in the numbers they are not going to approach you with any kind of proposition like running this gambling joint that nets like $3,000 a day. Once you have developed a reputation in a particular group of people you can't take that reputation and go out to some other area unless you have "your man" in that other area. Most of it stays right in the neighborhood and once you move out of that neighborhood then you've got to have contact or you are dead. [East Harlem]

The second major type of associational network we found was *the prison court,* where individuals within prison band together along very strict racial lines and form strong bonds with each other. In addition to racial segregation these prison courts are characterized by strong leadership and a sensitivity to being together under a coercive and authoritarian system. It was a major finding for us that these prison courts are far more important in the formation of networks in organized crime among blacks and Puerto Ricans than they ever were among Italian-Americans. One of our interviews in Central Harlem points to the difference between Italian-Americans and blacks and Puerto Ricans in organized crime.

What I learned when I went to prison was that there were more blacks and Puerto Ricans than anything else there and I didn't see many Italians.

What I did see were not big racket guys. Anybody among the Italian-Americans who was identified as a big racket guy always got special privileges and kept pretty much to himself. The word inside was that their families were being taken care of and that they could be sprung at any time if they wanted to. I also learned that they went to jail very little and that there weren't enough of them there to band together. Then, with the blacks and Puerto Ricans, it is very different. The Puerto Ricans stepped together and the blacks stepped together. When you went back from the court into your cells you went back with guys you could depend on and there was always somebody who would watch your back. When I got out of prison these were the guys that I knew and the ones that were from my neighborhood were closer to me. I knew these guys. I could trust them and they could trust me. I knew what they could do and they knew what I could do. We were the ones who always worked with each other. If I found something good I would cut them in on it because I knew they would do the same thing for me. When I got back to my neighborhood not all the guys I knew in the prison court were there, of course, but some of the guys in my neighborhood knew the guys in prison and I knew that I could depend upon them because their friends in prison had been friends of mine too. [Central Harlem]

There are numerous reasons why the associational ties developed in childhood gangs and in prison are so important in network formation among blacks and Puerto Ricans. Among blacks, the sociology of the black family points historically to a relatively unstable pattern of family relationships. While there is still some debate as to how unstable it is and how important this lack of stability is for developing personalities within the black family, there is little question that the more frequent absence of the male figure, the strong will of the mother, who is frequently out working and not at home, and the lack of a long tradition of family cohesion are characteristics of black families in the ghetto areas we studied. This lack of a strong sense of family cohesion and the consequent absence of a sense of rights from and responsibilities to something larger than the individual is greater in blacks than it was and is among Italian-Americans. Thus, the childhood gang or the prison court may well represent the first strong associational tie for the black youngster as he matures and may come to form the basis for his loyalties to other individuals.

Catholicism and the Latin ancestry of Puerto Ricans would suggest that among them the family is a strong unit, and we did find kinship more important among them than it was among blacks. But, at least among those individuals we studied in our networks, families are not that stable and strong because of the importance of shifting common-law relationships and especially because of the rapid and frequent movement of the members of the family back and forth between Puerto Rico and the United States. In any event we feel that the primary importance of prison in the formation of black and Puerto Rican networks is warranted by observation in each of the networks we have studied. In almost every case friendships were formed either in childhood gangs and subsequently validated in common prison experience or individuals made contact with each other for the first time when they were in prison. In the prison court, as was true in the childhood association, the relationships formed tend to be highly personalized and consequently tend to be very lasting. They have the character of partnerships since they do depend on mutual trust and responsibility as well as compatibility of the individuals. The prison court is not really a criminal network in the sense that we have used this term in our organized crime research. Although its members are convicted criminals, their participation in the prison network comes at a time when they are largely unable to commit the types of crimes classified as organized. While the chief purposes of the prison court do not include the commission of crime, there is impressive evidence in our data that prison activities are linked to external criminal activities and that base recruitment and basic relationships that structure organized crime networks in the post-release period are often first formed in prison courts. These prison courts are characterized (1) by a single strong leader and his followers, (2) by strict racial segregation, and (3) by extreme sensitivity to the closed environment of prison life. It is within these courts that the exchange of favors—described earlier as a mutuality of rights and obligations—seems to become well established. The possession, or lack, of material advantages is an important factor in the adjustment of relations within the prison court. Thus, the individual who is able to provide goods or services is able to achieve a leadership position with the in group. The relationships thus established become binding in the sense that there are expectations built up on both sides of each interpersonal relationship. Further, the members of the prison court form a bounded network within which norms and rules are established that govern life in the court structure.

The second type of behavioral organization we found in networks follows an *entrepreneurial model* and seems to be a more advanced one among blacks and Puerto Ricans than the associational model just described. It is the model of the small businessman, the individual entrepreneur, whose illegal activities are carried out through a network of individuals related to him in that activity for mutual profit. In many respects, these crime networks are similar or identical to the kind of network that would coalesce around an individual black or Puerto Rican who established his own small legitimate business. The pattern of this type of structure is quite familiar throughout our research and is found in networks ranging from Thomas Irwin's thieves through the gypsy cab industry. Its characteristics seem always the same. One man is basically in charge of the activity by virtue of the fact that he pays the salaries or commissions of the other men. There is not a great deal of hierarchical arrangement among the employees; most employees seem to have some direct contact with the boss and they identify with him more than they do with other members of the network except in those specific cases where we have seen direct partnerships or long-standing relationships among the employee-members. The boss or center of the network is in most cases the only one in the net who has accumulated any risk capital. In fact, if an employee does accumulate risk capital he is likely to try to go off and set up some enterprise of his own, as seems to be the case in Paterson with Calvin Horton seeking to break away from Bro Squires. Again it seems that the salaried or commissioned employees, even when they are out on the street, are likely to view their activities as little different from "a job." Similarly, the boss, if the business of the network is successful, is likely to have many of the traits of any good small businessman—economy, prudence, firmness, a sensitivity to when he is being cheated or lied to and status as a businessman in his neighborhood. It is this relationship between the illegal business set and the community that is most significant as we review the data in the various networks. There are probably no more secrets or confidences within the group of employees in these networks than there would be within any comparable group of employees in the legitimate small business. What is different is that despite the illegal nature of the activities many co-ethnics and neighborhood associates of members of these networks view them as legitimate if not legal.

The Code of Rules in Black and Hispanic Organized Crime Networks

Once we had identified the linkages—both the bonding ones that lead to the establishment of organized crime networks and the substantive criminal relationships that keep them functioning—and classified these into types of behavioral organization, we turned our attention to looking for the code of rules governing these black and Hispanic networks. By "rules," I mean a control mechanism that regulates and regularizes relationships within the network and between the network and the outside world. It is the "code" that keeps the network functioning and defines relationships within it. It also establishes who is inside the net and who is outside. Control systems of this sort begin with values that define what is "good" and what is "bad," what is expected in behavior and what is condemned. Ultimately, however, human behavior whether in organized crime or in legitimate enterprises is guided by *specific* rules that attempt to operationalize these values and apply them to everyday situations. Thus, while values give us some general sense of what is expected, the rule states which actions will be approved and which forbidden. Rules, since they specify a set of expected behavioral actions, also carry with them sets of sanctions to be applied when they are broken. Finally, rules do not stand alone but are usually grouped into codes or sets of rules covering specified classes of behavior—the rules of etiquette or the rules of good sportsmanship, for example. The rules that govern behavior in organized criminal networks follow all of these characteristics just as surely and direct behavior just as forcefully as do more legitimate codes, a fact to keep in mind as I describe the code of conduct found in black and Hispanic crime networks. Before doing so, however, it would be worthwhile to look at the descriptions that have previously been given of the general code of rules in organized crime and to comment on whether we found these rules to be present among blacks and Hispanics.

Like so much in the study of organized crime, rules of conduct for organized criminals have usually been derived by analogy—that is, rather than looking directly at the behavior of criminal syndicate members and extrapolating a code from their words and actions, investigators have tried to apply codes drawn from observations of other groups. One favorite source of analogies for rules of conduct in American criminal syndicates is the "Code of the Mafia," which originated in Sicily. The federal government's Task Force on Organized Crime set up in the mid-1960s, for example, points out that since "there is great similarity between the structure of the Italian-Sicilian Mafia and the structure of the American confederation of criminals, it should not be surprising to find great similarity in the values, norms, and other behavior patterns of the two organizations." [2] Continuing with this reasoning, the report then goes on to present two summaries of the Mafia code; one statement was made in 1892, the other in 1900. The 1892 version demands:

1. Reciprocal aid in case of any need whatever.
2. Absolute obedience to the chief.
3. An offense received by one of the members to be considered an offense against all and avenged at any cost.
4. No appeal to the state's authorities for justice.
5. No revelation of the names of members or any secrets of the association.

[2] The President's Commission on Law Enforcement and Administration of Justice, *Task Force Report—Organized Crime; Annotations and Consultant's Papers* (Washington, D.C.: Government Printing Office, 1967), p. 47.

The 1900 version adds some new rules:

1. To help one another and avenge every injury of a fellow member.
2. To work with all means for the defense and freeing of any fellow member who has fallen into the hands of the judiciary.
3. To divide the proceeds of thievery, robbery and extortion with certain consideration for the needy as determined by the *capo*.
4. To keep the oath and maintain secrecy on pain of death within twenty-four hours.[3]

Noting that the two statements of the Mafia code are quite similar and allowing for the fact that the code is nowhere written except in such summaries, the report then describes the Mafia code as quite similar to the tenets of American organized criminals: loyalty, honor, secrecy, honesty and consent to be governed, which may mean "consent to be executed." The reason for the similarity, suggests the report, is that organized crime in America is an offshoot of the Mafia. As the report freely admits, however, the Mafia code itself is also quite similar to those that govern any secret society, such as Mau Mau and the Irish Republican Army, that are opposed to the existing authority in power and seek to overthrow it.

Another favorite source for finding the rules that govern organized crime is the so-called "Prisoners' Code," an informal set of rules that operates among prisoners in American prisons. This unwritten but widely accepted code is best described in a paper published by the Social Science Research Council based on the work of the Conference Group on Correctional Organization (1956–1957). This report sees the prisoners' code structured into five major areas of concern:

1. There are those maxims that caution: Don't interfere with inmate interests . . . never rat on a con . . . don't be nosey . . . don't have a loose lip . . . keep off a man's back . . . don't put a guy on the spot . . . be loyal to your class—the cons.
2. There are explicit injunctions to refrain from quarrels or arguments

---

[3] *Ibid.*, p. 47. The first summary was taken from Ed Reid, *Mafia* (New York: New American Library, 1964), p. 31; and the second taken from A. Cutrera, *La Mafia edi Mafiosi* (Palermo, 1900).

with fellow prisoners: don't lose your head . . . play it cool and do your own time.

3. Prisoners assert that inmates should not take advantage of one another by means of force, fraud or chicanery: don't exploit inmates . . . don't break your word . . . don't steal from the cons . . . don't sell favors . . . don't be a racketeer . . . don't welsh on debts . . . be right.
4. There are rules that have as their central theme the maintenance of self: don't weaken . . . don't whine . . . don't cop out . . . don't suck around . . . be tough . . . be a man.
5. Prisoners express a variety of maxims that forbid according prestige or respect to the custodians or the work for which they stand: don't be a sucker . . . be sharp.[4]

Both Ralph Salerno and Donald Cressey, two leading experts on organized crime in America, describe the prisoners' code as similar to that found in organized crime, again recognizing the similarity of the prisoners' code to that of any other underground organization and its need for secrecy and control. They also see this code, like the Mafia code, as being an unwritten set of agreements that prisoners adhere to but that have no formal sanction by prison authorities. Finally, this code, like the Mafia code, draws together those maxims of behavior that members see as ideal and enforcement comes from general agreement to abide by the code.

While each of the major sources admits the absence of any written set of rules structuring behavior in Italian-American crime families, all present descriptive lists either are drawn from analogies to the codes just described or are abstracted from the experience of the writers in observing organized criminals. Cressey uses the so-called "thieves' code" as essentially the conduct code for Italian-American organized crime families:

1. *Be loyal to members of the organization.* Do not interfere with each other's interests. Do not be an informer.
2. *Be rational.* Be a member of the team. Don't engage in battle if you can't win.

[4] Gresham Sykes and Sheldon Messinger, "The Inmate Social System," in *Theoretical Studies in Social Organization of the Prison* (New York: Social Science Research Council, Pamphlet 15, 1960).

3. *Be a man of honor.* Respect womanhood and your elders. Don't rock the boat. This emphasis on "honor" and "respect" helps determine who obeys whom, who attends what funerals and weddings, who opens the door for whom, who takes a tone of deference in a telephone conversation, who rises when another walks into a room.

4. *Be a stand-up guy.* Keep your eyes and ears open and your mouth shut. Don't sell out. A family member, like a prisoner, must be able to withstand frustrating and threatening situations without complaining or resorting to subservience. The "stand-up guy" shows courage and "heart." He does not whine or complain in the face of adversity, including punishment, because "If you can't pay, don't play."

5. *Have class.* Be independent. Know your way around the world. Two basic ideas are involved here, and both of them prohibit according prestige to law enforcement officials or other respectable citizens. One is expressed in the saying, "To be straight is to be a victim." A man who is committed to regular work and submission to duly-constituted authority is a sucker. When one "family" member intends to insult and cast aspersion on the competence of another, he is likely to say, "Why don't you go out and get a job." [5]

Ralph Salerno derives his list from his experience in studying organized crime during a career with the New York Police Department, and it is generally very similar to Cressey's list. Salerno, however, describes the rules as being of American invention but based heavily on the attitudes and world view that southern Italian and Sicilian peasants brought with them to this country. Essentially, then, both Cressey and Salerno describe the current code of organized crime families as derivative from the "Code of the Mafia" but tempered by other codes such as the thieves' code and the prisoners' code.

Deriving rules of behavior by analogy, however, can only be a valid technique if the values of the organization or group being studied are similar to those of the organization or group from which the analog is borrowed. There is no certainty that present-day organized crime groups share the values of the Mafia in Sicily in 1900 or, for that matter, of prisoners and thieves. In my field study of the Lupollo family, we derived rules from observed behavior rather than

[5] Donald R. Cressey, *Theft of the Nation* (New York: Harper & Row, 1969), pp. 177–178.

by analogy. In that study, since we observed behavior within the Lupollo family, we based our derived code of rules on what we were able to see and hear. Our method was to observe and record social action and then to seek regularities in behavior that have enough frequency to suggest that the behavior results from the pressures of the shared social system rather than from idiosyncratic behavior. We also asked family members and others about rules, usually by asking why some member of the family behaved in a particular way. Thus, our reconstruction of rules of conduct came both from our own observations and from the explanations of the behavior we observed of the people living under those rules.

We found three basic rules that organize behavior in the Lupollo family: *(1) primary loyalty is vested in the family rather than in the individual lineages or families that make up the overall organization; (2) each member of the family must act like a man and do nothing that brings disgrace on the family; and (3) family business is a privileged matter and must not be reported or discussed outside the group.* These three rules were the basics for maintaining membership within the group, but there were a number of informal rules under each that explain why some members are more successful at playing the game than others.

In studying black and Hispanic organized crime networks, we again tried to extract rules from observed behavior rather than by analogy, even with what we knew from the Lupollos. We found that there is a similar but functionally different code of rules for each of the two forms of behavioral organization we found in our networks.

In the associational networks we found in prison and in the youthful partnerships, rules seem more likely to speak to intimate personal characteristics:

1. *Don't be a coward.* This rule, which is found in both the prison court and in the youthful networks, enjoins the individual to be a man but has a more physical connotation than we found to be true among the Italian-Americans. Essentially, it indicates that the individual is always willing to fight for his own rights and safety and to a lesser extent for those of his colleagues in the network.

2. *Don't be disloyal.* Here again, the injunction is less positive in terms of its relationship to the group than we found among the Lupollos. What is called for here is a feeling of membership in a group and a basic loyalty rather than the intensely socialized family membership code among the Italian-Americans. Loyalty in this context means acceptance of membership in a group with the consequent requirements that outsiders be rejected.

3. *Don't be a creep.* Here, the rule calls for a normalizing of behavioral relationships among members in the network. What this rule does is to exclude from membership aberrant individuals—those who are somewhat deficient or who cannot for some reason enjoy full membership—and consequently establish standards for behavior.

These rules are of course not written and they are usually expressed in terms of punitive or critical actions toward any behavior that violates them. No one says, "Be loyal," but when an act by a member of the network is perceived as disloyal by his fellows, he will be subject to verbal and sometimes physical abuse as well. Neither are these rules normally taught in any formal manner; they are learned by experience and taught by example. In effect what we found was that these are expected norms of behavior that are socialized into individual network members as a result of their day-to-day experiences in the network.

In prison perhaps more than in the youthful partnerships (and for obvious reasons) shrewdness and the capacity to keep calm seem to be required. Thus in the prison network we found greater emphasis upon a fourth rule:

4. *Be smart.* The individual is enjoined to learn to acquiesce to some regulations that cannot be ignored but at the same time to determine ways to beat the system as well.

This rule, which we found only in the prison networks, is also a rule in what we have earlier called the code of American prisoners. Prisoner-to-prisoner injunctions such as "don't whine . . . don't cop out . . . be tough . . . play it cool and do your own time . . ." are responses to the imposed authoritarian environment found in prisons but not in the youthful gangs.

In the small business networks rules speak much more to the impersonal requirements of activities of the network than to the personal qualities described in the prison and youthful gang networks. In these business-related networks we found three major rules:

1. *Don't tell the police.* This rule actually stretches beyond the injunction not to tell the police; it also includes the caution against telling anyone who is likely to tell the police either through malice or weakness. While the rule is strongest within the networks themselves we found that it reaches out beyond the networks into the community and that (just as we found among the Italian-Americans) there is a great reluctance on the part of the community to inform on organized crime activities. To some extent this is the result of fear but we feel certain that it also results from an antagonism toward the criminal justice system and the feeling of greater unity and identification on the part of the community members with their co-ethnics in the networks than with the police or other segments of the criminal justice system.

2. *Don't cheat your partner or other people in the network.* This rule establishes the necessary confidence within the network that individuals will be accountable to each other with some degree of certainty. The rule places a highly "moral" standard on interpersonal behavior within the network but does not carry outside that group. Thus, an individual is expected not to cheat with money inside the network but is not enjoined against doing it externally.

3. *Don't be incompetent at whatever you are supposed to be doing.* This rule sets standards of excellence within the network and again it establishes confidence among its members. What this rule suggests is that an individual—a thief, a numbers runner, a prostitute, a pimp, a locksmith, a dealer of stolen goods, a narcotics pusher, or a hijacker —should do his job well.

These rules, as I have said earlier, seem far less related to personal characteristics than they are to business relationships. This results, I believe, from the fact that in these entrepreneurial networks the relationships are more situational or episodic than those in the prison court or in the youthful gangs. Thus, individuals come together in these entrepreneurial models largely for mutual profit, and their dependence upon each other is related entirely to advancing that profit. In the prison court or youthful gang model, however, personal relationships develop out of long-term, intense interaction and are designed to build trust.

Although the rules that govern the prison court and youthful gang type of network as contrasted to the entrepreneurial type of network do differ, there is an important relationship between them. The more highly personalized associational rules take place within networks that might be considered training and testing grounds for the more profitable but also more demanding entrepeneurial networks of organized crime. The War Dragons and Santiago's prison court are to Bro Squires' crime empire and Roberto Mateo's numbers racket, for instance, as boot camp is to the Marines. That is to say, the youthful gang and the prison court both serve as preliminary training grounds in which an individual establishes his "rep" and learns the first rules of membership before moving into a more sophisticated network. In these early training experiences he can be observed and his reliability can be tested. Thus, recruitment of blacks and Puerto Ricans into sophisticated organized crime networks usually seems to come as a result of prior experience either in a youthful gang or in prison, where they are identified as promising individuals. Unfortunately our data about youth gangs and prison experience among Cubans is quite sparse and we cannot support similar observations there. We do know from Rolando Solis' story that Cubans must go through a preliminary street experience before they are accepted into more important positions. Among blacks and Puerto Ricans, however, we feel confident enough of this pattern to codify this inner connectedness by adding a fifth rule, a flexible but nonetheless subtly applied one, to be used as a general guide for the entrepreneurial type of network described earlier:

5. *Prove yourself.* In order to join the "organization" one must have passed through some kind of accredited criminal training course in

which it can be assumed that the personal qualities valued in organized crime were duly tested.

We also found some interesting differences in leadership roles in the various types of networks. Among youthful criminal partnerships, lines of authority seem, in general, to be poorly drawn—there is little sense of who is obliged to follow whose orders except in particular circumstances. This may, of course, only be true in the networks we happened to identify and consequently studied. Nonetheless, it was true in each of the networks we looked at. On the other hand, in prison and in the small criminal businesses, certain lines of authority seem to be clearly drawn. In prison, one man in each court is the leader, by virtue of personal qualities or their expertise in beating the prison system, and all of the others of the court are his followers. In the entrepreneurial network the authority pattern is simple: whoever pays the salaries gives the orders.

When this code of rules for the two types of black and Hispanic network structures we observed is compared with the code of the Lupollo family, there are some obvious similarities and some important differences as well. Both the Italian and the black and Hispanic codes establish who is inside the net and who is outside. Those rules demanding loyalty and secrecy serve to establish the boundaries of the network or family and set up behavioral standards as well. It is not surprising that an organization or network engaged in illegal activity should require that its members show their loyalty to the group by respecting its confidence and maintaining secrecy. Secret societies of any sort—whether criminal, fraternal or revolutionary—could not long survive without requiring both loyalty to the organization and some degree of secrecy. Thus, the similarity in the two codes results from the generic nature of organized crime as joint activity among a group of crime activists who must of necessity keep their activities to some degree hidden. The other similarity between the the two codes also derives from the nature of organized criminal activity. These injunctions, which are described in terms such as "be a stand-up guy," "be competent in what you do" or "don't be a coward," are rules that establish the fact that each member of the network or family can depend on every other member to maintain a standard of behavior that reinforces the feeling of trust among the members of the network. As in any group situation, criminals working together need to be able to predict with some accuracy what standards other members will adhere to or else there is small advantage to joining with others in criminal enterprises.

There were also some important differences between the codes. When the two codes are compared, it is interesting that while each of the major rules we found among the Lupollos is also found in black and Hispanic networks, these rules do not seem to operate with the same degree of force within the black and Puerto Rican organized crime networks we observed. The most important rule among the Lupollos—*primary loyalty is vested in the family and not in individual lineages or groups*—is present but in a somewhat different form in black and Puerto Rican networks. Most Italian-American organized crime families are much larger than the networks we studied. Such families may have hundreds of members, but most black and Puerto Rican networks are still small. Thus, loyalty is vested in a smaller group and often includes only a given number of associates within the network. Our field experience, however, presents striking evidence that this will not always be so and that increasingly larger networks are being formed among both blacks and Puerto Ricans and that they in time will probably reach the size of even the largest Italian-American families.

The second major injunction among the Lupollos—*each member of the family must act like a man and do nothing that brings disgrace on the family*—also differs in the black and Puerto Rican networks we studied. The concept of "acting like a man"—that is, presenting an image of strength and endurance as well as self-reliance—is present in each of the networks we studied. It differs from what we found among the Lupollos, however, in that it is highly individualized and the concept of bringing disgrace to a larger organization such as the "family" or the "network" seems to be absent among the blacks and Puerto Ricans we studied. Thus, among blacks and Puerto Ricans it appeared that each individual is *individually* responsible for presenting the image of "being a man" and does not receive any support in this venture from some larger group such as was true among the Lupollos. The third basic rule among the Lupollos—*family business is privileged matter and must not be reported or discussed outside the group*— is found in our networks as well. Here again the strength of the rule among the Lupollos emanates from loyalty to the family while among blacks and Puerto Ricans it appears that it is less social and more individual in its imperative. Thus, among blacks and Puerto Ricans, the function of secrecy is far less ritualistic than seems to be true among the Lupollos and seems to be more a matter of individual protection.

These answers to the first two questions we posed—how black and Hispanic crime networks are organized and what code of rules controls behavior within them—provide the basis for answering the next two questions: what is the organizing principle that establishes and maintains such groups and how do they relate to their communities and to American society? Before turning to those two questions, however, it would be useful to summarize what we have learned so far in looking at the first set of questions.

Essentially, we found that there are some similarities between how blacks and Hispanics seems to be organizing and what I learned earlier about the organization of Italian-Americans in organized crime. I sought to explain these similarities as growing out of the constant nature of organized crime as it has become institutionalized in American society and the fact that blacks, and to an even greater extent Puerto Ricans and Cubans, have learned some of their organizational patterns "on the street" from the Italians who are now just beginning to lose control of organized crime. There are, however, some important differences as well. First, while there are some interesting similarities between black and Hispanic crime organizations that emerge from the common culture of the urban ghetto, Hispanics, particularly the Cubans, seem closer to the Italian model of organization, with its affirmation of the kinship bond, than do blacks. In relation to this, we found that where kinship is present as a bond in

Hispanic organization (and also in the fewer cases where we found it to be so among blacks), the relationships tend to be in the same generation. Blacks, and to a lesser degree Puerto Ricans, also differ from the Italians in that women are often found in their crime networks, sometimes in positions of some authority. Very early, however, it became apparent that there is as yet no black or Puerto Rican equivalent for the Italian-American organized crime family. The period of black and Hispanic control over organized crime is still emerging and so the pattern of its organization is also emergent. Yet despite the apparent lack of organization among the various networks we observed some patterns of organization were found frequently enough to be defined as characteristic stages of development in black and Hispanic organized crime networks. The first stage of development is the establishment of associational networks, groups of individuals who come together as a result of relationships that establish trust and mutual dependence among individuals. These networks are formed in group situations in which close primary relationships are established. Among the Italian-Americans in organized crime these links were formed in the family and kinship system that dominates Italian culture and in the street society that results from groups of youngsters in the same neighborhood interacting in peer groups. Among blacks and Hispanics, the family seems much less important although this is less true of Puerto Ricans than blacks and even less so among Cubans. The childhood gang, however, is an important basis for the formation of associational links among blacks and Hispanics, and indeed street society seems more important here than it was among Italians. Prison experience seems to serve an important role in bringing black and Puerto Rican crime activists together far more frequently than was true among the Italians. Two reasons seem to be suggested here. The primary role of kinship as an organizer among Italians and its association with a cultural model—Mafia—established associational relationships among them early enough that it often precluded prison experience. Even when Italians did go to prison, they went, as we have seen earlier, as individuals. The widespread racial segregation in prisons, however, divides the prison population along racial lines and so, in the absence of strong family relationships, blacks and Hispanics found close associational relationships in the prison courts.

These associational networks among blacks and Puerto Ricans serve as training and sorting grounds for recruitment into the second stage of development, the entrepreneurial networks that are presently the highest stage of organized crime network development among these groups. The childhood gang is the initial training ground, and on the street youngsters establish the "rep" that brings them to the attention of older crime activists. Prison serves to reinforce those early experiences or in some cases to provide them initially. His dependability, silence and competence having been established during his apprenticeship, the individual is ready for recruitment into an entrepreneurial network.

The rules that govern behavior in black and Puerto Rican crime networks also follow this progression. The code of the streets and of the prison focuses on standards of personal responsibility: "don't be disloyal, don't be a coward and don't be a creep" and, in the case of prison, "do your own time." The rules of the entrepreneurial networks speak to competence in the business of the network: "don't inform," "don't cheat your partners" and "don't be incompetent." Here again, the code rules of the earlier associational networks are a primer for the later, more business-oriented rules.

Ethnic Succession and Urban Social Banditry

Up to this point, I have restricted my analyses to a rather cautious level of interpretation of the observed facts I have reported. Now, in order to describe what I think will be the future of black and Hispanic organized crime activities, I must go beyond these observations and speculate but always with reference back to the networks I have described, for the clues are there. We learned, from the networks, how organized crime activities are presently organized along both horizontal and vertical lines. Vertical patterns of organization run from the consumer groups on the bottom—addicts, numbers players, buyers of stolen goods—to the dealers, bankers, and suppliers at the top. Horizontal patterns are obtained among crime activists at similar organizational levels. Thus, pushers in and out of prison relate to one another, as do dealers, bankers and suppliers. What interaction there is among the various crime networks takes place in this horizontal axis among operatives at similar levels of their respective organizations. Thus, black pushers in different networks know each other and even Puerto Rican pushers, but they seldom know the "top men" other than their own immediate supervisor. These networks, however, could not be characterized as "big" operations, like Italian-American crime families, with many layers of authority and countless functionaries and associates, many of whom are not aware of the roles of the others. Black and Hispanic organized crime networks have not yet reached that level of development. We do, however, have enough data on hierarchical arrangements and placement within some of the networks to conclude that while they are growing in complexity, they are still dependent on external sources for supplies and protection. In the Paterson network, which is the most highly developed of the black networks we examined, the two lowest levels—the street operators who sell drugs, numbers or their bodies and their immediate supervisors, the numbers controllers, the pimps and the small-scale drug suppliers—are always black. It is the next, or "boss," level that now seems in ethnic transition as Bro Squires struggles to replace the Turk as the big man on the hill. Both Squires and the Turk, however, are still dependent on the Italians for police and political protection as well as for drug supplies. In Harlem and in Bedford-Stuyvesant, black networks seem to be free of such dependence on the Italians for protection but not as yet for drugs except in those cases where they are switching to the Cuban connection. Internally, these networks do not seem to have developed any new forms of hierarchical arrangement as yet. In the various numbers games we observed, the traditional pattern of the carefully articulated runner-controller-banker hierarchy, which is still in use by the Italians, is also used by both blacks and Hispanics. We are also told throughout the various networks, however, about those people who by virtue of their superior power and resources are often able to make or break a criminal operation. These are the wholesale drug suppliers, the lay-off bankers who protect the numbers "banks" against the possibility of a run on a particular number, and police officials and politicians who must protect or at least ignore the operations. As we followed the networks upward through the layers of individual black and Puerto Rican entrepreneurs, each with his own little entourage of employees and followers, however, it became obvious that while only in Paterson did we find a direct connection with an Italian syndicate, most of these individual entrepreneurs must relate to Italian families or to the Cuban connection for drug supplies and for other high-level services such as lay-off banking. Nowhere in our networks did we find blacks or Puerto Ricans who had risen to the point where they are providing major services to other criminals. Neither did we find any systematic pattern of exchange of such services among the various networks. Where we did find any contact among the networks, the individual entrepreneurs seemed to be connected to one another either through occasional joint ventures or through straight one-shot deals for sales or services.

This lack of organizational development in black and Puerto Rican criminal structures coincides with both the newness of blacks and Puerto Ricans in control positions and with the nature of the types of criminal activities we discovered in these networks. Just as the lack of a sufficient period of time in control positions has hindered any large-scale organizational development it has also tended to keep the networks and action sets we observed fairly specialized in specific types of criminal activities rather than maintaining hegemony over all organized criminal activities in some territory. Once again the only exception was in Paterson, where the Italians are still in control. Throughout the networks, however, there is evidence of some beginning diversity of criminal activity involved in the networks as black control is consolidated. The combinations seem to be fairly stylized: prostitution and drugs, theft and petty gambling, numbers and narcotics are typical patterns. We also found evidence that black crime activists are starting to acquire some legitimate fronts—Reggie Martin and James Mitchell's boutique, for example—to "shade" their illegal activities. Even in the gypsy cab network we described, which is furthest along in the movement toward legality, we found that the cabs are sometimes used for drug transactions and in prostitution.

Within this emergent system, mobility is based upon efficiency needs but also upon power through the accumulation of wealth and territorial control. There are a set of fairly strict rules and norms governing such movement. So it was among the Italians and the evidence suggests that it is becoming so among blacks and Hispanics in organized crime. Successful operations are gaining power increments over time through the scope, extent and intensity of their dealings. In crime organizations as in more legitimate business operations, small operations grow into larger ones and then join with other enterprises to maintain territorial control over rich market areas. The market for illegal goods and services is not restricted to the ghetto, but at present, with the exception of prostitution, the black or Puerto Rican organized crime networks are excluded from the larger markets, which are still dominated by Italians. This same condition prevailed among the Italians in the earlier part of the century until prohibition provided a source for extra-ghetto profit and power and allowed the Italian mobs to grow into control. But since the present networks among blacks and Puerto Ricans are still relatively small operations, they continue to specialize and have yet to develop into large empires or even interconnected baronies. There are a number of indications of connections among networks in the same line of business, and some of the activities we observed were on their way to becoming large. The evidence from our study, however, seems to indicate that the present pattern of loosely structured, largely unrelated networks has now reached its highest stage of development and that what seems to be necessary for these networks to become elaborated into larger combines, like those now present among Italians, is: (1) greater control over sectors of organized crime *outside* as well as inside the ghetto, (2) some organizing principle that will serve as kinship did among the Italians to bring the disparate networks together into larger criminally monopolistic organizations and (3) better access to political power and the ability to corrupt it.

The first of these conditions, monopolistic control over some sector or sectors of organized crime, can only come about by wresting or inheriting such control from the Italians or, alternately, by developing new forms of illicit goods and services for sale to the public. The current sectors of organized crime—drugs, stolen goods, gambling, prostitution and loan sharking—are each in a state of transition at the present time and their availability to blacks and Hispanics as a source of illicit profit differs. At present, the numbers game is the major organized crime sector coming into obvious and immediate control of blacks and, to a lesser extent, Puerto Ricans. But the short period of control by blacks in this area seems certain to come to an early end. The reasons for its demise are precisely the same as those in an earlier period when the game's popularity attracted the interest and attention of Jewish and Italian crime syndicates. Now it is the government that seems to be attracted to the immense profits that accrue in this form of gambling. Over the last decade a number of forms of gambling have been legalized, largely as a means of gaining additional revenue for near-bankrupt cities and for state governments as well. In New York, for example, the first step was the establishment of a lottery, ostensibly as a means of raising money for education. The success of the lottery, and the lack of a public outcry against it as immoral or illicit, led to the legalizing of gambling on horse races through the establishment of the Off-Track Betting system. Here, however, the ploy of using a socially constructive cause—education—as the supposed recipient of the revenues from an activity that had always been condemned as illegal was no longer necessary. Off-Track Betting was proposed simply as a means of diverting profits from gambling away from organized crime and directly into the public coffers.

Following up on the success of the Off-Track Betting system, there are now proposals in a number of cities to legalize the numbers as well. Here, however, the conflict between community sentiments and a revenue-hungry government is already beginning to emerge. When Off-Track Betting was established in New York, a number of spokesmen for the black community indicated that now the white middle class had managed to legalize its own preferred form of gambling and even added the convenience of placing the betting parlors throughout the city, doing away with the need to even go to the track. The numbers, however, was a black thing and it remained illegal. Thus, they said, it was illegal for blacks to gamble but not for whites. Evidence in support of this belief was not difficult to come by. By 1972, for example, despite the fact that blacks constitute only about 12 percent of the nation's population, over 70 percent of the persons arrested on gambling charges nationwide were blacks.[6] There are a number of reasons for this, in addition to the common problem of the seeming propensity of police to arrest blacks with greater frequency than other, less visibly different ethnic groups. One is that while the numbers game is played in white areas, it is overwhelmingly a black form of gambling. As a result, even where the game is controlled by whites, the street operatives or runners are almost always black or Puerto Rican. The arrest chances in any form of organized crime are inversely related to status; that is, the lower one's status and the closer one is to the actual street transaction, the higher are the risks of arrest. A second reason, however, is related to the legalization of other forms of gambling, which has reduced the illegal operations that used to flourish in those forms of gambling and so made numbers games even more vulnerable to the police. The ghetto dweller's sense of white establishment hypocrisy in legalizing most other forms of gambling while continuing to condemn the numbers is not difficult to understand. On March 6, 1973, the New Jersey edition of *The New York Times* ran a full-column story reporting a police raid on a Puerto Rican numbers operation in East Harlem. The article described the raid by more than forty policemen and detectives, the arrest of thirteen people and the confiscation of thousands of dollars'

[6] Washington Lawyers Committee for Civil Rights Under Law, *Legalized Numbers in Washington: Implications with Respect to Law Enforcement, Civil Rights, and Control by the Community* (Washington, D.C.: Washington Lawyers Committee, 1973), pp. 4–5.

worth of equipment. At the bottom of the column, there appeared the black-bordered box that is now present in every issue of the paper:

> The winning New Jersey
> daily lottery number
> yesterday was:
> 25113

The movement to legalize the numbers seems assured of success within the next few years, but once again the black community sees the hands of whites reaching into the ghetto to pluck out a lucrative black enterprise. Arguing that the state lottery, which was supposed to provide revenue to improve schools, has not made a bit of difference in the quality of urban education, most blacks see the moves toward legalization of numbers as another white takeover, and they oppose governmental control of numbers.[7] The proposal being advanced by a number of blacks is for a system of community control through licensing or franchising arrangements and even the granting of amnesty to present black numbers operators, who could run the legal numbers games. The chances for such community control are minimal, and even in the unlikely event that it does occur, the important point here is that the numbers, the present base for black organized crime that has the greatest return, will certainly disappear through legalization in the near future.

Prostitution, while predominantly organized by black pimps and already operating outside the ghetto, does not actually offer a large enough financial base for further expansion, so among the present forms of organized crime loan sharking, the theft and sale of goods, and drugs remain as possibilities. Loan sharking and the sale of stolen

[7] In Elizabeth Reuss-Ianni's study of community attitudes toward organized crime (*A Community Self Study of Organized Crime,* Criminal Justice Coordinating Committee, City of New York, June, 1973), out of 1,229 respondents in Harlem, 87 percent were in favor of legalizing the numbers with community control (as opposed to governmental control), and 65 percent of the respondents reported they would not play the numbers if it was under government control.

goods do not seem possible as means of expansion outside the ghetto for black crime activists. It is difficult to imagine that most white Americans would deal with a black salesman pushing stolen goods and even more difficult to envision whites borrowing money from black loan sharks. Thus, while these forms of illicit enterprise may well expand in the ghetto, is not very probable that blacks can use them as a basis for extending their control over organized crime outside it.

The one sector of organized crime that does seem to present some possibility for black and Hispanic monopolization as a basis for expansion both within and outside the ghetto is the drug traffic. The experiences of blacks like Henry Marzette, "Hollywood Howard" Munger and others who tried to establish their own import connections were precursors of growing black control of the drug traffic within the ghetto. Is it possible that they will come to control or at least dominate drug traffic outside the ghetto as well? There are indications that this could come about. First, narcotics and the drug traffic have the same pattern of relationships that surrounded alcohol and bootlegging during the prohibition era. Admittedly, there is not as wide public acceptance of or demand for drugs, and social disapprobation is stronger than was true of alcohol, but these are only questions of scale. All of the other conditions prevail. Drugs are illegal but in demand. In order for drugs to be produced and wholesaled, some safe haven is necessary for the crime operatives, a place in which they can be assured of at least tacit protection from police by their neighbors. The present movement toward tougher drug laws and stiffer penalties will reduce competition in the drug traffic so that blacks can begin to supply drugs outside the ghetto. Here, as in prostitution, the willingness of disfranchised blacks to take risks that other groups need not take to escape poverty will combine with the color blindness of the needs of drug users to break down the racial barriers in loan sharking and the sale of stolen goods.

Finally, there is the possibility of using drug monies to corrupt police and other governmental officials without whose protection no form of organized crime could long endure. When the numbers are legalized, the major source of police graft will disappear, leaving drugs one of the few remaining sources for the payment of substantial sums to police.[8] All of the conditions for control of distribution within the ghetto are now operative and all that seems necessary is for blacks and Hispanics to take over the sources of supply and then move into extra-ghetto distribution. As we saw in looking at the East Harlem–Brooklyn Hispanic network, the Cuban connection is already developing these sources. Since we gathered these data in 1970–1971, the importance of cocaine as a street drug has grown tremendously and the Cuban connection has grown apace.[9] Both the police and the underworld, until recently preoccupied with the heroin trade, are now realizing the enormous profits that can be made in cocaine. Its growing popularity among the affluent drug public in penthouses and luxury apartments as well as on the street is equally obvious today.[10] If blacks, either in concert or in competition with Hispanic groups, can take over control of this area then they can develop a national and even international base for operations. Then, as happened among

[8] Late in 1973, the New York Police Department released the results of an internal study which indicated that complaints against New York City policemen alleging corruption had been substantially reduced in recent years in all areas except narcotics, where allegations of illegal involvement had increased. *The New York Times* (December 28, 1973), 1.

[9] cf. Thomas Plate, "Coke: The Big New Easy-Entrance Business," *New York Magazine* (November 5, 1973).

[10] The Knapp Commission on Police Corruption in New York City reported that "in the five plainclothes divisions where our investigations were concentrated we found a strikingly standardized pattern of corruption. Plainclothesmen, participating in what is known in police parlance as a 'pad,' collected regularly bi-weekly or monthly payments amounting to as much as $3,500 from each of the gambling establishments in the area under their jurisdiction and divided the take in equal shares. The monthly share per man (called the 'nut') ranged from $300 and $400 in midtown Manhattan to $1,500 in Harlem. When supervisors were involved they received a share and a half. . . . Corruption in narcotics enforcement lacked the organization of the gambling pads, but individual payments—known as 'scores'—were commonly received and could be staggering in amount. Our investigation, a concurrent probe by the State Investigation Commission and prosecutions by Federal and local authorities all revealed a pattern whereby corrupt officers customarily collected scores in substantial amounts from narcotics violators. These scores were either kept by the individual officer or shared with a partner and, perhaps, a superior officer. They ranged from minor shakedowns to payments of many thousands of dollars, the largest narcotics payoff uncovered in our investigation having been $80,000." *The Knapp Commission Report on Police Corruption* (New York: George Braziller, 1972), pp. 1–2.

the Italians, they can take their profits and reinvest them in other illicit enterprises. Whether they can also follow the pattern of Italians and use these same monies as a basis for movement into legitimate areas is, however, another question and one to which I shall return later.

The second condition for the elaboration of black and Hispanic organized crime networks into larger combines, the development of some organizing principle that will coalesce them as kinship did for the Italians, is also visible in what we have seen in the networks. Hispanics in organized crime—particularly the Cubans—may well adopt and adapt the existing "family" model of organization used by the Italians. As we have noted, the bonds of kinship seem stronger in the Hispanic networks we observed than they did among blacks. In fact, there is growing evidence, since the completion of the field study, that Hispanics are working in concert with Italian families to a much greater extent than is true of blacks. In September 1972, for example, Cubans operated the gambling concessions at the San Gennaro festival, New York's annual Italian street fair. Until 1972, the gambling tables and wheels had always been operated by Italians. Obviously some arrangement must have been made for the Italians to allow the Cubans to operate, even under franchise, in the heart of Little Italy. While there is a cultural base for a family type organization among Hispanics, our field observations suggests that this is not true among blacks. There is increasing evidence, however, that there are developments that could lead to a high degree of organization of black crime networks in the next decade, an organizational strength that could equal and even surpass that of the Italians.

If drugs should serve blacks as alcohol did Italians—as a source of extra-ghetto profit and power in crime—this system's growth would provide only the *source* for power and profit and still not provide an organizing motif among blacks. What could serve to strengthen the organization of black organized crime networks and, more important, bring them together under one code of behavior, however, is black militancy. Previous ethnic groups involved with organized crime—

the Irish, the Jews and the Italians—were desperately trying to become "Americans." Now, however, the blacks are beginning to come into importance in organized crime at a time when being black, being a brother or a sister, serves to create a *family-type structure* based upon militancy. Even the terminology—"brother," "sister" —expresses a sense of rights and responsibilities to the "family of blacks." This militancy, then, might be strong enough to provide the necessary cement. More important, blacks involved in organized crime may rightfully feel themselves bound together by the oppressiveness of the system, which rejects their attempts at social and political mobility. Thus, during this period when much of black power is negative power—that is, demanded and given out of fear— banding together to beat the system by any means may serve as a powerful incentive and organizer.

There are a number of sources from which this militancy may develop. One is the black community itself, which sees the black crime activist as at once the victim and the protagonist of the white power structure. Patronage, acceptance and admiration toward black and Puerto Rican organized criminals define the attitudes of many of the blacks and Puerto Ricans we spoke with. The reasons are not difficult to find: black crime activists are "making it"—in spite of and in conflict with an oppressive white establishment. Also, the activities they engage in—gambling, boosting and fencing, prostitution and loan sharking—are not considered socially harmful by many ghetto dwellers or, indeed, by many nonghetto dwellers either. Community attitudes toward black crime activists change sharply, however, when the drug problem is discussed but black solidarity is even apparent here. The narcotics trafficker is universally detested in the ghetto. And yet the local pusher, even though he is black or Puerto Rican (perhaps because he is black or Puerto Rican), is often not held responsible for the problem of drug addiction. The community's attitude toward the drug pusher is ambiguous. On the one hand, he is a visible symbol of the narcotics traffic and as such becomes an easy target for verbal, sometimes physical abuse. People living in the community, overwhelmed by the magnitude of the drug problem and not knowing how to deal with it, identify the problem with the pusher. The pusher comes to represent the narcotics problem and the shame and fear community residents feel about drugs. At the same time, community residents assign the responsibility for widespread drug addiction to forces operating on the community from the *outside*. A conspiracy theory of ghetto drug abuse is widely held in the black and Puerto Rican communities. According to community residents, the widespread use of drugs in the ghetto is the result of a white establishment plot to kill off black and Puerto Rican youths by allowing or even encouraging drugs in their areas. The role of Italian-American criminal syndicates in narcotics importing and sale is also widely accepted in the ghetto. Community people believe it is Italian-Americans, not blacks and Hispanics, who profit most from the drug trade. Again, this belief mitigates the community's attitude toward the local pusher.

As one observes the streets in the ghetto it is obvious that a fair number of the brightest young men in black and Puerto Rican communities do go into organized crime and that a number of the wealthiest and best-known men in these communities are actively involved in organized crime. Community respect for black and Puerto Rican organized crime activists is high, extending even to those involved in narcotics operations, just because of their success. Thus, not only does the street society serve as a locus of recruitment into organized crime but, on those same streets, the message of militancy encompasses the crime activist as well as the noncriminal because both are considered victims of white oppression. The message is reinforced in the prison courts we examined, which, because of the informal policy of racial segregation, have made militancy a rallying point for prisoners.

Why are blacks and Puerto Ricans sympathetic to, and even envious of, the blacks and Puerto Ricans who have achieved success in organized crime? First of all, organized crime is accurately viewed by them in many ways as merely one end of the American business and industrial structure and, as such, is viewed more as a business venture than as a moral evil. Although organized crime is an illicit enterprise, it follows many of the same rules as the American business

system. Ghetto dwellers view organized crime from the same perspective many Americans adopt when they regard the American system of
business enterprise. That is, they envy it and criticize it at the same
time. The line between sharp business practice or successful political
machination and crime is thin and can scarcely be distinguished by
many Americans.

It is poverty and powerlessness that provide the moral climate
leading to acceptance of organized criminal activities in the ghetto.
Like most Americans living in our consumer society, ghetto dwellers
are hungry for money and for the goods and services it can procure.
They have accepted the American achievement model of striving for
success and security. Yet they are cut off from many legitimate ways
of obtaining financial security, and, at the same time, they have
fewer ways than white Americans to achieve the psychological security that can reduce the incidence of crime. When a man is financially secure, is happy and secure in his work, has a stable family life
and lives in a stable community, he has little reason to consider
criminal activity as a vocational possibility. But blacks and Puerto
Ricans like other ethnics before them see organized crime as one of the
few routes to success, to financial and thus psychological security,
open to them. In every society, criminals tend to develop when social
conditions seem to offer no other way of escaping bondage. Poverty
and powerlessness are at the root of both community acceptance of
organized crime and recruitment into its networks. Conditions of
poverty also nurture community desires for the services organized
criminal operations provide. Escapism accounts in part for both widespread drug use and numbers gambling; the resentment poverty and
powerlessness brings in the subordinated population makes drugs
and gambling attractive as mechanisms of rebellion. Organized crime
is esteemed for the very reason that society outlaws it.

It is important to note in this context of ethnic succession that none
of these characteristics of or attitudes toward organized crime is cul-
ture-bound: the structures of poverty and powerlessness, rather than
the structures of the black and Puerto Rican cultures, seem most
responsible. It is probable that certain subcultures are more prone to
certain kinds of specific behavior as a result of the normative struc-

ture of those cultures. As we observed among the Italian-Americans, for example, the cultural model provided by Mafia and other secret criminal organizations in southern Italy led to a high degree of organizational development in the criminal syndicates operating in the United States. Certainly if there is a movement toward higher organization within black and Puerto Rican networks, this movement will respond to the culture imperatives of those groups. This, however, is very different from a cultural propensity toward organized crime. Organized crime involves a calculated pattern of offense to one or more of a culture's norms. Its presence is perhaps predictable whenever one culture in a dominating way holds such norms over the heads of a lively and energetic dominated subculture. In such a situation, organized crime will probably persist until an adequate degree of assimilation and accommodation takes place. In effect I am suggesting that organized crime results from a conflict of cultures and I am further hypothesizing that organized crime as we know it in the United States requires an underclass of minority status ethnics in order to be operative.

There seems to be little question that assimilation and accommodation with the larger American societies are the chief aims of black and Puerto Rican organized crime activists. This is not to suggest that they are not criminals and that they are not involved in illegal activities but rather that, as was true of the Italians, the Jews and the Irish before them, the greater motivation is to achieve social, occupational and residential mobility. Even while they themselves might never articulate such aims, even when their goals are limited by the scope of their own neighborhood, nevertheless they still exhibit single-minded striving for the material wealth and social security that motivates others in society as well. If Luis Santos or Harold Robinson or Bro Squires cannot themselves quite imagine movement toward respectability and security, then certainly they want this for their children and their children's children.

Another source of militancy in crime is the prison, where, as we have seen, the predominantly black inmate population is becoming increasingly politicized—not only in search of improved prison conditions but against racist social conditions outside the walls as well.

This growing protest is marked by a good deal of self-education in political and revolutionary literature, black-history study groups and a new sense of identity as blacks. Thus, in the prisons, where institutional racism brings blacks together in the courts, the lessons of the street are reinforced and the crime activist-become-revolutionary is a growing pattern. As often happens, the image becomes part of the popular culture as well and the new cinema crime heroes—*Shaft, Superfly* and a growing host of others—are as militantly black as they are violently criminal.

Then there are the black revolutionaries themselves; groups ranging from the Muslims and Panthers to the Black Liberation Army are becoming increasingly paramilitary in structure and in the use of uniforms and arms as well as in their aims. Drawn from the same ghetto street society as the black crime activists, they are also the frequent targets of police harassment and often view themselves as essentially defense organizations against white oppression and open hostility. It is not too improbable to imagine that whether on the streets or in the prisons, there will be increasing contact between militant crime activists and revolutionaries. This becomes particularly probable when one assumes, as we must, that unlike previous generations of immigrants who used organized crime as a means of escaping the slum and gaining some access to social mobility, blacks will very probably not be permitted to take that route. Cut off from the "normal" process of transition into the legitimate world, black organized crime activists could become increasingly militant and even revolutionary and the vast sums that accrue from organized crime could be diverted to financing liberation movements. It might be well, at this point, to remember Rolando Solis' observation about the penchant of Cuban crime activists for purchasing military supplies to "liberate" their homeland.

Eventually, all these factors could serve to bring together the presently scattered black organized crime networks into a classical Mafia. Eric J. Hobsbawm, the eminent British social historian, has studied Mafia not as a specific organization but as a universal code of behavior that develops in societies lacking a strong social order and in which an oppressed group within that society sees the authorities as wholly or partly hostile and unresponsive to their needs. He has described Mafia in Sicily and elsewhere as a form of *social banditry* that seeks to overcome oppression and poverty through collective rebellion against real or imagined oppressors, which in time develops into "an institutionalized system of a law outside the official law." [11] While Hobsbawm was studying and so speaking primarily of peasant rebels who resort to social banditry as a reformist movement, the characteristics he cites are easily recognizable in the urban social banditry that could form among blacks. Mafia is, first and foremost, a form of social protest that can, like the classical Mafia in Sicily and its counterpart among the earlier Italian immigrants to the United States, use crime as a weapon of protest.[12] This protest is expressed in a general attitude toward the law that tends to develop where that law is considered unresponsive or hostile and alien to the culture of the rebellious group, and so they develop their own code of rules to regulate and regularize relationships between and among themselves and in their relationship with the larger society. In this sense, Mafia becomes a network of gangs held together by a common code. Hobsbawm also points out that such "Mafias" tend to develop in societies where there is not an effective social order and where Mafia provides a parallel machine of law and organized power that in time, so far as the people in the areas under its influence are concerned, becomes the only effective law and power.[13] Each of these conditions exists in black ghettos today, and the coalescence of the presently scattered networks into a black Mafia held together by a rudimentary ideology of black power is a distinct possibility within this decade. The emerging militancy of the black Mafia may provide an even more cohesive organizing principle for blacks than kinship was for the Italians and may well develop into a revolutionary social movement by joining with other militant aspirations and groups. Kinship-based clannishness comes out of a rural primitive tradition of bonding that cannot resist the social forces of the city and cannot

[11] Eric J. Hobsbawm, *Primitive Rebels* (New York: Norton, 1959), pp. 5–6.
[12] See Francis A. J. Ianni, *A Family Business: Kinship and Social Control in Organized Crime* (New York: Russell Sage–Basic Books, 1972), pp. 53–54.
[13] Hobsbawm, *op. cit.,* p. 35.

support it. Militancy, however, does have an urban base, and while social and economic mobility of Italians destroyed the "family structure," the resistance to such mobility on the part of blacks will serve to reinforce their militant base in the ghetto. The new black mafioso will, in fact, be an urban social bandit.

Finally, there is the condition of better access to political power and the ability to corrupt it as a prior factor in the elaboration and extension of black organized crime outside the confines of the ghetto. The evidence here is more difficult to deal with because it is, to some extent, contradictory. On the one hand, it is well established in the social history of the city that ethnic groups succeed to power in politics as they do in crime and that the two forms of mobility are often connected. There is evidence that blacks are moving ahead in politics in the large urban areas just as they are in organized crime. What is less evident is that the necessary connections between politics and its corruptability and black movement in organized crime will coincide. It is a maxim in the underworld that graft and corruption are color-blind and that the police and politicians will take graft regardless of the color of the hand that delivers it. It is difficult to imagine, however, that blacks will be able to insinuate themselves into the kinds of social relationships with white politicians that are the environment within which deals are made, bribes are offered or sought, and protection developed. Again, the black movement in both politics and crime, like so many other processes of social advancement among them, comes at a time when much of the power and profit has already been milked from the system by the groups that preceded them. The rampant corruption of our political system, reaching up to and including the White House, could raise the costs and risks of corruption to a prohibitive point. This already seems to be the case in New York City, where the revelations of the Knapp Commission on bribe taking by the police seems to have *doubled* the costs of bribery in just one year's time.[14]

While the growth of a black Mafia is fairly well known or at least perceived in black and Puerto Rican neighborhoods, it would not be

[14] *The New York Times,* September 24, 1973, p. 36.

unfair to say that, aside from the occasional newspaper headlines, there is little public knowledge that it is going on. To judge from its actions, the greater society seems to consider black and Puerto Rican organized crime as one of the small prices it must pay for the continuance of the many psychological and economic comforts that accrue from the existence of an ethnic underclass. Indeed, when measured against the cost of eliminating such crime, the costs are small. The most visible cost—from the thefts and muggings of narcotics addicts—touch only a few people in the large urban areas. In many respects there is also a continuation of that traditional attitude of the criminal justice system: so long as ghetto dwellers keep their crimes within the ghetto and do not spill outside, leave them to themselves. It is when the muggings and the robberies reach the nonghetto areas that there is a strong outcry. This attitude, which has traditionally been part of our law enforcement value system, allows organized crime to thrive within the ghetto. Once the organized crime networks find profitable sources of revenue outside the ghetto, then the growing economic, political and social impact of organized crime becomes a matter of public interest and social policy. In the meantime, blacks and Hispanics must continue to face the same basic dilemma that confounded earlier generations of Irish, Jews and Italians: *How do you escape poverty through socially approved routes when such routes are closed off from the ghetto?* Crime resolves the dilemma because it provides a quick if perilous route out.

Some Implications for Social Policy

There are, I believe, a number of important implications of this study for the criminal justice system. Generally, I would classify them into two broad categories. One of these grows out of the research methods we have used. This is our second major study using anthropological field work techniques to research organized crime in the community where it operates. As a result of this experience we are convinced that looking at organized crime as an institution in American society is an important and promising approach to studying, understanding and eventually controlling organized crime in the United States. There is now a beginning appreciation in the criminal justice system that interdiction and apprehension of individual organized crime figures is a necessary but insufficient method of organized crime control. Yet both research and intelligence operations related to organized crime remain unchanged and there also remains an overemphasis on the guillotine approach: if we knock off the head, the rest of the organization will fall apart. We have been knocking heads off with some frequency recently, but as I pointed out in the opening pages of this book, organized crime not only survives but seems to be thriving. The reason, of course, is that organized crime groups do not commit the kinds of crimes that the police attempt to solve. Strategies developed for the control of street crime are unsuccessful in organized crime because they are oriented toward criminal acts rather than these transactive group processes. In organized crime, it is the combination of capital, corruption and coercion that produces results. Law enforcement agencies have committed a major portion of their organized crime efforts in the apprehension of individual mobsters with little obvious payoff, a fact that is not lost on the public in general and the ghetto dweller in particular. There is now abundant evidence that organizational intelligence and analysis (rather than individual case development) could dramatically improve the ability of the criminal justice system to identify the social, cultural, political and economic factors that allow organized crime to develop and prosper and that there exists within the social sciences both the methodology and the manpower to develop such an approach. But a first requirement is an understanding that organized crime is a feature of the social, economic and political structure of American society and that it can only be understood in those contexts.

The second, and I think major, implication of this study for the criminal justice system complements this approach of understanding organized crime as an organizational entity that is symbiotically rather than parasitically associated with American society. If we are to control and hopefully eradicate organized crime, there must be a reconnection between the community and the criminal justice system and some attempt must be made to influence and refocus our social attitudes toward *prevention* of organized crime by attacking the social, political and economic problems that produce the conditions under which organized crime develops.

We are a society made up of a number of subcultures, which hold different values and attitudes toward proper behavior. These differences are sometimes significant and they mold the behavior of the individuals who make up the subcultures. This cultural pluralism produces many benefits for our society but it also makes the task of law enactment and enforcement a complex one. We are all aware that the law changes more slowly than public morals and that often it represents an antedated perspective on social behavior. It is in this context that organized crime develops when the wants and desires of a people, or some large segment of them, for goods or services are thwarted by legal sanctions against such felt needs. Where group attitudes and enacted law coincide, the disparity between the criminal justice system and the community is minimal; where they do not, the tension between the two is mutually dysfunctional. Organized crime could not survive without corruption in government and industry, nor could it thrive without community support. The reconnection of the community and the criminal justice system is the essential first step in the development of a sound social policy toward organized crime.

APPENDICES

A. A NOTE ON THE METHODS USED
IN THIS STUDY

In the final chapter of *A Family Business,* the book reporting on my study of the Lupollo organized crime family, I explained how my interest in the structure and function of secret societies and in the process of acculturation led rather naturally to the study of organized crime in America.[1] I also explained the various research techniques I used and how I analyzed the data, and, since it was a participant observation study, I spent some time describing my own background, training and experience. In the two years since that book appeared, organized crime has become a major cultural phenomenon as well as a social issue in American life. Any number of films and books punctuated by real-life gangland killings have reawakened the popular view of organized crime as a romantic, if deadly, ghetto western. But organized crime is more than that. It is an integral part of the American social system, involving a public that demands illicit goods and services, corrupt officials, and organized groups of ghettoized crime activists who supply the public demand while paying tribute to the corrupt officials. Social history indicates that every major ethnic group—the Irish, Jews, Italians and, most recently, blacks and Hispanics—has faced the basic dilemma pointed out in the final chapter of the present book: *How can a ghetto dweller escape poverty by socially approved routes when such routes are often foreign to ghetto life?* Organized crime frequently resolves that dilemma by providing a quick if perilous way out.

[1] Ianni, Francis A. J., *A Family Business: Kinship and Social Control in Organized Crime.* (New York: Russell Sage–Basic Books, 1972).

Although this process has been known to criminologists for some time, the knowledge has never had any effect on law enforcement programs. There are a number of reasons for this seeming oversight. To some extent it results from the insistence of many law enforcement officials that organized crime is really an Italian import and that Mafia and organized crime are one and the same thing in America. These same officials also maintain that at the heart of organized crime is a vast conspiracy, a conscious plot on the part of these same *mafiosi* to infiltrate and corrupt American government and legitimate business for their own illicit ends. But probably the most important reason is that no one has ever systematically and seriously studied organized crime as a way of life in America. There have been many studies of organized crime but inevitably they have drawn their information from the files of government law enforcement agencies. These files, however, were never intended as research sources; they are police intelligence files focusing on the types of information necessary to seek indictments and hopefully obtain convictions of individual criminals. They tell little about how crime activists organize themselves and nothing of the relationship between organized crime and other sectors of American society. As a result, law enforcement agencies continue to seek out individual organized crime figures in much the same way that they seek out perpetrators of street crime. Yet organized crime is different from street crime because it *is* organized, and understanding how it is organized and how it relates to American society is critical to the development of a sound national strategy for prevention and control. Donald Cressey, the criminologist who has frequently been a consultant on organized crime for law enforcement agencies and the Congress, has said that this reliance on law enforcement information and the absence of any research data on how organized crime and criminals operate is the principal handicap to understanding and controlling organized crime.

There are a number of obvious reasons why social scientists have not gone out into the field to study organized crime. Research in the field, out among organized criminal bands, is both more difficult and more hazardous than research in the file rooms of the Justice Department. As Cressey points out, informants are not readily available and observing the interaction of criminals with each other is no easy task. Even the clients or victims of organized crime are reticent.[2] These problems have always kept us from asking the right questions about organized crime in the only place where we can find the real answers: out in the world of organized crime among its producers, marketers and consumers.

Late in 1967, Francesco Cerase, an Italian sociologist, Elizabeth Reuss, an American anthropologist, and I decided to do just that and began a two-year field study of criminal syndicates in Italy and in the United States. Our immediate interest was in observing one or more Italian-American organized crime families to see if we could determine how they are organized, what holds them together and how they relate to the communities in which they operate and to American society. Since government reports invariably point to some link between crime families in this country and the Sicilian Mafia, we wanted to look at Mafia in Sicily as well and then try to determine what is "Italian" and what "American" about organized crime here. Cerase, Reuss and I spent time in Italy studying Mafia and other secret criminal societies in the south of Italy. My major task, however, was to observe behavior and social relationships in an Italian-American crime family.

We assumed from the beginning that organized crime families here and in Sicily behaved as a group in pretty much the same way as other social groups do: seeking common goals, making rules to guide members' behavior, rewarding those who follow and punishing those who disobey these rules. Obviously some of the methods they use to attain those goals are defined as illegal by the larger society, but then crime families such as the Lupollos learn some of their behavior, derive some of their motives and judge some of their actions by a different set of standards and so a different code of rules than most other Americans do. It has always seemed to me that the key to understanding how the Lupollos or any other group functions is to learn

[2] Donald R. Cressey, "Methodological Problems in the Study of Organized Crime as a Social Problem," *The Annals: Combating Crime,* 374 (November 1967), p. 109.

what those standards are and what rules they produce, where the rules come from and how they are enforced, and how members relate to each other and to outsiders. Any organization, whether criminal or legitimate, is, in short, really organized by a code of behavior, a structured set of rules of the game that regulate and regularize all social action within that organization. I understand what any organization is like far better if I know the rules by which its members live than I do from some elaborate organization chart that describes how the organization is supposed to be structured but tells me little about how it operates. And the best way to learn what those rules are, how they are made, which ones are followed and which ignored and how they are changed over time is to observe them in day-to-day operation. What we were really interested in learning from studying the Lupollos were some beginning answers to the illusive question "What is the code of rules shared by members of Italian-American organized crime families and how do their members learn to play the game?"

Since we assumed that the Lupollos operated by rules just as other groups do, we planned to learn what those rules were and how they were enforced through the same technique of participant observation —living among a group of people and observing and recording what they say and do—as we had used in past studies of groups ranging from African tribesmen to American schoolchildren. The process is not an elaborate one but it is exacting and time consuming; we attempt to learn the rules that structure and motivate behavior by observing how members of groups behave toward each other and listening to their own explanations for that behavior. We record all of this as accurately as we can and hope to approximate the reality the natives see and feel rather than impose our own. To really understand the culture and behavior of a people, it is necessary to live among them to learn their language and their customs, to understand their problems and their aspirations and to record carefully all that you see and hear. This is what we did in Sicily and among the Lupollos here in the United States.

We think that we learned a great deal about the structure and characteristics of Italian-American organized crime families and something about organized crime as a way of life in the United States by studying the Lupollos. In Italy we learned that whatever else they may be—social bandits or criminal bands—secret criminal societies such as the Mafia are clans, associated groups of families tied together for mutual protection and gain. Throughout Italy, but particularly in the south, from which the Lupollos and virtually every other Italian-American known to be involved in organized crime originates, the family is the only viable social unit. Neither the Church or the state has ever successfully challenged that supremacy. The family demand's each man's first loyalty and within it he practices all of the virtue and self-sacrifice that other men save for religious faith or patriotism. This rustic code dominates all social relations and behavior in the south; breaking the laws of the state or even of the Church is no great matter, just keep the laws of the family. Favors within and between families become obligations, and wrongs against any member of the family become debts that demand redress by any other member of that family: *"Si moru mi voricu; si campu t'allampu* ("If you kill me they will bury me; if I live, I will kill you"). It is this family-oriented code of rules and the consequent kinship model of organization that ties Mafia to the Sicilian social structure and has underwritten its survival over the centuries.

In this country we found that this same kinship model of organization structures the Lupollo "family." They have used this traditional Mafia model of organization to establish and maintain an intricate network of legal and illegal activities now worth over $30 million. The most obvious manifestation of this heritage and the Lupollos' secret of success is the close relationship between family and business. They are practically synonymous. The Lupollo family business, both legal and illegal, is controlled by a managerial cadre of fifteen men, all related by blood or marriage. All members of the central group are involved in all of the businesses and business relationships mirror family relationships. Joe Lupollo heads the family and he heads the business. Those with the most power in the business are those who are most closely related to Joe.

This same basic pattern of kinship organization occurs in every major Italian-American syndicate family we have looked at in this country. Not only are individuals within families related, there is widespread intermarriage among families throughout the country. Of the more than sixty "Mafia bosses" identified as participants in the famous Appalachian meeting in November 1957, for example, over half were related by blood or marriage and the percentage goes up dramatically if godparenthood is included as a kin relationship.

It is these bonds of kinship and the rules of behavior that grow out of them—not crime or some network of conspiracy—that tie the Lupollos and other Italian-American crime families together and to each other. Certainly the Lupollos are involved in criminal activity and just as certainly they conspire in order to conduct those enterprises, but what has made the Lupollos such a formidable group is the strength of their bonds to each other. Over the past seventy years they have become intricately bound to one another through a network of marriage ties and ritual kin associations so that they and other organized crime families have formed their own social system structured and regulated by the mutual obligations and rights of kindred. It is impossible to understand the nature and character of the Italian-American period in American organized crime without first understanding this pattern of organization and the rules that activate and sustain it. Yet as the inevitable force of assimilation into American society erodes the southern Italian values that have nurtured and sustained familialism among Italian-Americans, defections from the family are inevitable. Among the Lupollos, all male members of the first and second generations went into the family business and were involved in its illegal as well as legal enterprises. By the third generation, a number of the sons entered independent business and professional fields. Now, as I mentioned at the outset, in the fourth generation only four out of twenty-seven males are involved in the family business organization. The rest are doctors, lawyers or college teachers or run their own businesses. The movement of the younger generation of the four lineages out of the family business supports the point that, for Italian-Americans as for previous ethnic groups, organized crime has been a way station on the road to ultimately respectable roles in American society. If the Lupollo family is a fair example, and comparative studies we have done with similar crime families convince us that it is, it is predictable that fewer and fewer young Italian-Americans will be recruited into criminal syndicates of the future.

What we learned about and from the Lupollos presents a totally different picture of how Italian-American crime families are organized and a new perspective on what Mafia is and isn't in the United States. This in itself was an important contribution of the research and a strong endorsement of the use of anthropological field methods in the study of contemporary social problems. But as the research progressed, I began to sense that we were learning a good deal about organized crime as an aspect of American society as well. When I talked to "Uncle Phil" or other Lupollos about their early years it was obvious that they had learned the basic patterns of the operation from the Jews who preceded them just as they were now, no matter how grudgingly, teaching the blacks and Puerto Ricans who will replace them.

In the introduction to this book, I explained how my field experience with the Lupollos led me on to examine emerging patterns of organization among black and Hispanic crime activists and how they relate to society and to their communities. I also explained some of the differences between this work and the Lupollo study, some of which need elaboration here. The first and most fundamental problem was to identify the unit of analysis in black and Hispanic organized crime. There has been within the social sciences a growing tradition of comparative examination of total institutions. Any number of such institutions—armies, asylums, concentration camps, prisons—have been studied as unique social worlds which present distinctive sets of values, norms, sanctions and roles to those within their social boundaries. In studying organized crime, however, I have always had some difficulty in determining the totality of the institution involved. As I point out with some frequency throughout this book, standard definitions of organized crime, which focus on the criminals themselves while ignoring their clients and protectors, lose the total institutional context which is critical to understanding how any social system operates. My solution has been to look for definition in the *social boundaries* of organized crime rather than in the behavioral and cultural "stuff" enclosed within those boundaries. Thus I have tended to look at ground-level behavior to determine whom the known members of organized crime groups identify as insiders and outsiders; to find out what shared understandings operate among the insiders; and then to attempt to deduce the code of rules which indicates to the insiders that they are fundamentally playing the same game. Once these networks are identified, it should then be possible to ascertain how they are articulated and how they build into a total institution. How such boundaries are first established and then maintained is of more than academic interest. There are important social uses in identifying the prison "court" or the childhood gang as a bounded network within which criteria for judgments of value and performance may be developed. If these networks now operate as conduits through which their members acquire a socially dysfunctional construct of reality, there is no reason why they could not be put to socially constructive educational uses as well.

While I did have the difficulty of identifying the total institutional context of organized crime in studying the Lupollos, I at least knew what the ground-level unit of analysis was. As I have said, I already knew who and what the Lupollos were, who was in the family and who was not. In the present study, however, I have had to construct the unit of analysis, and so, as I have explained, I used network charting as a boundary-setting device.

In effect, we used this technique as a means of setting up parameters or boundaries so that we could delimit a particular group of people for observation. Since we did not have an established group structure to work within, we used network charts as a basis for forming quasi-groups. The way in which we did this was to gather data on the everyday life of the people who were involved in organized crime activities in the various areas of the ghettos we were observing and to attempt wherever possible to describe as much of the total social-behavioral field of that world as we could.

Then, through constant analysis of these reports, we began sketching out patterns of relationship, the kinds of situations under which they emerged, the regularity of interaction, closeness of ties and how people entered and left the network. As I mentioned earlier, we used these to build the network charts. Then by using these charts as boundary-setting devices—that is, as a means of focusing in on a particular net of relationships—we went back into the field and started to identify the dyadic contracts—the specific patterns of rights and obligations that existed between any two people connected in a network chart—that related people to each other. We then proceeded to build up from these dyadic contracts a pattern of social relations sets in the network—patterns of relationships that involved more than two people—until we had filled in the entire network. It was from these completed charts that we began the process of comparing the various networks we constructed to look for patterns of interaction that seemed to come up in the various networks with some frequency. It was out of these comparisons that we developed tentative models of black and Hispanic crime networks and some beginning theory on ethnic succession in organized crime by putting our questions to this model.

The foundation for all anthropological field work lies in the complex relationship between the anthropologist and his informants. His task and his skill are in describing the social behavior of a people as exactly, as meaningfully and as intelligibly as possible. To do so requires that he understand their life style in a way that approaches their own definition of reality. As a result, it is essential that he establish a really satisfactory and amicable relationship with the people among whom he is going to live. All of these conditions were in my favor when I studied the Lupollos. I shared their ethnicity, spoke their language and knew them even before I began the study. None of this was true in the new study.

Although finding and recruiting the field assistants was the first and most monumental problem, others were to come up constantly. My first meeting with the group lasted five hours, most of which was spent in discussing the ethics of what they (and I) would be doing, since, I explained, we would be working as a team. The first question they asked was the obvious one: why did I want this information and what did I intend to do with it? I explained that as a social scientist I was interested in organized crime as a social phenomenon in America and not in apprehending individual crime activists or exposing any group. I explained the concept of ethnic succession in organized crime and they began to give me examples of its reality out in the streets, and we spoke at some length about the need for looking at organized crime as it functions in the community and not as it is popularly portrayed. Their role would be to observe behavior and social relations in organized crime activities in their neighborhoods and to record their observations on life style, individual behavior and people in interaction with each other. Whenever possible—and we agreed that it would probably not be very often—they would interview crime activists about their life experiences, their social attitudes and any other information they could obtain. In some cases, particularly those that dealt with early experiences of childhood gangs or reports of prison experience and its relationship to organized crime, the field assistants reported on their own lives in crime. Where the information I report here is autobiographical by one or more of the field assistants I have indicated it as part of the narrative.

My own role would be to train the assistants in the skills necessary to gather information in the field, to do whatever observing and interviewing I could and then to work with them in putting the information they were gathering into some coherent form. Finally, after all of the data had been gathered and we had jointly discussed what it meant, it would be my responsibility to try to analyze the data and fit them into answers to the questions we were posing.

After considerable discussion, which included a long description on my part of my credentials and previous research (the Lupollo study helped rather than hindered their acceptance of me), we struck a bargain. They were willing to be informants in the anthropological but not in the police sense. They would gather the information I required if I would assure them that there was no way in which the individual crime activists they described or interviewed could be identified. We worked out at that meeting a system in which they would report information on individuals without naming them. Each field informant was given a code letter and he then would use that code letter and number sequentially for each person he described as involved in his area. Field assistant A, for example, would identify the first person he described as A-1, the second as A-2 and so on. I then assigned pseudonyms to each person described or reported on and we kept a running record of what information we had on each person. This allowed me to ask specific questions about particular people who seemed important or interesting without knowing their real names. The field informants were paid for the time they spent observing and recording and for attendance at group meetings, which were held once a week.

The field assistants were trained for two weeks in observation and recording techniques in group sessions. During these training sessions they carried out actual field assignments and the information they gathered was used to identify those areas of the city where the research could be conducted and to develop a basic set of items to look at, which each field assistant would use to ensure that we were getting comparable data. During the training period one field assistant quit and I had to drop another because he missed three of the training sessions in a row. In our group meetings we would discuss any problems they had encountered during the previous week. They experienced all of the problems that any field researcher encounters—some people refused to talk to them and some were openly hostile, they forgot to record some piece of information and so an hour or more of work was useless, the tape recorder didn't work properly and so an hour of field notes was lost to us—but these were eventually resolved. Because of who they were and what they were doing, however, the field assistants encountered some special problems. On the fourth day of the training session, Al, a Puerto Rican field assistant, announced that he was quitting. When I asked him why, he explained that his parole officer had told him that his field work was a violation of his parole. Al was dumbfounded since the parole officer had been encouraging him to get a job, improve his education and learn some specialized skills, and it seemed to him that he was doing all of these in the research project. The parole officer went on to explain that the conditions of parole specifically require that parolees should avoid all contact with known criminals and here Al was consciously seeking out criminals to talk with every day. Al was adamant in his decision to quit and as we all discussed the problem it became obvious that the other field assistants had no intention of continuing either. We adjourned the meeting with the decision to meet three days later to see if I could convince the parole authorities to exempt the field assistants because of the importance of the research they were doing. As he left the room, Al suggested that maybe I should talk to the Lupollos since they probably had some contacts with the parole authorities and they could maybe use that influence to our advantage.

I didn't call the Lupollos but I did contact the office of the Commissioner of Corrections for New York in Albany and explained my plight to his deputy. He was sympathetic and I sent him a copy of the original proposal for the study and a copy of the book we had done on the Lupollos. I never heard from him again but four days later all of the field assistants were back at work and the incident was never mentioned again.

Other problems came up from time to time. Sandy, one of the black field assistants, had his tape recorder stolen twice by his brother, who was a junkie. One of the other black field assistants began turning in recorded field notes that were bizarre, containing characters who were from other planets and situations that included bloody, almost ghastly, acts of violence. I asked him to remain after one of our group sessions and began to ask him about the field notes. His attitude was openly belligerent, almost threatening, and it was soon obvious to me that he was back on drugs. Uncertain as to what to do and, frankly, somewhat apprehensive about what he might do, I decided to bring the issue up with the entire group. At the next training session, at which he was present, I went over his last set of field notes, indicating that while there was some obviously valuable information in them, the fantasies and distortions made them useless since I now had no confidence in my ability to separate fact from fiction in his notes. At first the group was silent but then the silence was followed by a few statements in his defense; he was one of them and I was not and the meeting began to get out of hand as some of the issues I thought we had resolved earlier began to resurface. Had I not told them that one of the things I would do for them in exchange for their help would be to train them as field assistants and to help wherever I could with any problems? Yet when one of them had missed three training sessions I had peremptorily dropped him without really looking into why he had missed the sessions. Now here I was again making a judgment and ready to take an action without really understanding what the life of an ex-con was all about. Were we or were we not working as a team? Defensive now, I tried to explain that I *had* talked to the absentee; he had explained that he had another job and, when I said that the research required full-time attention, he had agreed that this would be impossible and seemed to accept the fact that he couldn't continue. Then, at the point when I was about to blurt out that the real problem *was* apparent to me and that I knew this guy was back on drugs, Budha, one of the black field assistants who had gradually been emerging as a leader in the group, finally suggested that perhaps I should leave the room while they rapped about "the crisis." I left, discouraged, certain that it was all over and despairing of ever being able to find and train a new staff. About forty-five minutes later I could stand it no longer and I returned to the seminar room to find the drug user gone but the others still there. They never explained to me what had happened and I did not ask, but after some discussion we agreed that we should destroy all of his field notes but pay him for the rest of the week. On Friday, which was the day on which the field assistants turned in their field notes and picked up their money and more recording tape, he appeared with the rest, picked up his pay and turned in his tape recorder. I never saw or heard of him again. From that point on, I always made certain that I honored my rather cavalier statement about our being a team and discussed with them, or at least with Budha, who now was their spokesman, any decisions that had to be made.

Then, in the middle of the first of our periods of field work, a black gunman shot and almost killed reputed Mafia boss Joe Colombo at an Italian-American civil rights rally. The police theory was that Joe

Gallo, Colombo's arch rival for control of the rackets in the Red Hook section of Brooklyn, was behind this shooting as the first step in a full-fledged gang war. The street talk was that Gallo had recruited blacks into his organization while he was in prison and that he was developing his own form of ethnic succession in organized crime by integrating them within his gang. This incident and its aftermath provided the basis for some interesting discussions with the field assistants but also created a major problem. Our two field assistants in Brooklyn reported that interviewing and observation there—particularly in Red Hook—were impossible. The place was swarming with police who were spying from rooftops, masquerading as postmen and hot dog vendors, making flash raids on known hangouts of crime activists and stopping anyone who had any criminal background. One of the field assistants reported that he had been stopped and rousted by the police four times while walking three blocks to buy a newspaper. No one in Brooklyn would talk to anybody about organized crime under these circumstances, and so we halted all field work there for a period of two weeks. At the end of the two weeks the tension seemed to have disappeared as quickly as it had come up and we had no trouble there after that.

Finally, there is the problem of credibility. A major question for me throughout the research, and one that must have struck the reader, is, given the nature of the research and means by which the data were gathered, how is it possible to assess the reliability or truth and the validity or accuracy of the information presented here. Reliability and validity are age-old problems in field research but they were particular problems here because we were using informants as observers so that data were always one step removed from my own control and experience. Our solution was to establish a standardized system of assessing both the validity of the data we were gathering and the reliability of the individuals who were gathering it. This system, which I had used previously in studying the Lupollos [3] is based upon separate judgments of how reliable each informant is and what evidence—documentation, my own checking

---

[3] Ianni, *op. cit.*, pp. 187–188.

out of the information, internal consistency and corroboration by other informants—there is that any particular piece of datum he is reporting is accurate or valid. In preparing the analyses upon which the descriptive material on crime networks is based, I did not use any information that did not pass the validity and reliability tests we established. In some of the chapters of this book in which I draw conclusions from what we found out about black and Puerto Rican organized crime, I included some quotations that did not pass our tests but which I feel shed particular light on some issue or question. Where I have done so, I have specifically cited my lack of certainty as to its reliability or validity.

B. NETWORK CHARTS AND
CASTS OF CHARACTERS

CENTRAL HARLEM NETWORK

CAST OF CHARACTERS

Reginald "Reggie" Martin, black male, twenty-eight years old, is a New York pimp. He lives in Harlem but his prostitutes work downtown.

Ginger Allen, white female, twenty-two years old, is a prostitute who works for Reggie Martin.

Debbie, white female, is a prostitute who was dropped from Reggie Martin's "stable" for using heroin.

Lucy Greer, deceased black female, was the prostitute who on account of her love for Reggie Martin first brought him into "the Life." She died of a drug overdose.

Patricia Quinn, white female, twenty-one years old, becomes one of Reggie Martin's prostitutes upon emerging from the Women's House of Detention.

Robert "Bobby Hassan" Lewis, black male, native of Detroit, is a Harlem street pusher and himself an addict.

James "Jimmy Brown" Mitchell, black male, is a large-scale Harlem narcotics dealer who operates boutiques on the side. He is a childhood friend of Reggie Martin.

Thomas Irwin, black male, forty-five years old, is a Harlem entrepreneur some of whose enterprises are legal and some illegal. He stumbled almost inadvertently into his illegal ventures.

Cleveland Dukes, black male, forty-four years old, is a heroin addict who "boosts" for Thomas Irwin. He is Elizabeth Dukes' husband.

350

CENTRAL HARLEM NETWORK

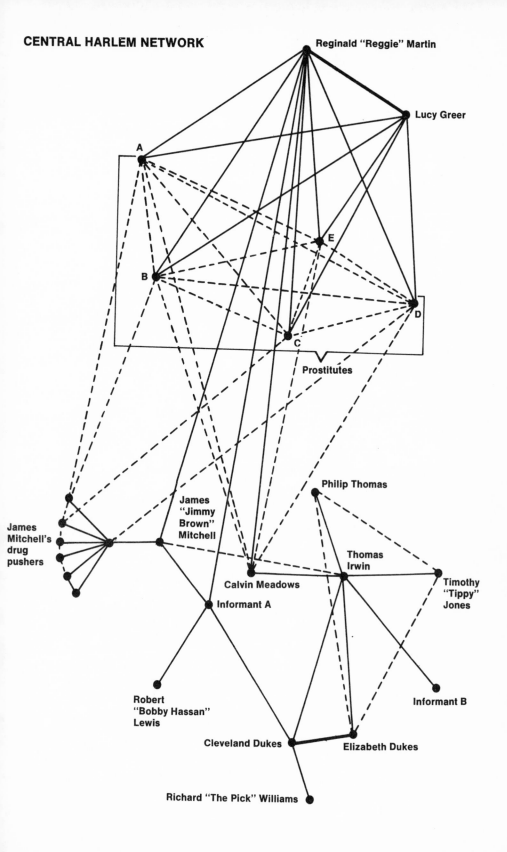

Reginald "Reggie" Martin

Lucy Greer

A

E

B

D

C

Prostitutes

Philip Thomas

James Mitchell's drug pushers

James "Jimmy Brown" Mitchell

Thomas Irwin

Calvin Meadows

Informant A

Timothy "Tippy" Jones

Robert "Bobby Hassan" Lewis

Informant B

Cleveland Dukes

Elizabeth Dukes

Richard "The Pick" Williams

Elizabeth Dukes, black female, forty-one years old, is a heroin addict who like her husband, Cleveland Dukes, "boosts" for Thomas Irwin.

Timothy "Tippy" Jones, black male, age thirty-seven, working with Cleveland and Elizabeth Dukes as partners, "boosts" for Thomas Irwin.

Calvin Meadows, black male, is the manager of a Harlem after-hours club owned by Thomas Irwin. He is a childhood friend of Reggie Martin.

Philip Thomas, black male, is the "booster" who first introduced Thomas Irwin to dealing in stolen merchandise.

Richard "The Pick" Williams, black male, owns a New York hardware store and will supply master keys to thieves.

PATERSON, NEW JERSEY NETWORK

CAST OF CHARACTERS

Joseph "Joe the Turk" Hajar, white male of Syrian extraction, dominated organized crime—the numbers, prostitution, loan sharking and finally, narcotics—in the Temple Hill section of Paterson, New Jersey, for many years.

Horace "Horse" Jackson, black male, is an employee of Joseph Hajar.

Albert Montgomery, black male, works for Joseph Hajar in Paterson as a numbers controller and as a supervisor of Hajar's loan sharking operation.

Tommy Washington, black male, is a barkeeper in a Paterson, New Jersey, establishment owned by Joseph Hajar.

Elsie Payne, black female, is a Paterson, New Jersey, prostitute and sometime mistress of Joseph Hajar.

Tommy "Tommy Egan" Velia, deceased white male, was the head of the Italian crime syndicate in Bergen County, New Jersey, for many years.

Angelo "Ponzi" Ponzillo, white male, was at one time Tommy Velia's "man" in Paterson, New Jersey.

Franklin "Bro" Squires, black male, brother of the murdered Willie C. Squires, heads a black criminal organization in Paterson that has challenged Joseph Hajar's control there.

Willie C. Squires, deceased black male, forged a partnership with his brother Franklin Squires to oppose the organized crime hegemony of Joseph Hajar in the Temple Hill section of Paterson, New Jersey. Willie C. Squires was found murdered, "gangland-style" in November 1970.

Runny Brown, black male, works for "Bro" Squires as a bodyguard.

Roy Howards, black male, works for "Bro" Squires as a bodyguard.

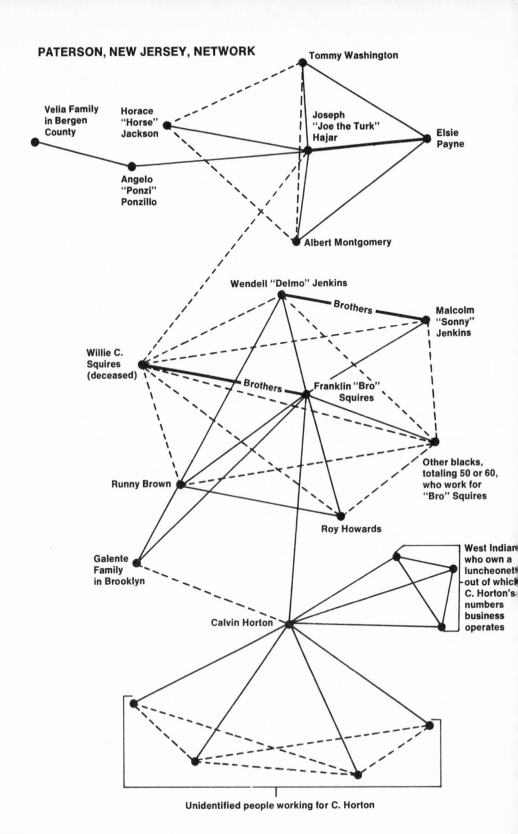

PATERSON, NEW JERSEY, NETWORK

Tommy Washington

Velia Family in Bergen County

Horace "Horse" Jackson

Joseph "Joe the Turk" Hajar

Elsie Payne

Angelo "Ponzi" Ponzillo

Albert Montgomery

Wendell "Delmo" Jenkins

Brothers

Malcolm "Sonny" Jenkins

Willie C. Squires (deceased)

Brothers

Franklin "Bro" Squires

Other blacks, totaling 50 or 60, who work for "Bro" Squires

Runny Brown

Roy Howards

Galente Family in Brooklyn

West Indians who own a luncheonette out of which C. Horton's numbers business operates

Calvin Horton

Unidentified people working for C. Horton

The Galentes are an Italian crime family based in Brooklyn. They supply quantities of drugs to the black man "Bro" Squires in Paterson.

Malcolm "Sonny" Jenkins, black male, is a Harlem hustler and "Murphy man" who taught the Squires brothers of Paterson some tricks of the trade when they were still teenagers. He is the brother of Wendell "Delmo" Jenkins, with whom he has often operated in tandem.

Wendell "Delmo" Jenkins, black male, brother of "Sonny" Jenkins, is like his brother a Harlem hustler and "Murphy man." Like his brother, he helped educate the young Squires boys.

Calvin Horton, black male of Jamaican origin, is a former employee of the Squires organization who has recently tried to set off on his own.

THE WAR DRAGONS NETWORK

CAST OF CHARACTERS

Harold "Manchu" Robinson, black male, forty-one years old, served as unofficial leader of the War Dragons, a Bedford-Stuyvesant, Brooklyn, youth gang of the early 1950s. He is today a successful numbers operator in his old neighborhood.

William "Tiny" Smith, black male, thirty-eight years old, was a member of the War Dragons. He now works in the numbers under Harold Robinson.

John "Sugar" Johnson, black male, thirty-eight years old, was a member of the War Dragons. He subsequently became a heroin addict and is now serving time in Attica on an armed robbery conviction.

Timothy Minton, black male, thirty-eight years old, was a member of the War Dragons. He is today attending college in Manhattan, while continuing to earn money by working in the numbers.

Theodore "Teddy" Stevens, black male, thirty-nine years old, was a member of the War Dragons. He still works in the numbers game, under Harold Robinson.

Ray Ballantine, black male, forty years old, was a member of the War Dragons. He is now a fairly well-known Brooklyn crap game hustler.

Michael Herlihy, white male, was in 1951 a police lieutenant in the Brooklyn neighborhood where the War Dragons were growing up.

George Gordon, black male, fifty years old, was throughout the 1950s a fence, shylock, and numbers operator in the Grand Avenue neighborhood of Bedford-Stuyvesant, where the War Dragons were growing up. He also owned a bar there, known locally as "the whorehouse."

Cynthia Brown, black female, in her late forties, during the 1950s worked as a prostitute in the bar owned by George Gordon known as "the whorehouse."

THE WAR DRAGONS

Bedford-Stuyvesant Section, Brooklyn

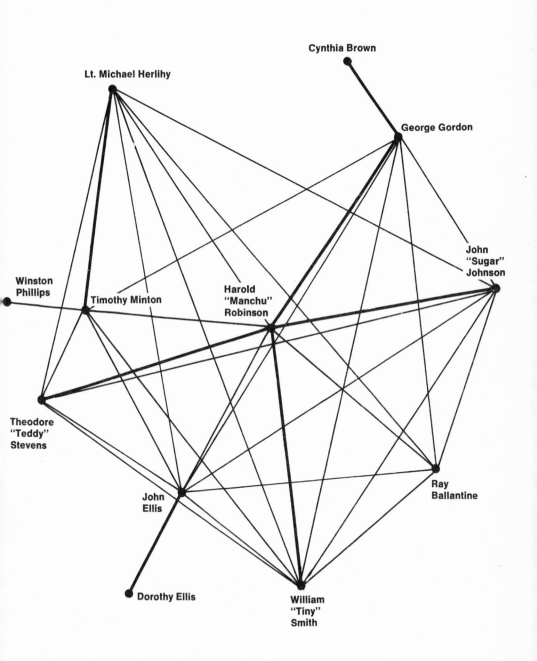

Cynthia Brown

Lt. Michael Herlihy

George Gordon

John "Sugar" Johnson

Winston Phillips

Timothy Minton

Harold "Manchu" Robinson

Theodore "Teddy" Stevens

John Ellis

Ray Ballantine

Dorothy Ellis

William "Tiny" Smith

Winston Phillips, black male, was the bartender at George Gordon's Bedford-Stuyvesant bar in 1951.

Dorothy Ellis, black female, mother of John Ellis, made her living in 1951 by working for George Gordon's numbers operation in the Grand Avenue neighborhood of Bedford-Stuyvesant.

John Ellis, deceased black male, was a member of the War Dragons. He was killed by police in 1971 while, with other members of a militant political group, he was attempting to rob a bank.

THE PRISON NETWORK

CAST OF CHARACTERS

Luis Santiago, Puerto Rican male, in his late thirties, has spent fifteen to twenty years of his life in New York State's prisons and is currently a leader among the Puerto Rican inmates of one of them.

Angel Parilla, Puerto Rican male, in his late twenties, works in the bakery of the prison where he is incarcerated. He is a follower of Luis Santiago.

Pascual Colon, Puerto Rican male, in his twenties, is a friend of Angel Parilla and a follower of Luis Santiago in the New York State prison where they are all incarcerated.

Jesus Hernandez, Puerto Rican male, in his late teens, is a relative of Luis Santiago who finds himself incarcerated with Santiago. He receives protection from, and has been adopted as *compadre* by, Santiago.

Jose Rivera, Puerto Rican male, in his late teens, incarcerated, is a member of the Young Lords youth gang and has tried to politicize Jesus Hernandez, Luis Santiago and his followers.

Juan Rocque, Puerto Rican male, in his twenties, is an incarcerated heroin addict who performs communication functions for Luis Santiago.

Billy Reagan, white male, in his twenties, is an inmate in state penitentiary. He is a pill freak and a friend of Juan Rocque, their shared addictions transcending ordinary racial barriers.

Trenton "Mau-Mau" Williams, black male, in his thirties, is a "jailhouse lawyer" who when his prison erupted in rioting a few years back was one of the inmates' leaders. He is highly respected both by his fellow inmates and by the prison administration. On the street he was once a highly successful hustler.

Frankie Henson, black male, in his twenties, serves in prison as a homosexual prostitute. He treats Raymond Atkins as his pimp.

359

A NEW YORK STATE PENITENTIARY NETWORK

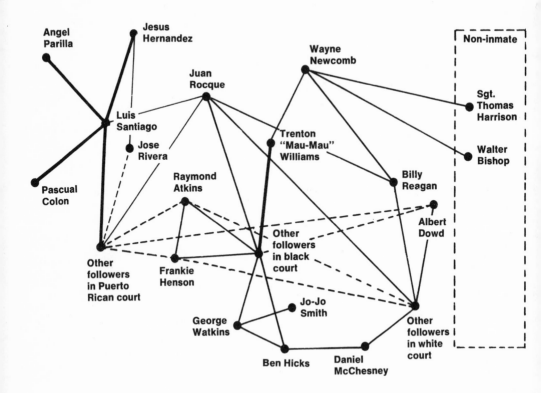

THE PRISON AT THE TIME OF THE UPRISING

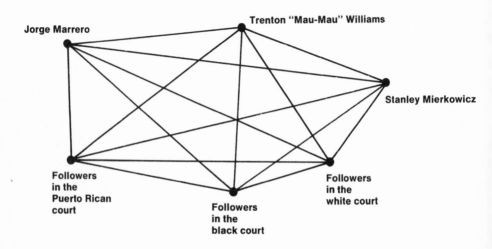

Raymond Atkins, black male, in his thirties, is a so-called prison "bandit," an aggressive homosexual. He has attempted to assault Jesus Hernandez, among others.

Ben Hicks, a black male, in his thirties, incarcerated, takes advantage of the mobility that his job as a prison porter offers him to help George Watkins in his winemaking.

Jo-Jo Smith, black male, in his late twenties, incarcerated, is a friend of George Watkins who intends to operate in Watkins' neighborhood when he is released on parole.

Daniel McChesney, a white male, in his twenties, incarcerated, works in his prison's warehouse. He is a "snitch." He supplies apples to George Watkins and Ben Hicks for their winemaking.

Wayne Newcomb, black male, in his twenties, has set up prison heroin deals while out on parole.

George Watkins, a black male, in his thirties, is a winemaker and entrepreneur in the prison where he is incarcerated.

Sergeant Thomas Harrison, white male, in his late thirties, is an ambitious prison guard who supplies heroin to certain of his prisoners.

Walter Bishop, black male, in his twenties, is a friend of Wayne Newcomb and an outside contact man for heroin traffic within a New York State penitentiary. He has himself served time in the prison that he supplies with drugs.

Joseph "Crazy Joe" Gallo (not a pseudonym), deceased white male, was a well-known Italian-American organized crime leader who was gunned down in Little Italy in 1972. During his stay in a New York penitentiary, he made numerous acquaintances among the black inmates.

Albert Dowd, older white inmate, instructs other inmates in various criminal techniques and skills.

Jorge Marrero, Puerto Rican male, in his thirties, was transferred from one prison to another for his aggressive role in a prison riot a few years back and is now in solitary confinement. At his old prison, he was one of the most respected Puerto Rican inmates.

Stanley Mierkowicz, white male, in his twenties, is a prison inmate who during the riots at his penitentiary was a leader of the white prisoners.

THE CUBAN CONNECTION

CAST OF CHARACTERS

Luis Santos, Puerto Rican male in his late twenties, member of a childhood gang that included Antonio Rivera, Angel Rojas, Juan Rios, and Rafael Quintero. He is the informant that first introduced us to the network that includes the Cuban connection.

Rafael Quintero, Puerto Rican male in his late twenties, was a member of a small East Harlem youth gang (among whose members was Luis Santos) that tried unsuccessfully to gain control of the narcotics trade in their own 109th Street–Lexington Avenue neighborhood.

Juan Rios, Puerto Rican male in his late twenties, was a member of the same gang.

Antonio Rivera, Puerto Rican male in his late twenties, also a member of this gang.

Angel Rojas, Puerto Rican male in his early twenties, was a member of Santos' childhood gang in East Harlem.

Carmine "the Hook" Grazioli, white male, lives near 109th Street and Lexington Avenue in East Harlem and is the wholesale narcotics distributor in his immediate neighborhood for an Italian crime family.

Clemente Sanchez, Puerto Rican male, thirty-one years old, friend of Luis Santos since childhood, is a very successful East Harlem drug pusher who has also managed to give himself the beginnings of a liberal education.

Hector Sanchez, Puerto Rican male, seventeen or eighteen years old, works in his brother Clemente's narcotics operation.

Jorge Sanchez, Puerto Rican male, twenty-four years old, formerly worked in his brother Clemente's narcotics operation but is now in prison.

362

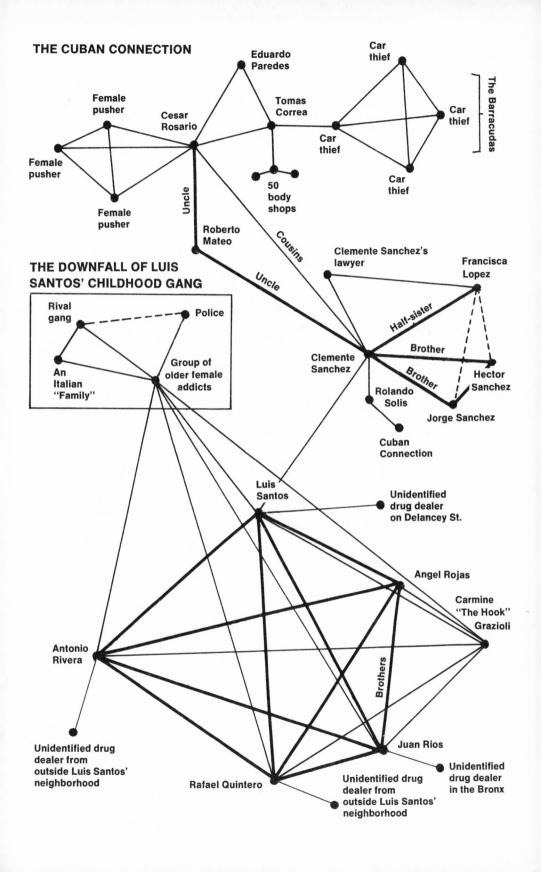

THE CUBAN CONNECTION

Eduardo Paredes

Car thief

The Barracudas

Female pusher

Cesar Rosario

Tomas Correa

Car thief

Car thief

Female pusher

Female pusher

Uncle

50 body shops

Car thief

Roberto Mateo

Cousins

Clemente Sanchez's lawyer

Francisca Lopez

THE DOWNFALL OF LUIS SANTOS' CHILDHOOD GANG

Uncle

Half-sister

Brother

Rival gang

Police

Clemente Sanchez

Brother

Hector Sanchez

An Italian "Family"

Group of older female addicts

Rolando Solis

Jorge Sanchez

Cuban Connection

Luis Santos

Unidentified drug dealer on Delancey St.

Angel Rojas

Carmine "The Hook" Grazioli

Antonio Rivera

Brothers

Unidentified drug dealer from outside Luis Santos' neighborhood

Juan Rios

Unidentified drug dealer in the Bronx

Rafael Quintero

Unidentified drug dealer from outside Luis Santos' neighborhood

Francisca Lopez, Puerto Rican female, twenty-two years old, is the half-sister of Clemente Sanchez. She is a Lesbian and has been addicted to heroin on and off for the last ten years. She occasionally works for Clemente in his drug "factory."

Roberto Mateo, Puerto Rican male, in his late forties, is a numbers operator of some stature in the Red Hook section of Brooklyn. He is the uncle of both Clemente Sanchez and Cesar Rosario.

Rolando Solis, Cuban male, twenty-seven years old, supplied us with much of our information regarding the so-called "Cuban connection." He is a friend of Clemente Sanchez. He both deals narcotics and works as a waiter in a Cuban restaurant.

Cesar Rosario, Puerto Rican male, twenty-one or twenty-two years old, is in the automotive business. He hires thieves to steal cars for their high-performanc? equipment, which he in turn sells, along with phony auto insurance cards. He is a cousin of Clemente Sanchez, from whom he purchases narcotics, which he employs three young women to sell.

Tomas Correa, Puerto Rican male, operates a car shop in Brooklyn out of which he sells stolen automotive parts that for the most part he has acquired from a gang of young car thieves called the Barracudas.

The Barracudas, Puerto Rican males, under twenty years old, steal cars to order for Tomas Correa, Cesar Rosario and others.

Eduardo Paredes, Puerto Rican male, is a car painter who specializes in quick jobs done on stolen autos.

"El Hombre," Cuban male, is an established leader in Cuban crime circles who gave Rolando Solis his start.

THE GYPSY CAB NETWORKS

CASTS OF CHARACTERS

THE SUPERFAST CAB COMPANY

James Taylor, black male, is an owner/driver for, and co-founder of, the Superfast Cab Company of Manhattan's West Side.

Edward Wilson, black male, is an owner/driver for, and co-founder of, the Superfast Cab Company.

Frank White, black male, is an owner/driver and co-founder of, the Superfast Cab Company of Manhattan's West Side. The car he drives was purchased from Tomas Correa of Brooklyn.

Ramon Suarez, Puerto Rican male, is an owner/driver for the Superfast Cab Company. He was formerly a yellow cab driver.

William Prentice, black male, is an owner/driver for the Superfast Cab Company of Manhattan's West Side. He once served prison time with the company's founders.

Jose Rodrigues, Puerto Rican male, is an owner/driver for the Superfast Cab Company.

Kenny Rivers, Puerto Rican male, is an owner/driver for the Superfast Cab Company.

Robert Quevedo, Puerto Rican male, owns a large garage in upper Manhattan through which he supplies stolen automotive parts to a variety of customers, among them some of the drivers of the Superfast Cab Company.

Rafael Pagan, Puerto Rican male, is a narcotics addict and thief who supplies Robert Quevedo with automotive parts.

Tomas Correa, Puerto Rican male, operates a car shop in Brooklyn out of which he sells stolen automotive parts that he often acquires from a

THE SUPERFAST CAB COMPANY AND CRIMINAL CONNECTIONS

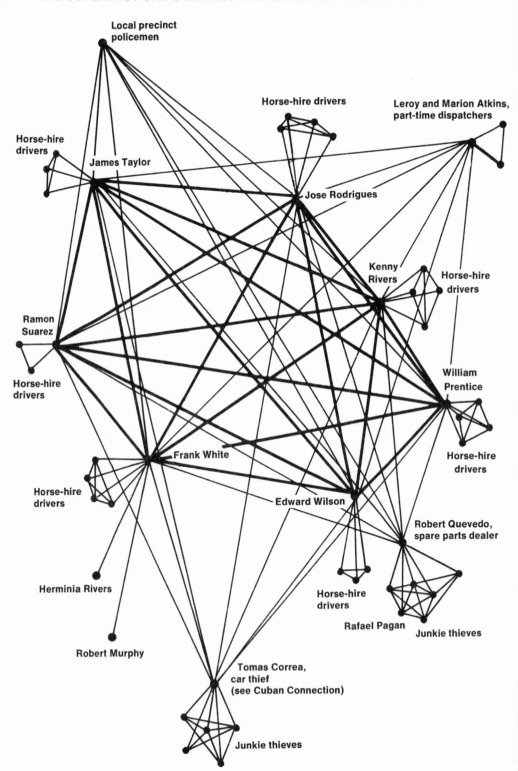

gang of young car thieves called the Barracudas. He is also involved in the Cuban connection.

Robert Murphy, white male, is a heroin addict and small-time pusher who occasionally horse-hires the cab of Frank White in order to peddle drugs out of it.

Herminia Rivers, Puerto Rican female, is a prostitute who often uses Superfast cabs to get from one appointment to another.

Leroy Atkins, black male, does the radio dispatch work for the Superfast Cab Company, along with his wife, Marion.

Marion Atkins, black female, wife of Leroy Atkins, helps him with radio dispatching for Superfast.

THE BLACK DIAMOND NETWORK

Theodore Huntington, black male, thirty-six years old, life-long resident of Harlem, is the heart and soul of the Black Diamond Special Omnibus Insurance Company.

Etta Brown, black female, was injured when a taxi in which she was riding and which was insured through the Black Diamond Special Omnibus Insurance crashed. She was the mother of Marvin Brown, who was riding in the same cab.

Marvin Brown, black male, a young boy, was killed when a taxi in which he was riding and which was insured through the Black Diamond Special Omnibus Insurance Company crashed. He was the son of Etta Brown.

Louise Franklin, black female, was injured when a taxi in which she was riding and which was insured through the Black Diamond Special Omnibus Insurance Company crashed.

James Strickland, black male, was injured when a taxi in which he was riding and which was insured through the Black Diamond Special Omnibus Insurance Company crashed.

VICTOR HIDALGO

Victor Hidalgo, Puerto Rican male, thirty-five years old, founder and owner of the Look Smart Livery, is a rising businessman with political aspirations.

Jorge Hidalgo, Puerto Rican male, forty-two years old, is the older brother of Victor Hidalgo. He has spent his whole adult life working in the numbers game.

THE BLACK DIAMOND NETWORK

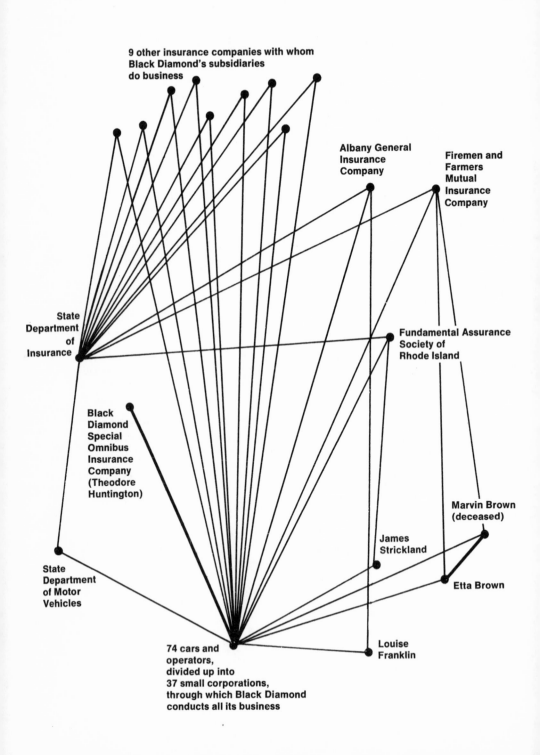

9 other insurance companies with whom
Black Diamond's subsidiaries
do business

Albany General
Insurance
Company

Firemen and
Farmers
Mutual
Insurance
Company

State
Department
of
Insurance

Fundamental Assurance
Society of
Rhode Island

Black
Diamond
Special
Omnibus
Insurance
Company
(Theodore
Huntington)

Marvin Brown
(deceased)

James
Strickland

State
Department
of Motor
Vehicles

Etta Brown

74 cars and
operators,
divided up into
37 small corporations,
through which Black Diamond
conducts all its business

Louise
Franklin

THE WORLD OF VICTOR HIDALGO

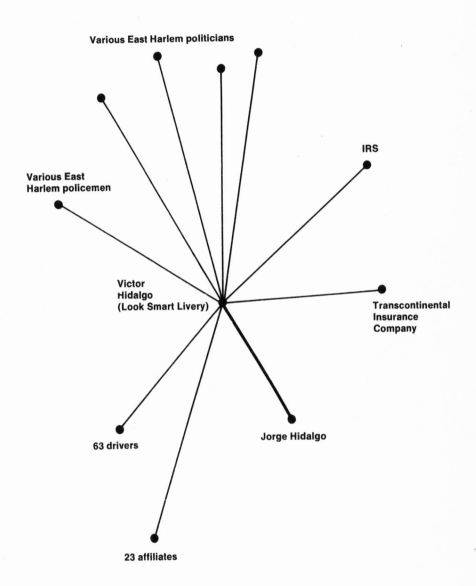

Various East Harlem politicians

IRS

Various East
Harlem policemen

Victor
Hidalgo
(Look Smart Livery)

Transcontinental
Insurance
Company

63 drivers

Jorge Hidalgo

23 affiliates

SELECTED BIBLIOGRAPHY

Albini, Joseph L. *The American Mafia*. New York: Appleton-Century-Crofts, 1971.

American Academy of Political and Social Sciences. "Combating Organized Crime," *The Annals*, 347 (May 1963).

Anderson, Robert T. "From Mafia to Cosa Nostra," *American Journal of Sociology*, 61 (November 1963), 302–310.

Barzini, Luigi. *The Italians*. New York: Bantam Books, 1969.

Becker, Howard S. *Outsiders: Studies in the Sociology of Deviance*. New York: Free Press, 1963.

Cressey, Donald F. "The Functions and Structure of Criminal Syndicates," Appendix A to the President's Commission on Law Enforcement and Administration of Justice, *Task Force Report: Organized Crime*. Washington, D.C.: Government Printing Office, 1967.

Gardiner, John A. *The Politics of Corruption*. New York: Russell Sage, 1970.

Hall, Susan, and Bob Adelman. *Gentleman of Leisure*. New York: New American Library, 1972.

Hobsbawm, Eric J. "The American Mafia," *The Listener*, LXXXII (November 20, 1969), 2121.

————. *Primitive Rebels: Studies in Archaic Forms of Social Movement in the 19th and 20th Centuries*. New York: Praeger, 1963.

Ianni, Francis A. J. *A Family Business: Kinship and Social Control in Organized Crime*. New York: Russell Sage–Basic Books, 1972.

————. "The Mafia and the Web of Kinship," *The Public Interest*, No. 22 (Winter 1971).

————, Suzy Fisher and Jeffrey Lewis. "Ethnic Succession and Network Formation in Organized Crime." Report prepared under grant NI-71-076-G from the National Institute of Law Enforcement and Criminal Justice, 1972.

The Knapp Commission Report on Police Corruption. New York: George Braziller, 1972.

Knight, Etheridge. *Black Voices From Prison*. New York: Pathfinder Press, 1970.

Landesco, John. *Organized Crime in Chicago*. Chicago: University of Chicago Press, 1929.

Lewis, Oscar. *La Vida*. New York: Vintage Books–Random House, 1965.

Morris, Norval, and Gordon Hawkins. *The Honest Politician's Guide to Crime Control*. Chicago: University of Chicago Press, 1970.

Mosca, Gaetano. "Mafia," *Encyclopedia of the Social Sciences*. Vol. X (1933), p. 36.

National Council on Crime and Delinquency. "Organized Crime: A Symposium," *Crime and Delinquency*, 8, No. 4 (October 1962), 321–407.

New York State Identification and Intelligence System. *Notes on the Second Oyster Bay Conference on Combating Organized Crime*. Albany: NYSIIS, March 1966. (Mimeographed minutes.)

New York State Investigations Commission. *An Investigation of the Loan Shark Racket*. New York: SIC, April 1965.

Padilla, Elena. *Up From Puerto Rico*. New York. Columbia University Press, 1958.

The President's Commission on Law Enforcement and Administration of Justice. *The Challenge of Crime in a Free Society*. Washington, D.C.: Government Printing Office, 1967.

Reuss-Ianni, Elizabeth, and Jeffrey Lewis. "A Community Self-Study of Organized Crime." Report prepared under grant #C58834 from the Criminal Justice Coordinating Council, City of New York, June 1973.

Salerno, Ralph, and John S. Tomkins. *The Crime Federation*. New York: Doubleday, 1969.

Sexton, Patricia Cayo. *Spanish Harlem: Anatomy of Poverty*. New York: Harper & Row, 1965.

Smith, Dwight C., Jr., and Ralph Salerno. "The Use of Strategies in Organized Crime Control," *Journal of Criminal Law, Criminology and Police Science*, Vol. 61. No. 1 (March 1970).

Steward, Julian (ed.). *The People of Puerto Rico*. Urbana: University of Illinois Press, 1956.

Suttles, Gerald D. *The Social Order of the Slum*. Chicago: University of Chicago Press, 1968.

Thomas, Piri. *Down These Mean Streets*. New York: Knopf, 1967.

Whyte, William Foote. *Street Corner Society*. Chicago: University of Chicago Press, 1943.

Wotzel, Robert K. "An Overview of Organized Crime: Mores versus Morality," American Academy of Political and Social Science *The Annals*, 347 (May 1963), 1–11.

INDEX

ABOUT THE AUTHOR

FRANCIS A. J. IANNI is Professor and Director of the Horace Mann-Lincoln Institute at Teachers College, Columbia University. He has been on the faculty at Yale University; University College, Addis Ababa, Ethiopia; the University of Florence, Italy; and Russell Sage College, Troy, New York.

From 1963 to 1965 he was Associate Commissioner for Research in the United States Office of Education. He has made extensive field trips in Ethiopia, Southern Italy and Sicily and has carried out a number of anthropological field studies in this country. His most recent research was a field study of *Mafia* in Sicily and an Italian-American organized crime family in New York City, which was reported in his first book on organized crime, *A Family Business,* published in 1972. The book was also published in Great Britain, France and Italy.

Mr. Ianni is a Fellow of the American Anthropological Association and of the African Studies Association and a member of the American Psychological Association. He is also a member of the Task Force on Organized Crime of the Criminal Justice Coordinating Council of New York City and served as a consultant to the National Advisory Commission on Criminal Justice Standards and Goals.